Setting Safety Standards

Setting Safety Standards

Regulation in the Public and Private Sectors

Ross E. Cheit

UNIVERSITY OF CALIFORNIA PRESS
Berkeley · Los Angeles · Oxford

University of California Press
Berkeley and Los Angeles, California

University of California Press, Ltd.
Oxford, England

© 1990 by
The Regents of the University of California

Library of Congress Cataloging-in-Publication Data

Cheit, Ross E.
    Setting safety standards : regulation in the public and private
sectors / Ross E. Cheit.
        p.   cm.
    Includes bibliographical references.
    ISBN 0-520-06733-9 (alk. paper)
    1. Product safety—Standards—United States.   I. Title.
TS175.C44   1990
363.19′0973—dc20   89-20339
                                                                            CIP

Printed in the United States of America
1   2   3   4   5   6   7   8   9

The paper used in this publication meets the minimum requirements of
American National Standard for Information Sciences—Permanence of Paper
for Printed Library Material, ANSI Z39.48-1984. ∞

To Budd and June

Contents

Illustrations and Tables

Technical Drawings by Jean Sanchirico, Rhode Island School of Design.

Abbreviations

AGA	American Gas Association
ANSI	American National Standards Institute
ASME	American Society of Mechanical Engineers
ASTM	American Society for Testing and Materials
CPSC	Consumer Product Safety Commission
FAA	Federal Aviation Administration
FTC	Federal Trade Commission
GAMA	Gas Appliance Manufacturers Association
NAS	National Academy of Sciences
NBS	National Bureau of Standards
NFPA	National Fire Protection Association
NGFA	National Grain and Feed Association
NTSB	National Transportation Safety Board
OMB	Office of Management and Budget
OSHA	Occupational Safety and Health Administration
UL	Underwriters Laboratories

Acknowledgments

This project would not have been possible without the cooperation of countless individuals in the public and private sectors. All of those listed in the appendix provided valuable information and were generous with their time. Hank Collins of Underwriters Labs and Don Mackay of the National Bureau of Standards were extraordinarily cooperative and deserve special thanks.

Friends and colleagues at the Graduate School of Public Policy at the University of California, Berkeley, provided assistance and encouragement of all sorts. I am grateful to Allan Sindler for arranging financial support from the Sloan Foundation, and to my fellow doctoral students for reading the roughest of drafts and providing encouraging criticisms. Glenn Shor and Fritzie Reisner were unusually helpful in both regards. I am also indebted to Martin Trow and Martin Shapiro for their service on my doctoral committee.

John Braithwaite and David Hemenway contributed thoughtful comments on early portions of this work, and Phil Harter was remarkably helpful at a surprising number of stages. I thank John Mendeloff for providing prompt, thorough, and fruitful comments about the entire manuscript in the style of our mutual dissertation advisor, Gene Bardach.

Many colleagues at Brown learned more than they ever wanted to know about grain elevators and woodstoves. Roger Cobb, Jim Morone, Mike Rich, Darrell West, and Alan Zuckerman provided useful suggestions for improving the manuscript. I am particularly grateful to Tom Anton, director of the Taubman Center for Public Policy and American Institutions at Brown, for his advice, encouragement, and support. Jason Grumet provided extraordinary assistance in the final stage of this project.

I am forever thankful to my parents for their generous support and genuine interest, and to Kathy Odean for just about everything else that helped make this book a reality.

Most of all, I want to thank Gene Bardach for providing the inspiration for this study, for carefully and critically reading the manuscript several times, and for lending the ideal combination of guidance and encouragement along the way.

PART ONE

Introduction

ONE

Protective Regulation and the Impasse Between the Public and Private Sectors

The rise and fall of government regulation challenges both sides in the debate over the proper role of government and business in protecting people against various risks. Leaving business to its own devices is suspect for reasons suggested by horror stories such as the exploding Ford Pinto. The "failures" of the free market are well recognized. Consumers frequently lack information. Businesses often lack the incentive to internalize "external costs" such as pollution. The costs of organizing collective interests can be prohibitive; and without the watchful eye of regulatory inspectors, the unscrupulous lack a powerful reason for self-restraint. But, as the revolt against regulation reveals, government regulation has its own serious shortcomings. As Charles Wolf points out, the "failures" of nonmarket arrangements parallel those of the free market.[1] Many regulatory agencies are plagued by adversariness and delay. Regulations are often slow in coming but quick to court. These regulations can be inflexible and unreasonable. As a result, the political debate over protective regulation has reached an impasse. Proponents of government regulation appeal to well-founded fears of laissez-faire arrangements, while supporters of the private sector appeal to similarly substantiated concerns about regulatory bureaucracy.

In the heyday of protective government regulation, the late 1960s and early 1970s, nearly two dozen new federal agencies were created, including the Occupational Safety and Health Administration (OSHA), the Consumer Product Safety Commission (CPSC), and the Environ-

3

mental Protection Agency (EPA). These agencies were born of an "entrepreneurial politics" that, according to James Q. Wilson, capitalized on general antibusiness sentiment and specific "horror stories" from the private sector. Unlike the traditional "captured" agencies, which exist largely for the benefit of the regulated, these new agencies, according to Wilson, generally choose "stricter and more costly standards over more lenient, less expensive ones."[2]

But as their performance fell short of expectations, these agencies fell from grace. OSHA damaged its reputation by adopting wholesale and enforcing almost indiscriminately scores of private standards for everything from toilet seats to stepladders. The CPSC looked similarly foolish devoting substantial resources to regulating matchbook covers and swimming pool slides. Several studies have since documented the economic burden of other government regulations that became excessive. Government regulation has also proven to be time-consuming and adversary in nature. Most CPSC and OSHA rules end up in court; few survive the challenge.

Enthusiasm for protective regulation waned further in the wake of "deregulation." The original targets of this movement were independent regulatory commissions engaged in economic regulation (for example, regulation of prices or terms of entry) where there are powerful arguments against stifling competition in the name of the public interest. Promising to "get government off our backs," President Reagan advocated several controversial proposals to leave protective regulation to the private sector. But the "policy consensus" that facilitated deregulation in interstate trucking and airlines is lacking in the fields of environment, health, and safety regulation.[3] By some measures, there is continuing popular support for certain types of social regulation. By historical account, however, this support vacillates. There have been three waves of government regulation this century, and a fourth may be in the making.[4]

The options for the future are often described in stark terms, favoring either government or business. As Wilson describes the political prospects, "One [option], favored by liberals, is new constitutional or legislative devices that will allow the government to be both active and uncaptured. . . . The second, favored by conservatives, is to have the government do less, thus leaving a greater variety of decisions to the market and to private lawsuits."[5] These alternatives reflect a rigid conception of the public and private sectors. The public sector is cast as hierarchical and political, the private sector as decentralized and market-based. But this conception does not do justice to the range of institutional arrangements available for protective regulation.[6] Rather, it obscures important similarities between public and private institutions, leaving no room for one of the most intriguing but misunderstood alternatives to government regulation: private standards.

This failure of political imagination has been observed elsewhere. In the context of social services, Lester Salamon notes that "the prevailing conception of the welfare state has left little room for a vibrant non-profit sector or for a blossoming government-nonprofit partnership."[7] The underlying reasons are ideological. Conservatives tend to exaggerate the threat of government power; liberals minimize the accomplishments of the private sector. Yet, as Salamon demonstrates, nonprofit organizations play a much more important role in providing social services than is normally acknowledged.

The same is true in protective regulation. The prevailing conception of the regulatory state ignores significant activities in the private sector. Private standards are not even considered in many discussions of protective regulation. And when they are mentioned, ideology often clouds reality. Private standards have been promoted in the name of deregulation, even though they are obviously a form of regulation. But this position is based on ideology rather than on any specific understanding of how these obscure standards actually work.

The Vast Unknown World of Private Standards

Gas stoves, extension cords, x-ray equipment, and automobiles are among the thousands of items regulated in the United States by industrywide safety standards. Yet remarkably little is known about the institutions that generate the overwhelming majority of standards. These institutions, many will be surprised to learn, are private, not public. In the list above, only automobiles are subject to safety standards written by the public sector—and even so, private standards developed by the Society of Automotive Engineers play an integral part in the government's regulatory scheme. In significant product categories, such as gas and electric appliances, virtually all existing safety standards are developed by the private sector.

The National Bureau of Standards (NBS), recently renamed the National Institute of Standards and Technology,[8] estimated that there were thirty-two thousand private standards in 1983. The bulk of these regulate uniformity or interchangeability and are not particularly important or controversial.[9] The number infused with significant implications for the public interest is probably in the thousands. These standards aim to promote social goods such as fire safety and product safety. Many are written by traditional trade associations—membership organizations with relatively homogeneous memberships. Others are written by little-known groups such as Underwriters Laboratories (UL) and the American Conference of Government Industrial Hygienists (ACGIH; a prominent private organization, despite its name). At least half of the top twenty standards-setters in the private sector are organized along professional lines or as "independent" entities (see table 1). More detailed background information about these private standards-setters appears in chapter 2.

Private standards raise many significant policy questions for government. First, public agencies must decide when (if ever) to defer to these standards or incorporate them into law. The Office of Management and Budget (OMB) issued a circular in 1982 to encourage federal agencies to use private standards, but the policy is vague and has not been implemented effectively.[10] Second, agencies must decide when and how to participate in private standards-setting. A controversial issue within the CPSC is whether government representatives should vote on private standards-setting committees. Third, government must consider how (if at all) it can improve private standards-setting. Finally, government must decide when (if ever) to ban private standards. The FTC and the courts have addressed this issue over the years in the context of antitrust law.[11]

The literature on private standards-setting is long on anecdotes but short on systematic analysis and evidence.[12] Public standards-setting, by contrast, has received far more scrutiny, even though the size of the undertaking pales in comparison to the private sector. The CPSC, for example, has adopted about a dozen product safety standards since 1973, several of which were struck down in court; UL, on the other hand, has over five hundred published safety standards currently in force.[13] Yet there are books, dissertations, and countless articles about the CPSC. The only published works about UL, a few scattered articles, were written mostly by UL staff members. David Hemenway's *Industrywide Voluntary Product Standards* provides a helpful analysis of the various types of private standards, but it says little about the "quasi-political" process through which these standards are developed.[14]

The Presumption Against Private Standards

Given their disputed, but potentially important, role in public policy, there is surprisingly little information about the actual performance of

TABLE 1   THE TOP TWENTY NONGOVERNMENT
STANDARDS-SETTERS

Organization	Number of Standards
American Society for Testing and Materials	7,200
Society of Automotive Engineers	4,200
U.S. Pharmacopeia	2,900
Aerospace Industries Association	2,800
Association of Official Analytic Chemists	1,500
Association of American Railways	1,350
American National Standards Institute	1,330[a]
Cosmetic, Toiletry, and Fragrance Association	630
Factory Mutual	600
American Society of Mechanical Engineers	550
Institute of Electrical and Electronics Engineers	500
Electronic Industries Association	480
Underwriters Laboratories	527[b]
American Railway Engineers Association	400
American Petroleum Institute	350
American Association of Cereal Chemists	350
American Oil Chemists Association	330
American Association of Blood Banks	280
Technical Association of the Pulp and Paper Industry	270
National Fire Protection Association	260

SOURCE: U.S. Department of Commerce, National Bureau of Standards, *Standards Activities of Organizations in the United States*, NBS Special Publication 681 (Washington, D.C.: Government Printing Office, August 1984), 2.

[a]Published and copyrighted by the American National Standards Institute.

[b]Does not include draft or unpublished standards.

private safety standards. Nevertheless, there is widespread belief that these standards are more lenient and are developed through procedures less formal and less solicitous of due process than those of government. Various conclusions might follow from this conventional wisdom. Informality might be favored over formality, as it increasingly is in the resolution of civil disputes. Leniency might also be favored, depending on whether government regulation is really as burdensome as often claimed. But those interpretations, however plausible, are rarely applied to private safety standards. Rather, suspicion of private regulation is so high that there is practically a prevailing presumption against using private standards for public purposes.

The Federal Trade Commission (FTC) was so concerned about private standards during the Carter administration that it proposed to regulate the entire enterprise. That effort was not ultimately successful, but neither was President Reagan's subsequent effort to increase public use of private standards. The OMB circular advising the use of voluntary standards "wherever possible" is ignored by agencies that harbor popular doubts about the desirability of private standards. Similarly, the CPSC, in the face of intense opposition, backed away from a proposal to "recognize" selected private standards.[15] The presumption against private standards stems from (1) the voluntary nature of these standards and (2) the political pressures that are thought to control their development.

The "Voluntary" Nature of Private Standards

Private standards are initially suspect because they appear to be "voluntary" in nature; at least they are frequently described that way. This label suggests the kind of decentralization intrinsic in market arrangements. In Albert O. Hirschman's useful terminology, it suggests the importance of "exit."[16] As an organizing force, exit can precipitate a distinct logic of institutional control. In the area of education, for example, Terry Moe and John Chubb argue that public schools, which respond more to politics (voice) than markets (exit), are "quite literally at a systematic disadvantage" compared to their private counterparts.[17] Because parents can remove their children from private schools, they argue, the teachers and administrators are more responsive than in the public sector.

Applied to the area of private safety standards, "exit" suggests a serious problem. To extend the analogy with education, manufacturers and other business interests apparently take the place of interested parents as the primary influence on program administrators. These participants, seemingly concerned more about self-interest than about the interest of others, might "exit" if they do not approve of the regulatory product. In other words, they might refuse to participate in the process and boycott any standard developed in their absence. This suggests a bias in favor of the largest firms, those whose "exit" would most damage the enterprise.

A related hypothesis is that private standards-setters simply seek the "lowest common denominator." This downward pressure is thought to stem from rules requiring private standards to reflect a "consensus" of the participants. This does not usually mean formal unanimity, but the reality of private organizations is that "the fear of disintegration is frequently the decisive factor in the framing of governing institutions."[18] The implication is that the demands of organizational maintenance generally override the possibility that private standards will be more stringent than desired by nearly all the participants. As a result, George Eads and Peter Reuter have hypothesized, private standards-setters probably "water down" their safety standards to appease potential dissenters.[19]

These hypotheses seem most appropriate for trade associations, but they do not appear to fit a legion of other private standards-setters. Scores of so-called voluntary standards are actually coercive. They exist by demand on the part of more than just the regulated. Many of these standards have the force of law. UL standards, for example, are frequently incorporated into law through municipal building codes. Powerful nonlegal forces also compel compliance with various "voluntary" standards. Gas utilities generally will not install or service a gas appliance unless it is certified as complying with the safety standards of the American Gas Association (AGA) Laboratories. Major retailers such as J. C. Penney incorporate private safety standards into their purchase orders, helping to explain a popular observation by those familiar with private standards: "It is impossible to market an electric appliance in this country that is not UL-listed." These various forces call into question whether "exit" dominates private standards-setting. They also limit the application of George S. Stigler's theory that regulation exists primarily to satisfy demands of the regulated.[20]

Private Power and Public Safety

Recognizing that private standards cannot be dismissed as "voluntary" leads directly to larger concerns about the coercive use of private power. As Grant McConnell argued in *Private Power and American Democracy,* it is "unreasonable to assert that private associations are both important to general policy and yet so unimportant that their political life may be ignored."[21] McConnell described as "orthodoxy" an "unstable amalgam of very different ideas" *favoring* the exercise of private power in America. While that "orthodoxy" certainly favors the basic elements of a vibrant market economy—McConnell wrote about the modern corporation, agriculture, and labor—the argument does not carry over to private safety standards. There is tremendous skepticism about private regulation in this country.

First, the United States has a strong legal tradition that embodies a liberty-based concern for the protection of individual interests against the exercise of "police powers." The legitimacy afforded private action in the business world, where social arrangements are more consensual than coercive, simply does not extend to actions perceived as "regulatory." Concerns about the due process of private standards-setting are widespread. These concerns were fundamental to the FTC's effort to regulate private standards-setters. Lacking the constitutional order of public government, these groups appear particularly vulnerable to Robert Michels's "iron law of oligarchy"—the tendency of organizational leaders to acquire and promote interests different from those of their members.[22] The tendency of private organizations to develop "internally nondemocratic and bureaucratic structures" is "generally accepted as fact by social scientists."[23] Although the FTC did not adopt the process-based regulations, it retains legal jurisdiction, and its attorneys retain heightened interest, in pursuing complaints concerning private abuses of due process.[24]

The second argument against private standards is more substantive. The political critique of pluralism suggests that when private groups dominate the policymaking process, the results are rarely (if ever) in the public interest. "The most entrenched, the best organized, and frequently the oldest" interests are likely to benefit most from the resulting policies.[25] This criticism need not imply bad motives or exclusionary practices on the part of private standards-setters. Even organizations that encourage participation of various groups are unlikely to hear from some interests. The "logic of collective action" suggests that consumer and other diffuse interests will often be underrepresented, whatever the forum.[26] These interests might be galvanized effectively (but temporarily) by a catastrophe, but in the long run the concentrated interests of the regulated are likely to prevail.

The argument is familiar in the public sector, where agencies are often thought to favor the interests of the regulated. Based on observations about the Interstate Commerce Commission, the Civil Aeronautics Board, and the Federal Communications Commission, for example, Grant McConnell argued in 1966 that "accommodation" with private interest groups tends to "eliminate public values from effective political consideration."[27]

Theodore Lowi has argued more recently that the "parceling out" of public policymaking to private interests is "co-optive" and destructive of public values. Private safety standards appear to be the ultimate extension of this phenomenon. Lacking the presence of outside interests, private regulatory institutions seem nothing more than a variation of the fox guarding the chicken coop. Lowi makes specific reference to private standards in the second edition of *The End of Liberalism,* condemning these arrangements as "prime examples of the continuation and reinforcement of 1960s liberalism applied to public policy."[28]

Beyond "Capture" Theory: Toward an Institutional Perspective

But private regulation, like public regulation, varies in so many respects, internal and external, that no single theory fits all forms. Just as capture theory has limited application in the public sector, particularly in the area of protective regulation, there is reason to question its universal application in the private sector. The politics of private regulation appear to be far more complex than capture theory admits. The mixture of motives and interest groups in the private sector is wide-ranging and unpredictable. Internal factors, such as administrative procedures and organizational self-interest, further complicate the picture. Each suggests reasons why capture theory apparently fails to chart the most important differences between public and private standards-setters.

Who Benefits from Private Safety Standards?

Private standards-setters are widely assumed to be "captured" by business interests. Suggesting otherwise would, under this view, be as naive as indulging the notion that public agencies simply carry out their statutory charge to act "in the public interest." But developments in the public sector suggest that capture theory does not fit protective regulation nearly as well as it fits economic regulation. The classic statements of capture theory—Samuel P. Huntington's "administrative marasmus," Marver Bernstein's "life-cycle theory," and Stigler's "theory of economic regulation"—stem from agencies that regulated prices or terms of entry.[29] There is little justification for such regulation, the kind long performed by the Interstate Commerce Commission ("the most studied of all agencies" when McConnell and Lowi wrote about government regulation).[30] But protective regulation is different. It is economically defensible in various (arguably frequent) instances of market failure.[31] And, at least in the public sector, protective regulation does not come about through the demands of business. More often it is adopted over their objections. "Only by the most extraordinary theoretical contortions," Wilson concluded, can this regulation be explained "by reference to the economic stakes involved."[32]

Protective regulation in the private sector is similarly complex. Business interests are neither unitary nor necessarily opposed to the public interest. Some forms of private standards-setting, typically those sponsored by trade associations, are controlled entirely by the regulated. Others are more independent, offering services such as "third-party certification." The mission of these organizations resembles those of the public agencies charged with protecting health and safety. Their status is unclear, however, and this lack of clarity has given rise to several disagreements about motives. UL lost a legal battle with the Internal Revenue Service in 1943 when a federal court decided that "testing for public safety" is a business, not a charitable undertaking.[33] A private standard developed by the National Sanitation Foundation was upheld in a recent case partly because the court considered the organization to be "independent."[34] How to characterize the American Society of Mechanical Engineers (ASME) was the source of strong disagreement in a recent Supreme Court case, with one side calling it a "scientific" group and the other side alleging it is "dominated by commercial interests."[35]

To be sure, there is a rich tradition of using "self-regulation" to stifle competition. This includes standardization of sizes and shapes, practically a prerequisite to effective price-fixing.[36] But safety standards are different. Granted there are some anticompetitive ones masquerading as safety standards, but there are also genuine safety standards that, although not necessarily as strict as what government would adopt, certainly benefit the diffuse interests of consumers.

These private standards-setters do not fit easily into the existing understanding of private organizations. In their landmark study of formal organizations, Peter Blau and W. Richard Scott classified organizations "on the basis of the *cui bono*—who benefits."[37] In his book *Who Profits*, Robert Leone suggests looking at regulation in a similar way.[38] Either way, private standards-setters are far more complicated than generally appreciated. In Blau and Scott's terms, private standards-setters are likely to be considered "mutual-benefit associations," organized primarily for the benefit of membership. But that analysis fits the trade associations much better than the "independent" organizations. The membership of, say, the National Fire Protection Association is so large and diverse that the "mutual-benefit" theory clearly does not fit. The members are not the primary beneficiaries of most standards. And many organizations, such as Underwriters Labs, do not even have members.

These groups might be considered "service organizations" because they have clients. But that description is also inappropriate, because product testing and certification appear to be directed at third parties, including insurance companies, wholesale buyers, and individual consumers. This leaves the most nebulous category of all: the "commonweal" organization, whose prime beneficiary is the public at large. While this term undoubtedly describes some private standards-setters, it is not clear whether "commonweal" private standards are likely to be better or worse than the public alternatives.

Several political scientists have condemned private standards in any case. Lowi declared private safety standards guilty by association with the old National Recovery Administration (NRA). Calling these standards "indistinguishable" from the old NRA codes, Lowi marveled that "there is so little suspicion as to their constitutionality" under the nondelegation doctrine.[39] Others have invoked the ghost of Herbert Hoover—the engineer turned secretary of commerce intent on a grandiose plan of economic "standardization"—to belittle private standards.[40]

These arguments are not convincing. In contrast to Lowi's interpretation, Donald Brand has recently argued that "ideology and the institutional interests of the state played a more important role in determining the behavior of those administrators than special interest demands."[41] Moreover, just as it would be inappropriate to judge the Environmental Protection Agency based on the performance of the Interstate Commerce Commission, it is inappropriate to judge private safety standards as if they were akin to the NRA's "codes of fair competition" (in other words, economic regulation).

Lowi's argument also misrepresents the role of the public and private sectors by suggesting that government is preeminent in protective regulation. By framing his argument in terms of "delegation," Lowi implies that these functions are somehow inherently public. This conception is not supported by history. The private sector was in the business of product safety decades before the Consumer Product Safety Commission was created in 1972. The American Gas Association Labs started regulating gas appliances in the 1930s, and Underwriters Laboratories was certifying electrical equipment before the turn of the century.

These arrangements are far more complicated than capture theory admits. Undoubtedly, some private standards-setters are mainly self-serving. But others probably promote the public interest to a significant degree. When OSHA adopted hundreds of private standards, the problem was not that they were private; it was that the agency acted indiscriminately.[42] Some of those standards were essentially defunct, like old statutes never removed from the books. Others were more desirable. Unfortunately, OSHA did not distinguish between the two. In 1988, however, without any measurable opposition, OSHA adopted a more carefully selected group of private safety standards.[43] Certainly the public benefits to some extent from these standards, although the magnitude of the benefit and its corresponding cost must be examined before reaching any broader conclusions.

Bringing the Bureaucracy Back In

A second major problem with existing theories of private standards-setting is that they do not account for organizational interests or administrative procedures. Agencies should not be "mistaken as passive tools yielding to the strongest pressure of the time."[44] Organizations have their own interests, although these are often overlooked in theories that emphasize compromise among outside interests. Bringing the bureaucracy back into the consideration of private standards challenges the conventional wisdom in two ways. First, it demonstrates that private administrative law is similar in many ways to traditional administrative law. Second, it identifies several unexpected manifestations of organizational self-interest.

Private Administrative Procedure.   The rules of administrative procedure, the stuff of administrative law, are recognized as an important influence on agency decisionmaking in the public sector. Although the content of administrative law is controversial, it is widely assumed that the tradition of constitutionalism it reflects sets the public sector apart from the private. By affording certain due process protections, enforcing notions of interest representation, and holding agencies accountable through an appeals process, administrative law shapes and legitimizes agency decisionmaking. Private forms of governance, by contrast, are more consensual, minimizing the rule of law and, according to Lowi, favoring large, well-organized groups.

But the private sector is not without administrative rules and legal norms. In fact, there is a surprising degree of similarity in procedural requirements in the public and private sectors. The precepts of due process are enshrined in the by-laws of most private standards-setting organizations. Simple notice and comment procedures are commonplace. And the opportunity to appeal exists in many organizations. The Board of Standards Review, for example, hears appeals concerning any of the thousands of standards sponsored by the American National Standards Institute (ANSI). Committee membership in several private organizations is subject to rules against "domination" by any single interest. Some private standards-setters encourage outside groups, including consumers, to participate in their proceedings. The extreme example, the American Society for Testing and Materials (ASTM), even pays such groups to participate in the development of certain standards—a practice that has been discontinued in the public sector.

This is not to say that various private organizations protect individual interests to the same extent as public organizations; only that they apparently do more than is generally recognized. Of course, more is not necessarily better when it comes to procedural "protections." As Ronald Braeutigam and Bruce Owen point out: "This jurisprudentially laudable set of constraints on agency behavior has an interesting side effect, which is the creation of substantial delays and legal expense."[45] Such costs might be worthwhile. But, as Lawrence Bacow observes, divisive proceedings might hinder compliance.[46] Overly formal proceedings might also limit "the rich set of informal contacts" that would otherwise enhance decisionmaking.[47] Therefore, the private sector might even hold an advantage over the public if its administrative procedures strike a better balance between providing meaningful procedural protections and minimizing the undesirable side effects of due process.

Organizational Self-Interest.   Conceiving of standards-setting solely in terms of the regulated also overlooks the recognized importance of organizational self-interest. Agencies do not just respond to exterior pressures; they have interests of their own. Although there is no clearly articulated theory of organizational self-interest in the public sector, it is widely assumed that the interests of private regulators diverge significantly from the public interest. Much has been made of Michels's "iron law of oligarchy," the tendency of organizational leaders to acquire and promote interests different from those of their members. McConnell went so far as to argue that "the sweep of [Michels's] work extends by implication to all organizations in which membership could be said to exist."[48] Michels's conclusions stem entirely from a 1913 study of political parties in Germany, however, and in all likelihood the operation of this "iron law" varies significantly with such variables as organizational purpose and structure, not to mention larger differences in political culture and history.[49] Even if Michels's hypothesis is fitting, what ultimately matters is the *nature* of the interests pursued by the leadership of private standards-setters.

One of the few studies of private safety regulation, Michael Hunt's examination of the Association of Home Appliance Manufacturers, suggests that the leadership might pursue policies more enlightened than those favored by the membership. Hunt found that the AHAM staff had "a substantially different set of preferences from the member companies" and used it to achieve "stricter" results than would have been supported by the membership![50] Steven Kelman's comparison of public regulation of the workplace in the United States and Sweden is similarly suggestive. Kelman concludes that these two seemingly different regulatory regimes produce surprisingly similar outcomes. He attributes this largely to the influence of safety professionals.[51] Wilson's study of public regulation concludes that the motives of various types of government employees help explain outcomes that cannot be explained by capture theory. Similar influences probably exist in the private sector. To the extent that they do, private standards are more desirable than generally recognized. In short, Michels could be right about the significance of organizational self-interest, but Lowi could nonetheless still be wrong about the undesirable nature of the resulting outcomes.

There are several other reasons aside from the influences of professionalism why private standards-setters might adopt standards much stricter than expected. One is the desire to forestall government action. This incentive might actually lead the private sector to adopt *stricter* standards than government would have done.[52] Another possible reason is liability law. In the case of product safety standards, for example, strict standards may minimize liability costs or reduce the cost of liability insurance.

This is not to say that private standards are generally better or worse than public ones. Insufficient information is available to reach a conclusion. There are reasons both to doubt and to believe the conventional wisdom about public and private regulation. What is needed is more detailed information about the similarities and differences between standards-setting in the public and private sectors.

Research Goals and General Findings

This study seeks to provide the basis for a better understanding of the relative merits of public and private standards-setting in the area of safety regulation. Given limited knowledge of private-sector efforts, however, the first goal is to determine how private organizations actually work. What Wilson said about studying public regulation is equally true of private: "There is a need to go beyond an account of the newsworthy scandal to an exposition of how [agencies] ordinarily operate."[53] This inquiry is well suited to the case-study method. Two lines of analysis are suggested in the literature. The first concerns administrative law and procedures. Little is known about how private organizations actually achieve "consensus," respond to negative comments, or handle appeals. Proponents of private standards claim these procedures work well; critics charge they paper over fundamental flaws in private decisionmaking. An analysis of specific cases should shed some light on this dispute. The other obvious avenue for inquiry is political. Critics argue that the interests represented in private standards-setting are heavily biased in favor of business. This hypothesis is plausible, but, as indicated above, there are also reasons to doubt it. The case-study approach allows a detailed examination of the nature and balance of participating interests in a specific context.

The ultimate aim of this study is to evaluate the *relative performance* of public and private standards-setting. How well does each sector regulate safety? This study consists of four *pairs* of case studies. In each instance, both the public and private sectors have adopted safety standards in the same general area, and the study concentrates on organizational differences between the two sectors. The form of inquiry is decidedly institutional. Its main contribution is in identifying the comparative institutional advantages of the two systems.

Looking ahead to the analysis and conclusions, these case studies suggest that the difference between public and private standards-setting is not just a matter of degree, but one of kind. The analysis reveals important differences in how public and private standards-setters (1) estimate costs and benefits, (2) resolve philosophical questions about the appropriate scope of safety regulation, and (3) act over time and in the context of a larger regulatory program. Is the public or the private approach generally better? No simple answer to the question is possible, because the two sectors do not only favor different outcomes; they have different ways of looking at problems as well.

The analysis of outcomes partially confirms the conventional view that public standards are stricter than private ones and more prone to overzealousness. But there are contrary indications as well, suggesting that the private sector is more diverse than often presumed. Although the range of the interests represented on most private committees is limited by the absence of bona fide consumer representatives—an interest not necessarily better represented in public proceedings—the cases identify several important, but unappreciated, advocates of safety in the private sector. On occasion these forces combine to exhibit a surprising tendency toward strictness. Private standards should not, therefore, be rejected on the argument that they are intrinsically underprotective.

The differences between public and private approaches are not just in *what* should be done about a problem, but in *whether* anything should be done. Some "solutions" that are never seriously considered by one sector are routinely favored by the other. For example, public agencies are more willing than private ones to select early compliance deadlines, require use of unproven technologies, and regulate in a manner that interferes with traditional notions of managerial discretion. But these differences do not all cut along ideological lines. In surprising ways the private philosophy also encompasses public safety goals. Two institutional features appear to shape these regulatory philosophies: professional norms and the regulatory environment.

The significance of the former was suggested by Wilson, whose study of public regulation notes that professionals in different fields "often have distinctive ways of thinking about problems." This is particularly significant in comparing public and private standards-setters, because engineers dominate most private organizations, while lawyers play a leading role in the public sector.

The law is also a powerful external influence that constrains decisionmaking in the two sectors. Only private standards-setters are subject to the antitrust laws, and they frequently cite these laws as a reason for taking various actions. Liability law is seldom cited as an official reason for doing anything in the private sector, but the case studies suggest it is a more significant factor than antitrust law in explaining regulatory behavior. Liability concerns help explain why certain provisions are vague while others are relegated to an appendix. More generally, liability law seems to explain the reluctance of the private sector to address issues of consumer misuse or embrace certain new technologies. Public agencies, on the other hand, are subject to more frequent and intrusive judicial review of their regulatory decisions. These differences in regulatory environment help explain other differences in regulatory philosophy.

At least as important as these static differences is how the organizations change over time. Aaron Wildavsky has stressed the importance of "resilient" approaches to safety regulation.[54] Others have emphasized the advantages of "flexibility" and "responsiveness."[55] These concepts place standards-setting in an evolutionary context. What matters is not so much how individual cases are resolved, but how results change over time. Again, the case studies suggest important difference between the public and private sectors. Private standards-setting is prospective and ongoing, while public efforts tend to be corrective and singular. Private standards-setters tend to intervene relatively early in the life cycle of an issue, adjusting the subsequent standard over time. Public standards-setters, by contrast, are likely to get involved later in time, often after a major disaster, and to adopt a "one-shot" standard that is not subsequently revised.

Chapter 12 offers several suggestions on how to take advantage of these differences. One approach is for the public sector to stress "public" values. In other words, it should emphasize strategies shunned by the private sector. Second, government should identify niches where public standards are likely to complement private ones. A particularly promising strategy is filling "holes" in private standards. Finally, the importance of alternative policy instruments must not be overlooked. Standards-setting in both sectors is affected by a variety of "external" factors that are subject to influence by government action. Several of these alternative policy instruments hold the promise of improving standards-setting in ways that could never be mandated directly. For example, altering product liability law and improving the education of engineers could both lead to significant improvements in standards-setting. Recognizing these subtle influences and pursuing strategies that build on the complex interaction of public and private safety standards is the key to an intelligent and productive standards policy.

TWO

Background and Research Design

The universe of private standards is massive and mysterious. There are literally tens of thousands of these uncelebrated standards. In contrast, public standards seem better understood and more commonplace. Agencies such as the Consumer Product Safety Commission, whose standards often generate significant media attention, have been the subject of countless studies. Most private standards-setters operate in relative obscurity. This chapter presents some general background about both universes, public and private. It also provides a précis of several important, but not well known, private standards-setters. The chapter concludes with an explanation of the research design of this study, consisting of four comparative case studies of setting safety standards.

Private Standards and Public Interests

According to the most extensive directory of standards-setting organizations, compiled in 1983 by the National Bureau of Standards, based on information submitted by private organizations, approximately 420 nongovernment organizations maintain thirty-two thousand standards in the United States.[1] These standards facilitate commerce in various ways, but most are not particularly important to public policy. Some set forth definitions such as size of screw threadings. Others facilitate the interchangeability of items such as flashlight batteries and automobile parts. An ANSI standard specifies the minimum requirements for the permanence of paper for printed library material (see the copyright page of this book). A small portion, consisting of at least one thousand standards, are infused with more significant implications for the public interest.

The largest component of this group involve matters of public health and safety. Private standards affect the public interest in other areas, of course, such as finance and communications. For example, the Financial Accounting Standards Board, an entirely private organization, develops the influential Statements of Financial Accounting Standards (SFASs) that form the bases of "generally accepted accounting principles."[2] Similarly, the National Advertising Review Board and, to a lesser extent, the National Association of Broadcasters privately regulate advertising. But this study focuses on private safety standards, a field that roughly parallels the distinct domain of public regulation often placed under the rubric of "environment, health, and safety" regulation.

The subset of private standards that directly concern public health and safety is fairly well delineated. The best measure comes from the American National Standards Institute, an organization that certifies standards written by other groups. For reasons discussed in later chapters, most, but not all, private standards-setters seek ANSI approval. ANSI classifies approximately 900 of its 8,500 certified standards under the rubric of "Safety and Health."[3] These standards cover a fantastic array from the obviously important (Criteria for Accident Monitoring Functions in Light-Water-Cooled Nuclear Reactors) to the seemingly trivial (Safety Standard for Christmas Tree Lights). Some of ANSI's safety and health standards are procedural (Storage and Handling of Mixed Fluid Fertilizers); others are substantive (Safety Requirements for Baling Equipment). A few are massive in scope. The Boiler and Pressure Vessel Code, for example, fills twenty-four volumes. Others take up just a page (Safety Standard for Agricultural Equipment), although obviously there is no way to tell from the name alone.

The ANSI list omits some significant private organizations involved in environment, health, and safety regulation. Building code organizations, for example, play a critical role in public safety. Building codes, which vary by region and by type of construction, make reference to countless ANSI standards. But the codes themselves are not certified by ANSI. Nor does ANSI list many safety standards developed in connection with the insurance industry. The Factory Mutual Research Corporation, for example, develops loss control standards for industrial and commercial policyholders insured by the Factory Mutual System. This extensive private regulatory system, founded in 1835, consists of hundreds of engineers and technicians, along with a cadre of inspectors who implement FM's "Approval Standards." In short, the ANSI estimate of nine hundred private "health and safety" standards includes many, but not all, of the relevant standards.

Private standards-setting occurs under several institutional arrangements. Four basic forms of organization account for nearly all private standards: (1) trade associations, (2) professional societies, (3) general membership organizations, and (4) third-party certifiers. These organizations have different forms of governance, and they rely on a variety of administrative procedures. But a few core concepts permeate these organizations: one is "consensus" decisionmaking; the other is due process.

Organizational Forms of Private Standards-Setting

Trade associations are probably the best known and the least trusted form of private standards-setting. Since trade associations are created to advance the interests of their (usually homogeneous) memberships, it is widely assumed that their standards will be anticompetitive or otherwise against the public interest. But only some trade association standards have significant implications for the public interest. Most facilitate commerce in a rather mundane fashion. The Diamond Walnut Growers, for example, develop standards for the size, color, and grade defects for in-shell walnuts. Other trade associations develop a full array of such relatively innocuous standards. The American Petroleum Institute, for example, maintains 350 standards concerning the transportation, refining, production, measurement, and marketing of petroleum products. Trade association standards are usually financed directly by the membership, reinforcing the concern that narrow private interests will capture the process. But trade associations account for only a small portion of ANSI-certified health and safety standards.

Professional societies and general membership organizations bring together a broader spectrum of participants than trade associations. Rather than being tied to one economic interest, the memberships of these organizations are diverse. There are numerous professional societies organized around the specialties of engineering. For example, the Society of Automotive Engineers (forty-four thousand members) maintains over a thousand standards for ground vehicles and several thousand more for aerospace applications. Similar organizations include the

American Society of Agricultural Engineers (167 standards), the American Society of Heating, Refrigeration, and Air-Conditioning Engineers (60 standards), and American Society of Lubrication Engineers (22 standards).[4] These organizations generally develop technical standards (for example, definitions, specifications, and tolerances), few of which are very controversial or significant to the public interest.

Membership organizations are broader in constituency, but not necessarily in purpose. They are more open than trade associations, often including participants from various professions and competing aspects of industry. The American Society for Testing and Materials, often called "the world's largest source of voluntary consensus standards," has almost thirty thousand members and seven thousand standards. Most of its standards resemble those of an engineering society. In other words, very few have significant implications for public policy. The National Fire Protection Association (NFPA), by contrast, has a similar number of members and about one-thirtieth the number of standards (approximately 250), but *all* NFPA standards concern public safety. One important feature that membership organizations have in common is loose reliance on the market demand for their standards: 77 percent of ASTM's budget comes from publication sales; NFPA derives two-thirds of its income from the sale of standards.

The final form of private standards-setting is so different from the others that it is often given a separate name: certification.[5] "Third-party certifiers" test products against standards. They collect a fee for certifying compliance, which is usually signified by affixing a label or seal to the product. While some testing laboratories rely on standards developed by other organizations, the most significant product certifiers are also standards-setters. The most prominent of these organizations is Underwriters Laboratories, a nonprofit organization with the motto Testing for Public Safety. In-house engineers develop UL's standards. Less well known organizations engaged in third-party certification include the National Sanitation Foundation (which certifies restaurant equipment) and the International Association of Plumbing and Mechanical Officials (a model building code organization that certifies compliance of various products with the code). Some trade associations, such as the Association of Home Appliance Manufacturers and the Snowmobile Safety and Certification Committee, provide specialized certification services, which can generate significant income for them.[6]

A few administrative procedures characterize almost all of these organizations. One is "consensus" decisionmaking. The other, surpris-

TABLE 2   SELECTED FEATURES OF NINE
PRIVATE STANDARDS-SETTERS

	Founding Date	Standards Staff[a]	Active Standards
ACGIH	1938	2	600[b]
AGA Labs	1918	10	65
ANSI	1918	110	8,500[c]
ASME	1880	74	500
ASTM	1898	200	7,218
BOCA	1915	36	6
NFPA	1896	30	260
SBCCI	1940	10	7
UL	1894	50[d]	520

SOURCE: U.S. Department of Commerce, National Bureau of Standards, *Standards Activities of Organizations in the United States*, NBS Special Publication 681 (Washington, D.C.: Government Printing Office, August 1984).

[a]Organization staff only; does not include "volunteers," who, in many cases, actually write the standards.

[b]Threshold Limit Values cover this many chemicals.

[c]These standards are all developed by other organizations.

[d]Standards department only; does not include engineers and inspectors. The total number of UL employees in 1984 was 3,107.

ingly, is due process. These tenets form the basis for ANSI certification of private standards and are incorporated into the by-laws of many private standards-setting organizations. Although the extent of due process protections varies by organization, and the real-world implications of "consensus" decisionmaking are not clear, these concepts obviously play an important role in how these organizations define themselves.

Profiles of Prominent Private Standards-Setters

Lacking a more detailed description of the universe of private safety standards, perhaps the best way to understand this territory is through its major landmarks. Some of the most prominent private standards-setters in the field of public safety are described briefly below. These organizations vary significantly in age and size (see table 2). Four of them—ANSI, AGA Labs, NFPA, and UL—are examined in detail in later chapters.

ANSI.   The American National Standards Institute is unique among these groups, acting as an overall coordinator and certifier of the so-called voluntary national standards system. It is the trade association of the standards-writing industry. ANSI does not write standards. Other organizations, including ANSI committees—groups "accredited" by ANSI—submit their standards for approval as American National Standards. There are approximately 8,500 ANSI-approved standards (1,000 of which were developed by ANSI committees). The requirements for ANSI certification, discussed later in this chapter, are essentially procedural, not substantive. The Board of Standards Review hears complaints from anyone who objects to certification of a "national consensus standard." Appeals are infrequent, except in the area of "health and safety." Approximately 900 ANSI-certified standards are in this category. ANSI's membership consists of industry representatives and standards-setting organizations (including professional and technical societies, trade associations, and government agencies).

ACGIH.   The American Conference of Government Industrial Hygienists publishes an annual compilation of Threshold Limit Values— recommendations on airborne contaminants and physical agents in workplaces—for approximately six hundred chemical substances. These values influence industrial practice in the United States and in a host of countries abroad. Despite the implication of its name, ACGIH is a private organization with no formal links to the public sector. The organization was founded in 1938 by federal, state, and local health officials. Its committees now include academics and industry representatives. A recent study of "Corporate Influence on Threshold Limit Values" concludes that there are "104 substances for which important or total reliance was placed on unpublished corporate communications."[7]

AGA Labs.   The American Gas Association Laboratories, a division of the larger trade association, is sometimes referred to as "the UL for gas appliances." Founded in 1918, AGA Labs provides third-party certification for all gas appliances. It currently maintains sixty-five standards. Unlike UL's, these standards are not developed by in-house engineers. They are developed by ANSI-sponsored committees consisting of various representatives, largely from industry.

ASME.   The American Society of Mechanical Engineers is a nonprofit educational and technical organization with 110,000 members and nearly six hundred active standards. ASME's reputation is based almost entirely on one standard: the Boiler and Pressure Vessel Code, a compilation of safety and performance requirements for power and heating boilers, nuclear reactors and power plants, and pressure vessels, which is widely incorporated into law throughout the United States and Canada. ASME's image was tarnished in 1983 when, after it refused to settle an antitrust case involving a blatantly anticompetitive interpretation of the Boiler and Pressure Vessel Code, the Supreme Court upheld a $9.5 million judgment against the organization. ASME argued that it should not be responsible for the acts of volunteers acting in bad faith.[8]

ASTM.   The American Society for Testing and Materials, founded in 1898, is a nonprofit organization "to develop standards on characteristics and performance of materials, products, systems, and services." A staff of two hundred oversees the maintenance of 7,218 standards, most of them standards for uniformity. A few committees act in a more overtly regulatory fashion. The F-15 Committee (consumer products) has developed a dozen standards for products such as high chairs, cigarette lighters, and bathtub grab bars. ASTM standards are written by "volunteer" committees and subject to the approval of ASTM's thirty thousand members. ANSI has long been an organizational rival of ASTM's. The organizations trade allegations of "turf grabbing," and ASTM no longer submits its standards for certification as American National Standards.

Building Code Organizations: ICBO, BOCA, SBCCI.   Building codes, enforced by local building inspectors, are one of the most visible forms of government safety regulation. They are largely written, however, by a complicated web of overlapping private standards-setters. Four model code organizations dominate the field. The International Conference of Building Officials (ICBO) promulgates fourteen comprehensive codes covering various aspects of construction. These codes make reference to nearly one thousand ASTM, UL, NFPA, and ANSI standards. The best known, the Uniform Building Code, is enforced in jurisdictions from Michigan and Indiana to Alaska and Hawaii. The Southern Building Code Congress International (SBCCI) and the Building Officials and Code Administrators International (BOCA) each promulgate similar sets of building, plumbing, mechanical, gas, fire, and housing codes. The SBCCI codes have been adopted in over 1,600 communities in the Southwest, South, and Southeast; the BOCA codes cover fourteen states and 3,000 local governments in the East and Midwest. Finally, the Council of American Building Code Officials (CABO), created by the three major building code organizations, attempts to coordinate activities, particularly with regard to product certification. There are myriad other actors in the field of building codes, many providing specialized standards that are incorporated into building codes. The CABO One-and-Two Family Dwelling Code, for example, mandates, among other things, compliance with ANSI Z21.11.2 (the private safety standard for unvented gas space heaters, examined in chapter 6). The International Association of Plumbing and Mechanical Officals, author of fifty-seven product and installation standards, develops the Uniform Plumbing Code, adopted in the building codes of over 2,500 jurisdictions.

NFPA.   The National Fire Protection Association is a membership organization similar to ASTM. "Volunteer" committees write the 260 NFPA codes and standards, and the membership votes en masse at semiannual conventions. NFPA has over thirty-two thousand members, including architects, engineers, firemen, manufacturers, and representatives of insurance interests, labor, and government. NFPA standards are published as the National Fire Codes in a multivolume set consisting of over twelve thousand pages. Various NFPA standards are referenced by OSHA, the Coast Guard, the Veterans Administration, and the Department of Housing and Urban Development. Its best-known codes, the National Electric Code and the Life Safety Code, have the force of law in most jurisdictions. Other standards cover the fire risks at nuclear power plants, airports, storage tanks, and grain elevators.

UL.   The primary business of Underwriters Laboratories is product safety certification. UL evaluates products and monitors the quality control of their production. Manufacturers pay for the service, and if their products comply, they are entitled to display the UL label. There are other testing laboratories—most prominently, the American Gas Association Laboratories in the field of gas appliances—but many simply certify compliance to UL standards. The most important feature of UL is that it writes the standards it uses in testing. There are over five hundred published UL standards, covering such diverse products as microwave ovens, life preservers, kerosene heaters, fire extinguishers, and automated teller systems. UL maintains membership in five hundred committees of other private standards-setting organizations.

The Universe of Public Safety Standards

Public standards seem both more visible and more controversial than private ones. In the areas of environment, health, and safety, most of the federal agencies that develop standards are practically household names: EPA, OSHA, FAA, FDA. Other federal agencies, involved in similar missions, have less name recognition, but they are nevertheless well known for what they do. The National Highway Traffic Safety Administration (NHTSA), the Nuclear Regulatory Commission (NRC), and the Consumer Product Safety Commission, for example, all write safety standards in areas where public regulation is widely recognized and generally supported.

These agencies vary considerably in size. It is difficult to compare the number of standards they develop because public standards usually come in packages, rather than individually. Unlike the private sector, where separate committees develop discrete standards on a project-by-project basis, public agencies take a range of actions from the adoption of single standards to the implementation of complex statutes. The Code of Federal Regulations is not divided by individual standards. For example, the safety standards of the NRC comprise 850 pages in one title of the code, which by one count represents approximately 350 standards. In contrast, the subchapter of the code concerning biological products regulated by the FDA accounts for approximately 325 standards.[9] Lacking a comparable measure of actual standards-setting activity, the relative size of these agencies can roughly be gauged by their budgets and staff (see table 3).

These agencies also vary considerably in age, reflecting the three waves of public regulation this century. The Food and Drug Administration (FDA) and the Federal Trade Commission (FTC) are the oldest, reflecting the Progressive Era, when federal regulation began. The FDA was created in 1906, the FTC in 1914. The Federal Aviation Administration (FAA) evolved from a New Deal agency, the Civil Aeronautics Board (1938), created along with a host of agencies primarily engaged in economic regulation (for example, the Securities and Exchange Commission and the National Labor Relations Board). The most controversial federal agencies are also the youngest. These agencies spearhead the "new social regulation" movement, a grandiose agenda of environment, health, and safety objectives adopted about twenty years ago. The most prominent are the EPA, OSHA, NHTSA, NRC, and CPSC. Although other strategies would be possible, these agencies generally favor

TABLE 3   SELECTED FEATURES OF SIX PUBLIC
AGENCIES INVOLVED IN SAFETY REGULATION, 1988

Agency	Founding Date	Budget[a]	Staff[b]
CPSC	1972	32,696	459
EPA	1970	4,968,429	11,127
FAA	1958	2,367,778	46,811
FDA	1906	483,066	7,032
NHTSA	1970	62,534	503
OSHA	1970	235,474	2,532

SOURCE: *Federal Budget, 1988* (Washington, D.C.: Government Printing Office, 1988).
[a]Appropriate funds only; does not include highway or airport trust funds.
[b]Full-time staff only.

"command and control" regulation, which relies on standards, inspectors, and penalties to achieve social ends. One important feature common to all of them is the Administrative Procedures Act (APA), which describes two kinds of rulemaking, formal and informal. Most agencies favor the latter but implement it in a "hybrid" fashion that incorporates some due process protections beyond those demanded by the APA.[10]

Agencies concerned with environment, health, and safety regulation account for only a small portion of all federal standards. By one count, the federal government maintains more standards than the private sector. According to the National Bureau of Standards, there were forty-nine thousand standards in 1983.[11] As in the private sector, however, most of these are not particularly weighty. The overwhelming number are procurement standards adopted by either the Department of Defense (38,000) or the General Services Administration (6,000). The number of federal standards with significant implications for the public interest is minuscule by comparison.

In most areas involving the environment, health, or safety, there are far more private standards than public ones. Take consumer product safety, for example. Hundreds of private standards are developed by UL alone. In contrast, the relevant federal agency, the CPSC, had twenty-one active standards in 1984, many of which were carry-overs from old statutes.[12] A few others seem absolutely frivolous. Not coincidentally, these standards (matchbooks, swimming pool slides) were overturned in court. This leaves only a handful of safety standards actually developed by the CPSC—most prominently, standards for lawn mowers, gas-fired space heaters, electrical toys, and citizens band base station antennas.

In most areas that government seeks to regulate there are already so many private standards that interaction between the two sectors is inevitable. Model codes and use codes, including most standards developed by the National Fire Protection Association, contain repeated references to "the authority having jurisdiction." In other words, they are written in anticipation of adoption by government (usually at the local level). The federal agencies that regulate safety issues are also intertwined with the private sector. Many federal agencies rely directly on private standards to accomplish public purposes. The FDA, for example, has adopted over three hundred standards from private organizations such as ASTM, the American Public Health Association, and the Association of Official Analytical Chemists. The National Highway Traffic Safety Administration, by contrast, uses private standards (developed by the Society of Automotive Engineers) for test methods and other largely technical matters, while leaving basic safety questions to the public realm. Most agencies participate in private standards-setting activities. The CPSC, which originally had a procedure for private organizations to "offer" standards for agency adoption, has participated in the development of hundreds of private standards. The Nuclear Regulatory Commission participates on more than 150 private standards committees. Although interaction and coexistence prevail, there remain distinct areas of public regulation.

Research Design

Making a direct comparison of public and private standards-setting practically requires that the two sectors be active in the same area. Otherwise, whether outcomes or procedures are evaluated, case studies in either sector will leave the same lingering question: compared to what? The criterion of economic efficiency, often a useful benchmark, probably has limited potential. "Determining the proper level of product safety is next to impossible," note Eads and Reuter in the introduction to their case studies of corporate safety efforts.[13] Without independently conducting cost-benefit analyses, it is doubtful that existing information will facilitate anything more than a crude analysis of outcomes.

An obvious answer to the benchmark problem is to compare the private sector directly with the public. After all, the most important public policy questions about private standards are comparative. What really matters in assessing possible government action is how that action compares to the actual alternatives. One can only speculate whether public standards would actually be stricter in the thousands of areas presently regulated exclusively by private standards. But in the areas where public and private efforts overlap, outcomes can be evaluated comparatively.

If appropriate "pairs" can be found, the comparative approach has two obvious advantages. First, it solves the benchmark problem. Without a comparative framework, it is difficult to imagine how to evaluate either public or private standards in a fashion that will shed light on the other sector. The exercise would be entirely hypothetical: guessing what the other sector might have done. Second, the comparative approach might also facilitate broader generalizations by "controlling" for the idiosyncrasies of issues. It is frequently alleged that general theories of regulation are fruitless because circumstances such as industry profitability and structure, the quality of available information, and the mixture of political interests vary significantly by issue. A related argument, relevant to the study of public and private regulation, is that only certain types of issues are regulated by government. Government, the argument goes, regulates the issues that industry will not, making the public cases unique. Both of these arguments fade if the public and private sectors are active in the same area.

There are drawbacks, however, to studying only those cases in which public and private efforts can be paired. First, the universe of possible cases is very small. Public and private standards rarely regulate the same things. Moreover, when there is overlap, there is the attendant danger that the effects of their interaction will obscure the influences that might otherwise prevail. In other words, the observed outcomes might reflect "strategic behavior" more than they reflect the indigenous characteristics of either sector. If either sector acts strategically—that is, based primarily on the anticipated response from the other sector—then the pairs themselves might be idiosyncratic. In other words, special patterns of regulatory behavior might characterize such pairs. One likely pattern is "splitting the territory"—the strategy by which both sectors adapt their behavior to avoid direct overlap. This problem is not unique to actual pairs, however. Strategic behavior is considered a primary characteristic of most private standards-setting. The nature and significance of the pair problem is examined in chapter 8.

The possibilities for "paired" case studies are limited mainly by the comparatively narrow scope of government regulation. There are private safety standards in almost every field where there are government standards. With so little known about these standards and the organizations that write them, however, it is difficult to know how potential case studies from the private sector fit into the larger universe of standards-setting.

Several considerations guided the choice of cases for this study. First, in order to permit an actual comparison of public and private decision-making, the cases had to overlap in content but have some degree of independence in development. In some cases, similar content denotes a lack of independent effort. Sometimes, a government standard is nothing more than a private standard with the force of law. The HUD mobile home standard was originally written by NFPA. The FDA relies largely on UL to evaluate microwave ovens. In other cases, the overlap is in title only. With many of the automotive safety standards, for example, the private sector (the Society of Automotive Engineers) writes test methods in areas where government standards specify performance levels.

These considerations narrowed the apparent field of possible pairs considerably, leading to the second consideration: how "representative" the pairs would be of the public and private sector. Recognizing that it would be impossible to select truly representative pairs without knowing more about the universe, particularly on the private side, selection was based on reputation. A primary goal was to examine private organizations with the best possible reputations, a variation on deviant-case analysis. Examining "best case" examples should provide a basis for estimating the outer bounds of the private sector's potential. Conversely, it should avoid the criticism that the sample is tilted toward the "bad apples."

By this reasoning, the most suspect class of private standards-setting organizations—trade associations—was eliminated from further consideration. Trade associations seem least likely to advance public purposes because of the narrow scope of their interests. Although trade associations vary more than is often appreciated, few have sufficient independence from immediate membership demands to seek a more enlightened, long-term course.[14] The remaining organizations—professional societies, general membership organizations, and third-party certifiers—are not necessarily better, but their form of organization suggests greater potential for something beyond parochialism.

Within this grouping, UL clearly had to be one of the private organizations studied. It is not only the oldest and best-established private standards-setter; according to knowledgeable observers, it is also widely thought to be more independent and public-spirited than other private organizations. In addition, UL is most active in consumer products, an area in which standards policy may be most significant. Not coincidentally, there is practically no overlap between UL's standards and the few that have been successfully promulgated by the Consumer Product Safety Commission. UL actively seeks to keep the CPSC off its turf. The CPSC has considered getting involved in many areas regulated by UL, but the only case of dual standards is that of woodstoves. Accordingly, that is the first pair in this study.

The overlap between UL and the CPSC is minimal in the woodstove case. Instead of developing a product standard for woodstoves, the CPSC supplemented UL's product standard with a labeling standard—an unusual form of CPSC regulation. Therefore, although the woodstove case offers an opportunity to examine UL, it appears to provide a peculiar view of the CPSC. Selection of the second pair was motivated by a desire to balance the woodstove case with one in which the CPSC adopted a full-fledged product standard—its more usual role in regulation. Given the CPSC's relative inaction in recent years, there were only two possibilities: lawn mowers and gas space heaters. The private sector's lawn mower standard was adopted by an ANSI committee under the sponsorship of the Outdoor Power Equipment Institute; the gas space heater standard was also adopted by an ANSI committee, but under the supervision of the American Gas Association Laboratories. The latter was chosen for two reasons. First, the gas space heater case is more recent, minimizing the chance that subsequent changes in either the public or private sector would render the findings outdated. Second, the lawn mower case has been studied many times; gas space heaters have not.[15]

Desire for a "best case" example of public standards-setting motivated the selection of the remaining cases. The CPSC may provide close to the "worst case" example of government regulation. The agency's short history has been marked by failure and poor judgment.[16] (An American Enterprise Institute study in 1983 suggested abolishing the CPSC.)[17] In order to ensure that the pairs were more representative of the potential for government regulation, the remaining cases had to involve government agencies with better reputations.

The possibilities included automobile safety (where there is some overlap between NHTSA and the Society of Automotive Engineers), nuclear power safety, aviation safety, and grain elevator safety. The first two were eliminated for practical reasons—they appeared to require a researcher to have substantial engineering (and possibly physics) background. Accordingly, the remaining cases were selected as the third and fourth pairs. In aviation safety, the FAA's 1984 proposal concerning fire extinguishers and smoke detectors overlaps directly with an NFPA standard. Although the FAA is criticized occasionally for an inadequate inspection and maintenance program, the agency enjoys strong congressional support and a surprising level of industry support for its regulatory activities.

The grain elevator case involves an OSHA standard, also paired with an NFPA one. Although OSHA's reputation, unlike the FAA's, is only a little better than the CPSC's, this case study seemed appropriate for three reasons. First, it looked at "the new OSHA"—that is, OSHA under President Reagan. The grain elevator standard is one of only a few OSHA standards promulgated under the Reagan administration, and as such it might not be prone to the perceived excesses of previous OSHA standards. Second, like the CPSC, OSHA addresses the kinds of issues in which questions about the relationship between public and private standards are most likely to arise. Finally, the grain elevator case offered a research opportunity unavailable on the private side of the other selected cases: to observe the revision process in action. The NFPA grain elevator standard was due to be revised at a two-day subcommittee meeting in July 1985, offering an opportunity to observe the committee responding to comments and deliberating over specific language. This seemed likely to make possible a more complete and realistic view of private standards-setting than the other case studies (based as they are on documents and after-the-fact interviews).

Notes on Fieldwork

The fieldwork for the case studies was conducted from September to December 1984 in Washington, D.C., New York, and Boston, and from May to July 1985 in Chicago, Cleveland, New York, Washington, D.C., and Minneapolis. Seventy-two detailed interviews were conducted, approximately half of which were tape-recorded and transcribed (a list of these is given in the Appendix). Additional information on the research method is contained in notes that precede the bibliographies for each case.

A major problem encountered during the fieldwork, but not anticipated in designing the research, was access. As it turned out, initial
contacts with Underwriters Laboratories were met with suspicion and
an assertion that UL would not permit its engineers to be interviewed.
The NFPA, which professes openness, was also hesitant about providing certain documents and allowing attendance at subcommittee meetings. These organizations are more secretive than they appear. They are
sued with regularity and are not anxious to talk about it. Moreover,
they have been on the defensive since the FTC began its investigation of
standards and certification. Shortly before this fieldwork began, *Mother
Jones* magazine ran an article containing criticisms of UL.[18] A few years
earlier the "60 Minutes" television program did a critical story on the
American Gas Association Laboratory.

In both cases, personal contact eventually resulted in access: UL's
representative in Washington, D.C., arranged for access to UL's engineers, and after a lengthy personal meeting, an NFPA vice president
provided assistance in obtaining documents. Even so, a few NFPA committee members were unwilling to discuss their work in detail, and
several UL engineers were quite guarded in conversation. During the
course of the fieldwork, the FAA standard on fire extinguishers and
smoke detectors was approved. The OSHA standard on grain elevators
was adopted two years after conclusion of the fieldwork.

The other unexpected development during the course of the fieldwork involved revelations about the relationship between product standards and installation codes. An apparent advantage of the initial case
selection appeared to be the diversity of private standards-writers; the
four pairs involved three different organizations (UL, AGA, and NFPA).
It turns out that NFPA plays an important role in the standards of both
UL and AGA Labs. Accordingly, the case studies contain much more
information about the NFPA than originally expected. This points up a
potentially important distinction between codes and standards that was
not understood during the research design. The two are so different that
they are probably best studied separately. However, this discovery bears
out the decision to do case studies in order to identify such factors,
instead of doing a broader survey.

PART TWO

Case Studies

THREE

Safety Standards for Grain Elevators

Private regulation is often characterized as weak or diluted, a kind of lowest common denominator of prevailing business practices. Many private standards are considered largely defensive, motivated by the desire to forestall government regulation. Public standards, by contrast, are thought to be more stringent than their private counterparts, sometimes unreasonably so. Public regulation is also considered inordinately cumbersome, laden with procedural requirements and judicial appeals.

These conceptions of public and private regulation are borne out substantially in the case of grain elevator safety. The private standard (NFPA 61B) is generally lax, reflecting industry's desire to avoid meaningful regulation of dust-control practices. The public sector, on the other hand, developed a more demanding standard but spent almost ten years in the process. The Office of Management and Budget shares the conclusion of the National Grain and Feed Association (NGFA) that the OSHA regulation is burdensome and unreasonable. As with so many regulatory issues, however, the relevant data are weak and inconclusive. Proponents and critics advance plausible, but divergent, arguments, each as good as its unsure assumptions. OSHA's grain elevator standard, for reasons argued below, actually seems worthwhile. It fills the gap in existing practices and is likely to produce benefits in excess of costs.

The importance of this case is twofold. First, it contributes to the conventional wisdom by providing specific details about actual behavior and suggesting ways in which this behavior is affected by institutional design and external influences. Two popular explanations of public regulation—"capture" theory and Bernstein's "life-cycle" theory—have been discredited for their incompleteness. The "life cycle" is a vivid metaphor, but it lacks causal content about the force and nature of the regulatory "aging" process.[1] Similarly, capture theory has been challenged by the rise in social regulation, where government actions are opposed, not favored, by the regulated.[2] This case study illuminates several aspects of the conventional wisdom about public and private standards. For example, the enforcement ethic in the public sector tempered OSHA's willingness to adjust the regulatory burden on certain low-risk facilities.

Second, this case highlights an aspect of NFPA's behavior that does not fit the conventional image of private regulation. Several provisions in NFPA 61B are surprisingly strict. When judged by the criteria used to evaluate public regulation, a few NFPA provisions appear to be unreasonable. This suggests a previously unrecognized aspect of private regulatory behavior. Private standards-setting is not all "lowest common denominator" politics. There is a mixture of managerial behavior (marked by considerations of politics and economics) and technical behavior (permeated by the ethos of engineers). Managerial considerations explain the biggest weakness in NFPA 61B: favoring one regulatory approach to dust hazards (ignition control) to the complete exclusion of another technique (dust control). But some realms of private decisionmaking are dominated by technical, more than managerial, influences. The "technical" provisions in NFPA 61B are the most stringent. Technical influences help explain why NFPA 61B was developed more than fifty years before OSHA considered writing a standard. This case indicates how professional engineers alter the dynamics of private regulatory decisionmaking. These influences are sketched in greater detail in later chapters; but first the story of public and private efforts to regulate grain elevator safety.

Grain Elevators and the Explosion Problem

Grain elevators come in all sizes and shapes. Some are connected to processing facilities, others serve only as bulk storage. Bulk storage facilities are often grouped into three functional categories that roughly correlate with their size: country elevators (the smallest), inland terminals, and export terminals (the largest).[3] Differences in function, product, and capacity have all been urged as reasons for avoiding safety standards of general application. Feed mills, for example, have a much better safety record than bulk grain storage facilities.[4] Some "country elevators" handle grain only a few days a year, obviously minimizing the opportunities for accidents. The significance of these distinctions for safety regulation is unclear because throughput—the amount of grain moved through a facility—has a more direct bearing on safety than function or capacity.[5]

The Explosion Problem

Of all the hazards associated with grain handling, the most serious one is also the most difficult for those outside the grain business to understand. It is grain dust. This dust, generated whenever grain is handled, is easier to ignite and results in a more severe explosion than equal quantities of TNT. One insurance company distributes placards with the warning "Grain dust is like high explosives." Dust explosions account for the vast majority of personal injuries and property losses in grain-handling facilities. There are thousands of small fires in these facilities every year; estimates range from 2,970 to 11,000. But the twenty to thirty explosions a year account for almost 80 percent of the property damage and 95 percent of the fatalities[6] (see table 4). Making sense of these trends over time is complicated by the changing fortunes of the grain trade. The major explosions in 1977–78 coincided with tremendous increases in wheat exports (primarily to the Soviet Union). The comparatively low number of explosions in recent years, on the other hand, is attributable in part to decreases in grain sales.[7] Fluctuations in trade patterns notwithstanding, the explosion problem remains the most serious hazard in grain elevators.

Contrary to popular belief, explosions in grain elevators are not caused by spontaneous combustion. To cause an explosion, the dust must be mixed with air to form a dense cloud. (Layered dust only smolders upon ignition.) The airborne dust concentrations must also be above the lower explosive limit (LEL), a condition so opaque that visibility is minimal and breathing is difficult. Concentrations above the LEL occur regularly inside most bucket elevators (described below) but seldom elsewhere in a facility. Also contrary to popular belief, grain elevator explosions are not one big blast. They usually involve a primary explosion and a series of secondary ones.[8] The primary explosion generates shock waves throughout the elevator, often raising into sus-

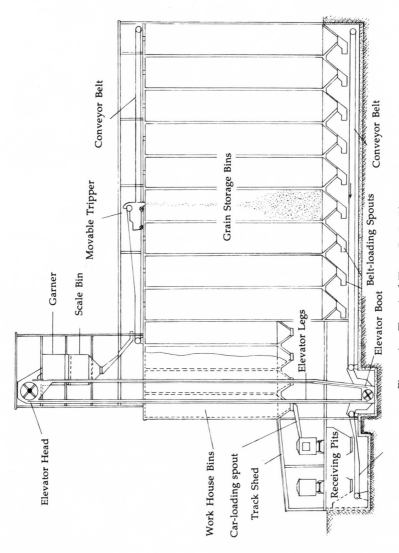

Elevator Head

Garner

Scale Bin

Movable Tripper

Conveyor Belt

Grain Storage Bins

Belt-loading Spouts

Conveyor Belt

Elevator Boot

Elevator Legs

Work House Bins

Car-loading spout

Track Shed

Receiving Pits

Figure 1. Terminal-Type Grain Elevator

TABLE 4   CASUALTIES RESULTING FROM EXPLOSIONS
IN THE U.S. GRAIN-HANDLING INDUSTRY, 1976–87

	Explosions	Deaths	Injuries
1976	22	22	83
1977	31	65	87
1978	20	8	46
1979	29	2	18
1980	45	10	50
1981	21	13	62
1982	14	11	32
1983	13	0	14
1984	20	9	30
1985	22	4	20
1986	21	2	14
1987	15	0	18
Total	273	146	474
Average/Year	23	12	40

SOURCE: "Some Impacts of a Proposed OSHA Standard in Grain Handling Facilities" (Report prepared by Booz, Allen & Hamilton, Inc., April 1984); Petition for Partial Stay of Grain Handling Facilities Standard, *In the Matter of Grain Handling Facilities*, March 21, 1988, 5 n. 5.

pension layered dust on walls, rafters, equipment, and the floor. Accumulations of as little as one-hundredth of an inch will propagate the flame from an initial explosion. In other words, layered dust provides the fuel to turn a primary explosion—often itself quite minor—into a major one.

There are two basic schools of thought about how to approach the explosion hazard: one, eliminate ignition sources; two, control airborne and layered dust. Although it seems obvious that neither strategy should be pursued exclusively, the debate over safety standards is often between groups that have a strong preference for one approach.

The Ignition-Control Strategy

Industry's inclination, according to a former USDA investigator, is to concentrate on ignition sources. Ignition occurs most frequently in the bucket elevator—a continuous conveyor belt with equally spaced buckets (often metal) that elevates the grain and discharges it into a spout (see figure 1). The top section of a bucket elevator, where the drive is located, is referred to as the "head." The bottom section, where grain enters the elevator, is known as the "boot." The "leg" connects the head and the boot.

Ignition sources are varied and often notoriously difficult to pinpoint. In a study of fourteen explosions, the USDA identified ten different "probable sources," the largest group (four) being "unknown."[9] Most studies agree that welding or cutting (also known as "hot work") is the largest known ignition source, accounting for perhaps 10 to 20 percent of all explosions. Other common ignition sources include electrical failure, overheated bearings, foreign metal objects sparking inside the leg, and friction in choked legs. "Jogging the leg"—trying to free a jammed bucket conveyor by repeatedly stopping and starting the driving motor—is a primary cause of friction-induced explosions.

Ignition-source control can take several forms. One is mechanical. Mechanisms including electromagnets and special grates can minimize the problem of metal objects entering the grain stream. Belt speed, alignment, and heat monitors can be used to detect hazardous conditions and shut down the equipment before suspended dust is ignited. The effectiveness of these devices varies, but quality has improved since their introduction to the grain-handling industry ten or fifteen years ago. Another approach to ignition control is behavioral. Employees are instructed not to jog the legs. Rules against smoking are strictly enforced. Permit procedures are instituted to ensure that hot work is done safely, and preventative maintenance schedules are instituted and implemented.

Whatever the combination of mechanical and behavioral requirements, ignition-source control has two limitations. First, there are countless potential ignition sources. The National Academy of Sciences (NAS) has reported the results of two surveys in which the ignition source remained unknown in over half the cases. Virtually every piece of equipment, as well as every grain transfer point, is a potential ignition source. Eliminating or controlling them all seems impossible. Second, as an NAS panelist put it, "ignition control is fine if you have perfect people; but people will make mistakes and then the equipment fails." A common example is jogging jammed conveyors instead of inspecting and digging out the elevator boot. This problem has been recognized for years, yet it persists largely unabated. According to an insurance representative, operators of some country elevators encourage this time-saving but risky practice. In short, everyone agrees that good operating procedures are a good idea. They are also inherently difficult to enforce. Since operational breakdowns are inevitable, critics consider this loss control method inadequate by itself.

The Housekeeping Strategy

The other school of thought about grain elevator safety is enamored of—some say preoccupied with—"housekeeping" (or dust control). The label can be misleading to the extent that it conjures up only images of brooms and vacuum cleaners. Dust control is aimed at both airborne and layered dust. Airborne dust can be removed by various systems of aspiration, also called pneumatic ("moved or worked by air pressure)" dust control. Pneumatic dust-control systems have four major components: hoods or other enclosures; ductwork; a filter, or dust collector; and an exhaust fan. Layered dust can also be removed automatically, but in all but the largest facilities it is removed manually: with vacuum cleaners, brooms, compressed air, and, in some cases, water.

Both types of housekeeping (pneumatic dust control and layered dust removal) are controversial, but in the first case the disagreement is mostly technical, while in the second it is largely a matter of economics. The technical potential of pneumatic dust control is highly disputed. One grain elevator insurance company touts a system it claims can reduce dust concentrations in the bucket elevator below the lower explosive limit. The technology was not proven to the satisfaction of a 1982 NAS panel, but panel members placed a high priority on continued research in this area.[10] Many in the industry still consider such technology unavailable. Others claim to have used it successfully.[11] Both are probably right, as the design of pneumatic dust-control systems is, according to a Cargill engineer, "more of an art than a science." Engineers cannot simply take specifications for the desired concentration of airborne dust (or rate of accumulation for layered dust) and design a system that will perform accordingly. The technology for removing airborne dust is too uncertain. Much depends on how the system is installed and maintained.

Layered dust poses much less of a technical problem. How to remove it effectively is not very controversial (although the virtues of vacuuming versus sweeping are a minor topic of disagreement). For large facilities, dust removal is usually part of normal operations. Sweeping is done at least once per shift at all export facilities. But for many smaller facilities, removing layered dust means hiring additional labor and slowing down operations when they are most profitable. Few quarrel with the conclusion of the NAS that housekeeping and maintenance are often given low priority and are usually the first tasks postponed when there is a rush of business.[12] A grain company representative on the NFPA Technical Committee on Agricultural Dusts concurs that "there are many, many filthy ones that get by." A less tactful USDA investigator describes the prevailing levels of housekeeping in grain elevators as "fair to abysmal." The main objections to stricter housekeeping rules is the cost. The controversy, in short, is managerial, not technical.

Trying to estimate the number of "bad apples" is difficult, however. "It depends on which day of the week you are counting," as one industry representative put it. There has been very little counting to date. No one even knows with precision how many elevators there are, let alone when they were all built and what kind of equipment they currently use. Harder still is determining the relative cleanliness or safety levels of grain-handling facilities. No industry group investigates or collects information on explosions. NFPA collects statistics through newspaper clippings and voluntary reporting from the fire service, but this information is hardly comprehensive. A USDA task force concluded that the NFPA estimate of annual fires in grain elevators may understate the actual situation by a factor of five.[13]

The NFPA Standard for Grain Elevators

Whatever the numbers, insurance companies have worried about grain elevators since a series of big explosions in 1919 and 1921. Responding to calls for an industrywide standard on grain elevator safety, NFPA appointed a Committee on Dust Control in Grain Elevators. Insurance interests have been major participants in NFPA's subsequent efforts. The committee, lacking sufficient information on certain aspects of the explosion problem, hired Underwriters Labs (another organization created by the insurance industry) to investigate methods of controlling floating dust in terminal grain elevators.

The results of the UL study formed the basis for the dust-control provisions in the early versions of the standard, which also contains general operation and design provisions. It has been revised at least five times since then, although many of the provisions in the most recent version can be traced back to 1953. The most significant changes were in 1970, when NFPA added country elevators (formerly governed by a separate standard) to the scope of the standard, and in 1980, when NFPA responded to the threat of imminent government regulation by strengthening the ignition-control requirements for bucket elevators.

The revision process began again with a meeting in July 1985 of the Technical Committee on Agricultural Dusts, and a revised version of NFPA 61B (hereinafter "61B") was adopted the following year.

The Agricultural Dusts committee, chaired for the past fifteen years by a representative of Continental Grain, has approximately two dozen members. Twelve to fifteen attend formal committee meetings, but all actions are subject to letter ballot by the full committee. The largest-segment of committee membership comes from the insurance industry—Industrial Risk Insurers, the Mill Mutuals, the Insurance Services Office of Nebraska, Kemper Insurance Co., and Factory Mutual Research Corp. are each represented. Two other organizations related to the insurance industry, UL and Johnson & Higgins (a brokerage firm), are represented on the committee along with Cargill, the country's largest grain company, and two major grain processors (Kellogg Co. and General Foods). Other representatives include those of a fumigant company, a fire equipment manufacturer, a manufacturer of grain-handling equipment, and several academics. Conspicuously absent from the committee roster is a representative from OSHA. "It wasn't for lack of trying," notes an NFPA staff member. Neither was it always this way. OSHA's policy on participating in private standards-setting activities has varied by administration and by issue.

Certain provisions in 61B have been a source of repeated debate over the years. Such issues, according to the current committee chairman, are brought up practically every time 61B is revised. Some of these largely technical issues are discussed below. But 61B is probably better known for what it does not cover than for what it does. Some provisions, including those on housekeeping, are so general that the standard quite literally requires nothing in particular. Additionally, owing to the retroactivity clause, most provisions apply only to new facilities, even though older facilities actually pose the most serious hazards.[14]

In its present form, 61B is a remarkably compact regulation, devoting no more than a page or two apiece to chapters on construction requirements, equipment, and dust control. Most provisions are as general as they are brief. "Extraneous material that would contribute to a fire hazard shall be removed from the commodity before it enters the [grain] dryer."[15] "Boot sections [of the elevator leg] shall be provided with adequate doors for cleanout of the entire boot and for inspection of the boot pulley and leg belt."[16]

NFPA 61B avoids almost all design details. The complex topic of explosion venting, for example, is addressed by reference to a separate NFPA venting guide that committee members agree is not particularly applicable to grain-handling facilities.[17] Similarly, dust-control systems are mentioned, but there are no performance requirements or construction specifications.[18] In contrast, the National Academy of Sciences has published a 116-page guide to designing pneumatic dust-control systems.

Housekeeping: A Gentlemen's Agreement

The most significant provision in 61B is the basic housekeeping requirement. Unlike the standard later adopted by OSHA, which contains specific action levels and alternatives for dust control, 61B dispenses with the topic by stating simply that "dust shall be removed concurrently with operations."[19] This language has been known to provoke a good laugh from Agricultural Dusts committee members pressed to explain what it really means.

Whatever it means, the provision is not enforceable. OSHA learned that when it tried to use 61B in support of citations issued after the 1977 explosions. The commission that reviews OSHA citations was unwilling to rely on such an ambiguous provision.[20] In actuality, the housekeeping provision is not a "requirement" at all. It is more of a gentlemen's agreement to recognize the problem but leave its solution entirely to the individual operator. "I think that you have to consider that people are going to be reasonable and rational about applying this," explained a Continental Grain representative at an OSHA hearing.[21]

Whether a more specific requirement would be desirable is the subject of considerable controversy. Leaving that question aside for the moment, the lack of specificity of the housekeeping requirement in 61B is not adequately justified by the reasons most commonly offered in its defense. "If someone can tell us how to be more specific and be scientifically logical" in establishing dust-control requirements, explains an Agricultural Dusts committee member from a major grain company, "we would buy it." Indeed, there is no way to do so—short of banning grain dust—if "scientific logic" demands total safety. Research sponsored by the NGFA indicates that a dust layer as thin as one-hundredth of an inch can propagate an explosion. The NGFA has been accused by its detractors of conducting this research precisely to bolster the "scientific" argument against any standard. But there rarely is a strong *scientific* basis for resolving complex problems involving the trade-off between cost and safety. If this call for greater scientific certainty applied equally to all standards-setting, it would largely paralyze the effort. There are too many variables interacting and changing over time to expect anything resembling scientific certainty for each one.

Guesses, commonsense judgments, and just plain arbitrary numbers adorn public and private standards alike. They have to. NFPA 61B is no exception. The requirement that grain driers be cleaned every 168 hours, for example, is not scientifically logical. As it turns out, 168 was chosen because that is how many hours there are in a week—a measure no more scientific than Continental Grain's policy of cleaning them every 48 hours.[22] Limiting the temperature of hot pipes to 160° F, prohibiting more than 25 percent of a roof from being plastic panel, and suggesting that motor-driven equipment be cleaned at one-hour intervals during operations are further examples of provisions in 61B that are equally susceptible to the charge of scientific infirmity.[23] In each case, the number is an admittedly arbitrary one, based on the consensus of committee members as to what constitutes a reasonable requirement.

In fact, scientific uncertainty did not prevent Continental Grain or the Factory Mutual Corporation from incorporating an "action level" of one-eight of an inch of layered dust into their own in-house standards for housekeeping.[24] So why does the NFPA Agricultural Dusts committee demand more of science? One possible reason is that the dust-control problem is more complicated than most issues. Hot pipes present similar hazards under a variety of circumstances; grain dust does not. Dust hazards depend, to some degree, on virtually every aspect of a grain-handling facility, including the product it handles, its sales and operation patterns, the general layout and date of design, and the effectiveness of existing dust-control equipment. In short, some facilities have much less need or ability than others to conduct housekeeping. The image of the "small country elevator"—a mom-and-pop operation with no hired hands, but a line of anxious farmers waiting to unload their grain before it starts raining—is often evoked in this line of argument. Some country elevators have little need for dust control because they have low throughput and no enclosed bucket elevators. Others, it is argued, lack the resources to purchase dust collection systems or hire additional labor. The appropriate action level, if there is such a thing, varies significantly by facility, and the small ones should, the argument continues, be spared the regulatory rod entirely.

This position on dust control contradicts the position taken elsewhere in 61B. The Agricultural Dusts committee has gone on record several times against the notion that differences in facilities render a general standard inappropriate. Separate NFPA standards for country elevators were combined with those for other grain-handling facilities in 1973, when the committee decided that "a distinction between types of grain elevators on the basis of capacity or shipping or receiving media is no longer practical."[25] Similarly, a committee member argued in July 1985 that motion switches should not be mandated on all bucket elevator legs because some country elevators "do not realistically need them." The committee rejected the argument on the grounds that motion switches were generally a good idea and it would be impossible to identify in a standard those situations in which they are not necessary.[26] The same could be said about dust-control requirements. "Facilities vary," notes a former USDA investigator, "but the hazard scenarios are the same."

The Unspoken Arguments: Liability and Retroactivity

So why is the housekeeping provision in 61B so vague? Two factors other than the limitations of science and the diversity of facilities are at play. One is specific to this issue, the other indicative of a larger force affecting the development of private safety standards. There is an unspoken belief that good housekeeping simply is not the answer. To some, it is a matter of practicality. It would require excessive effort, the argument goes, to keep an elevator clean enough to prevent explosions. "There is no such thing as a clean elevator," quipped one trade association representative. Perhaps the strongest explanation is that a specific housekeeping provision could be legal dynamite. Industry has learned that voluntary standards can and will be used against you in a court of law. Most explosions lead to litigation. According to a retired Cargill executive who testifies in such lawsuits, 61B and a host of related standards are raised in almost every case. The stakes can be very high. The two largest explosions in 1977 resulted in settlements of approximately $25 million each, and a jury recently applied the bane of the tort law—punitive damages—for the first time in a grain elevator case.[27] The vaguer 61B is on housekeeping, the less powerful a weapon it would be after an explosion.[28] Some of the vagueness, then, is simply an attempt to make the standard liability-proof. The ill-fated OSHA citations that relied on 61B are testimony to the effectiveness of this strategy.

Success, in this context, breeds more generalities. Substituting what Agricultural Dusts committee members refer to as "motherhood statements" for specific provisions is an increasing trend with 61B. Space heaters shall be located in "suitable places." Fire extinguishers shall be located in "strategic" places. A proposal that all bearings be properly maintained in accordance with the manufacturer's specifications was rejected by the committee in 1985 in favor of a requirement that "all bearings shall be properly maintained."[29] ("Let's see what a lawyer can do with that one!" mused a committee member at the July 1985 meeting.) Of course, the ability of lawyers to "do something" with the standard is probably equal to (or greater than) the standard's usefulness to its intended audience, grain elevator operators. Without guidance concerning the specifics of "proper maintenance," the lawyers will be as lost as anyone trying to glean any substance from the standard.

The extent to which 61B should contain such generalities appears to be the most significant issue facing the Agricultural Dusts committee. Some think that the committee has gone too far already. The president of one of the only two insurance companies presently underwriting grain elevators—major companies such as Cargill are self-insured—abhors the generality. He considers 61B so vague as to provide no real assistance in evaluating elevator safety. He does not even keep a current copy of the standard in his office. The technical director of the National Grain and Feed Association, on the other hand, considers such generalities the silver lining to an otherwise objectionable standard.

The generality problem indicates a more significant dilemma. The committee is trying to achieve two largely incompatible objectives: having a meaningful standard that can affect safety and provide helpful guidance to elevator operators *without* providing ammunition that will be used against you whenever an explosion occurs. Nowhere are the dimensions of this problem more accentuated than in respect to retroactivity.

By its own terms, 61B applies only to new facilities. This makes the most sense for design requirements. Compliance costs for many requirements are low in the design stage but very high after construction. Elevators used to be built with combustible materials, for example, and little consideration was given to minimizing ledges and horizontal surfaces or designing conveyors in a manner that would facilitate cleaning with portable vacuum cleaners. These things can easily be remedied in the design process. Correcting them retroactively would practically involve building a new facility.

In reality, 61B can, has, and will be applied to situations other than brand-new elevators. When issuing citations, OSHA often refers to 61B without regard for the date the facility was constructed. Plaintiff's attorneys are similarly inclined and have met with greater success. The retroactivity clause invites this attitude. NFPA 61B attempts to be unusually lenient in this regard. Unlike most building codes, it does not even require compliance in the case of major expansion or renovation—the vast majority of "new" construction. Moreover, the 1980 version also exempted from retroactive coverage a host of operational activities—such as hot-work procedures and housekeeping—that can be carried out without regard to the age or design of the facility.

The opposing viewpoints about retroactivity reflect deep-seated differences concerning the role and nature of private standards. Some of those favoring the broadest possible exemption from retroactive application "really do not want a standard at all," according to an Agricultural Dusts committee member at the July 1985 meeting.[30] This group is not insignificant. The National Grain and Feed Association, the largest trade association in the field, is unwilling to refer to 61B as a national consensus standard and refuses to participate on any of NFPA's agricultural dust committees.

The implications of this reticence are not lost on the Agricultural Dusts committee. Organized opposition can prevent or at least postpone proposals from being adopted in the NFPA system. Should this private standard become unpalatable enough to the NFPA, or if others in the industry actively opposed it, 61B might fall of its own weight. As one committee member said at the July 1985 meeting, "It behooves us to try and give some relief to those being sued." Nevertheless, most committee members realize that the only real "protection" against retroactive application is to abolish the standard. They understand that others will do as they please in interpreting the retroactive effect of 61B, so it is futile to attempt to prevent this from happening by tinkering with the retroactivity clause. These members also see the danger in exempting too many requirements from retroactive effect. "If this [standard] is too unattractive to the states," warned another committee member at the same meeting, "they might adopt their own requirements." Several proposals to strengthen the tone of the retroactivity clause were rejected in July 1985 primarily because they seemed pointless to the committee.

To the chagrin of those proposing the stronger exemption, the committee adopted a proposal by the representative from Continental Grain to narrow the scope of the retroactivity clause—that is, to make more provisions apply retroactively. The only provisions in the 1980 version with retroactive effect concerned fumigant usage. In seeking to identify appropriate candidates for retroactive application, the intent, according to the committee chairman, was to include "operational" requirements but not those requiring "even a dime of investment."

The results of the 1985 revisions are revealing because the committee chose to include the housekeeping provisions in the group to be given retroactive effect. This change appears to make 61B more credible. After all, shouldn't old and new facilities alike be expected to do proper maintenance or take precautions to ensure that welding is done safely? In light of the "not even a dime of investment" principle, however, the committee's action seems more significant for what it admits about the housekeeping provisions—that they do not require anything more than what an operator is already doing.

The Uneasy Solution: Change the Packaging

In an effort to placate those who would rather not have a standard, the Agricultural Dusts committee has done everything possible to make 61B a more agreeable document. These changes have largely been a matter of form, not substance. The language in 61B has been toned down considerably over time. References to such unpleasantnesses as "injuries to personnel" have been replaced with less specific references to hazards in general.[31] The introduction to the 1959 version of 61B warned that: "GOOD HOUSEKEEPING AND CLEAN PREMISES ARE THE FIRST ESSENTIALS IN THE ELIMINATION OF DUST EXPLOSION HAZARDS, CONSEQUENTLY THIS CODE IS NOT INTENDED TO LESSEN IN ANY WAY THE RESPONSIBILITY OF THE OWNER AND OPERATOR IN THIS RESPECT." This language was moved to the appendix in 1973, and the capital letters were replaced with regular capitalization. The statement was omitted entirely in the 1980 version.[32] Only the gentlemen's agreement remains.

Placing things in the appendix is a popular compromise. Fully one-third of the 1980 version of 61B is appendix material. The appeal of this compromise is clear: the individual in favor of the material gets it "into the standard" in some form, while those opposed to the specifics take considerable solace in the fact that it is "not a requirement." Employee health and safety, a subject avoided in many NFPA standards but favored by the labor representative on the 61B committee, is addressed in an appendix added in 1980.

The appendix also contains more specifics than the actual standard. For example, the standard requires that "horizontal surfaces shall be minimized," while the appendix indicates that the "suggested angle of repose is 60 degrees."[33] This is another tactic in the search for a liability-proof standard. The hope is that through the appendix the generalities in 61B can be given meaning in a nonenforceable manner. The official NFPA position, set forth in every standard, is that the appendix "is not part of the requirements . . . but is included for informational purposes only." Of course, one of the stated purposes of NFPA's "requirements" is to provide information.

The difference is really a matter of wishful thinking. All NFPA "requirements" are informational until an "authority having jurisdiction" chooses to enforce them. Moreover, the authority can choose to enforce the appendix as well as the "requirements" proper. An NFPA member who has worked with this committee confirms that appendix material is often treated by state fire marshals as having equal weight to the "requirements." The wishful thinking paid off, however, in the case of grain elevators. Some OSHA citations were overturned by the Occupational Safety and Health Review Commission precisely because they relied on material contained in the appendix of 61B.[34]

Technical Arguments, Surprising Results

This is not to say that 61B is all appendix and no substance. Nor is it to say that disagreements are foreign to the Agricultural Dusts committee. Certain provisions in 61B are specific and have been the source of repeated debate throughout the years. Should there be a vent between bins to allow dust generated during loading to settle into adjoining bins instead of blowing back up into the work area? To what extent is it possible or desirable to vent silos and elevator legs to relieve pressure from an explosion? Should compressed air be allowed, and under what circumstances, to "blow down" dust from walls and rafters?

The technical nature of these questions is not surprising. Private standards-setting is often described as technical. Esoteric questions such as those above seem to fit the bill. How the committee has handled these issues is more unusual. "Irrational," "unrealistic," and "unduly stringent"—criticisms often reserved for government regulation—are all strictures used by some NFPA members to describe the resolution of these issues.

For example, even though most insurance and grain company representatives privately concede that the requirement is irrational, 61B prohibits interbin venting,[35] and it is also accused of being unrealistic about explosion venting. (Explosion vents are movable panels designed to vent the pressure from an actual explosion; interbin vents, just discussed, are actual openings designed to vent airborne dust.)[36]

NFPA 61B includes several other provisions that are considered by many in the grain industry to be too stringent. Removing layered dust with compressed air is prohibited unless other equipment is shut off. The concern is that "blowing down" can create a combustible cloud. There are no known cases in which an explosion has occurred this way, and one insurance representative expressed serious doubts about whether compressed air could create dust concentrations above the LEL. The only explanation for this provision is that it represents a compromise between those who are opposed to blowing down on principle and those who think that it is never dangerous.

Requirements incorporating the National Electric Code's classifications for environments with agricultural dust are also quite strict. The code, written by NFPA, specifies two classes for such environments: Divisions 1 and 2.[37] Equipment certified for Division 1 must be tested under conditions in which dust concentrations regularly exceed the LEL. Equipment for Division 2 is tested under conditions in which such concentrations are "occasionally" encountered. Herein lies the controversy. Division 2 equipment is tested under extreme conditions compared to those normally encountered in those parts of a grain elevator where Division 2 equipment is required. The Division 2 test methods do not just represent the worst case, they represent an impossible case.[38] Not only does this provision increase the price of grain-handling equipment, but in some cases the required equipment is not available. The same arguments apply to Division 1 equipment if it is required in areas without explosive dust clouds. The NFPA leaves these implementation questions to "the authority having jurisdiction."

NFPA 61B is also stringent with respect to ignition sources in bucket elevators, but this is a recent development. Several requirements for bucket elevators were added in 1980, including (1) monitoring devices that cut off the power to the drive and sound an alarm when the leg belt slows down, (2) magnets or separator devices to minimize metal objects entering the grain stream, and (3) closing devices to prevent flame propagation through idle spouts.[39] These requirements did not generate the controversy produced by those discussed above. Neither were they really new; they were moved from the appendix to the body of the standard. This unusual move is best understood by the politics of the moment. The changes were suggested around the time OSHA initiated its Advance Notice of Proposed Rulemaking. Some committee members privately acknowledge that these changes were an attempt to forestall OSHA regulation. The changes certainly strengthened the standard, at least for new construction. But they did not forestall OSHA.

The OSHA Standard

Grain elevator operators did not have a very merry Christmas in 1977. Three grain elevators and two feed mills exploded during the third week of December, killing fifty-nine people and injuring forty-eight others. The Department of Agriculture, hit particularly hard because thirteen federal grain inspectors were killed in the explosions, established a Special Office for Grain Elevator Safety. OSHA was put on the spot. There was intense political pressure to do something about grain elevator safety, but OSHA had little experience with the issue. Lacking its own safety standard, the agency had only its "general duty" clause to back up any enforcement actions. Citations based on this clause require, among other things, proof of a "recognized hazard."[40] NFPA 61B came in handy, since one possible method of establishing a "recognized hazard" is to cite private standards. OSHA did so on numerous occasions after the 1977 explosions. Citations tend to evoke indignation, however, and these cases were no exception. Some of the citations lived up to the agency's reputation for unreasonableness—one firm was cited for an ungrounded coffee pot in an office building detached from the grain elevator, for example—but even those involving seemingly serious violations were met with hostility. Virtually every citation was contested, and OSHA lost almost every one on appeal: 61B was considered too vague in some instances; in others, the review commission that hears appeals from OSHA citations honored the "advisory" nature of the appendix. OSHA had to look elsewhere to advance its enforcement strategy.

To overcome its limited background in grain elevator safety, and in the hope of defusing an already politicized issue, OSHA contracted with the National Academy of Sciences to evaluate possible methods of preventing grain elevator explosions. The first of four NAS reports confirmed the inadequacies of OSHA's experience, criticizing the agency for emphasizing citations instead of investigating explosions sufficiently to understand the problem.[41]

OSHA adopted a cautious, if not timid, stance. In January 1980, the same month that the Department of Agriculture released its report "Prevention of Dust Explosions—An Achievable Goal," OSHA issued a "request for comments and information and notice of informal public meetings," which posed approximately two hundred questions for public comment.[42] Although it was widely assumed that OSHA intended to propose a grain elevator safety standard, the agency did not start drafting one for two more years. It was waiting for support from the NAS. Testing the political waters in the meantime, OSHA held hearings a few months later in Wisconsin, Louisiana, and Missouri.

The water was hot. The hearings opened an acrimonious debate that shifted locations over the years but never lost its political intensity. Several hundred comments were received in response to OSHA's request, and over two thousand pages of testimony were received at three "informal public meetings." Most of it was extremely negative. This hostility hindered the NAS, which noted the "reluctance of elevator management to cooperate" with their study.[43] The key report, "Prevention of Grain Elevator and Mill Explosions," was released in June 1982.[44] It identified as the two most significant issues in grain elevator safety (1) ignition sources in bucket elevators and (2) dust concentrations throughout facilities. With this background, OSHA began drafting a standard for grain elevators. Within a month, the head of OSHA told a House subcommittee that grain elevator safety was one of the agency's two priority projects, and that a rule would be completed by January 1983.[45] It took much longer than expected, but the agency eventually proposed a regulation, with fourteen basic requirements.[46] Many of these, particularly those concerning ignition-source control in bucket elevators, came directly from the NAS recommendations. One received practically all of the attention: the "action level" for removing layered dust.[47]

Hanging a Number on Dust Control

The action-level concept came from the NAS report, which proposed that corrective action should be taken whenever layered dust exceeded a specified depth (over a 200-square foot area). The NAS did what the NFPA would not: hang a number on dust control. "It was done to satisfy labor and other political groups who felt that without a definite figure you do not have a club," explains an industry member on the NAS panel. The panel chose one sixty-fourth of an inch as its "club."[48] The number was a compromise, plain and simple. Some panel members argued for one-hundredth of an inch, based on flame propagation experiments and without regard for economic feasibility. One-eighth of an inch, a figure already used in some proprietary standards, was also suggested. One sixty-fourth was somewhere in between.

OSHA engaged in its own search for an agreeable number. Again, the process was predominately political, not scientific. Under more pressure than NAS to take into account the economic impact of its proposals, OSHA considered a higher range of numbers. The argument was between one sixty-fourth and one-eighth. The former had newfound credibility thanks to the NAS; the latter had historical acceptance. OSHA chose historical acceptance.

The selected number appears to have been favorable to industry. The rejected figure (one sixty-fourth) was, after all, eight times stricter than the one chosen. One-eighth is considered by many to be not only lenient but downright dangerous. An elevator with an eighth of an inch of layered dust, according to an insurance representative, is "a bomb waiting to explode."

But appearances can be deceiving. Industry opposed one-eighth and one sixty-fourth with practically equal vigor. In reality, the disagreement was not about the best action levels; it was about whether to have action levels at all. OSHA wanted a number. Industry did not. "You've got to have a number for it to be enforceable," according to an OSHA official familiar with the agency's bad luck under the general duty clause. For related reasons, industry was opposed to any number. Although it cited the specter of dangerous facilities being in compliance with the rule—those with one-ninth of an inch of dust, for example—industry's real concern was the opposite: seemingly safe facilities being in violation. It is likely that even the best facilities would at some time, in some part of the facility, be in violation of the one-eighth-inch requirement. This would not be a problem if OSHA could be trusted to use good judgment in enforcing the rule. But most elevator operators did not have such confidence. As a result, unreasonable enforcement strategy was of much greater concern than the "false sense of security" some claimed would follow from an action-level approach.[49] The paramount concerns of the National Grain and Feed Association when it later petitioned for a partial stay of the OSHA regulation were the enforcement directives for implementing the housekeeping require-

TABLE 5   A COMPARISON OF OSHA AND NGFA COST
ESTIMATES FOR SELECTED PROVISIONS OF OSHA'S
PROPOSED GRAIN ELEVATOR STANDARD
(in thousands of dollars)

	Initial Costs		Recurring Costs	
Provision	*OSHA*	*NGFA*	*OSHA*	*NGFA*
Training	495	677	1,821	3,913
Permit System	584	584	114	114
Grate Openings	1,671	11,087	280	0
Housekeeping (one-eighth-inch action-level)	149,941	399,344	134,150	263,369
All 14	201,924	556,567	137,777	269,488

SOURCE: "Confidential Survey of the Grain Handling Industry" (report prepared by
G.E.M. Consultants, Inc., Overland Park, Kans., May 30, 1984).

ments.[50] Unfortunately, the enforcement strategy, including possible
methods for heading off unreasonableness, was never seriously discussed during the rulemaking proceedings. Instead, the debate was
dominated by a battle of the cost-benefit analysts. The issues they raised
were important, but so were many of the ones they ignored.

The Battle of the Cost-Benefit Analysts

The battle itself was costly. First OSHA hired a well-known consulting
firm (Arthur D. Little) to analyze its draft proposal. The resulting report
was riddled with errors and questionable assumptions.[51] It was so vulnerable to attack that OSHA hired a second firm (Booz, Allen & Hamilton) to massage the data. The NGFA subsequently hired a third consulting firm (G.E.M. Consultants) to attack the conclusions reached by
the first two.

On the cost side, estimates prepared for OSHA by Booz, Allen
pegged the total initial cost of the standard at $200 million, with annual
recurring costs of approximately $137 million. These estimates re-
flected a series of assumptions about the cost of each of the fourteen
provisions in the proposed rule.[52] Industry accepted the Booz, Allen
estimates for some of the minor provisions, such as permit systems for
hot work (see table 5), but it took issue with most of the others. By

making marginally higher estimates for almost every subsidiary assumption, industry argued that the cost of many provisions were understated by a factor of two.[53] Except for the housekeeping provisions, these differences of opinion did not add up to much. Hundreds of millions of dollars, however, separated the cost estimates for housekeeping. Some of these differences are impossible to evaluate.[54] Other assumptions made by OSHA's consultant seem more reasonable than the industry's.[55] Industry also offered some persuasive indictments of the OSHA estimates. The Booz, Allen study assumed that operators would purchase "dust-tight" vacuum cleaners, even though the National Electric Code requires the more expensive models certified for class (g) environments. In short, it seems safe to assume that the true cost of the rule would fall in between the estimates prepared by the two consultants.

On the benefit side, where estimates are normally subject to more uncertainty, the report prepared for OSHA took a realistic position. It was assumed that the housekeeping provision would prevent approximately 30–50 percent of all fires and 17–32 percent of all explosions. Through a series of calculations intended to gauge the "willingness-to-pay" to avoid property damage and personal injuries, these figures produced an estimated total benefit of approximately $286 million.[56] Industry did not take issue with the specifics of these estimates. Although it is always arguable that things will not work out as well as planned, the estimates prepared for OSHA were not vulnerable to the charge of overoptimism.

The battle of the cost-benefit analysts was not won clearly by either side. Assuming that actual benefits would be between 50 and 90 percent of OSHA's (possibly high) estimates, the rule would yield from $143 million to $286 million in total annual benefits. Estimates of annualized cost, based on the figures presented in table 5 and discounted to present value, ranged from $113 million (OSHA) to $240 million (NGFA). The true cost is likely to be somewhere in between. Therefore, the OSHA standard may or may not generate more benefits in excess of costs—a plausible case can be made for both propositions. Either way, the costs appear to be in the same ballpark as the benefits.

Country Elevators and Distributional Effects

Aside from cost-effectiveness, the standard was controversial for distributional reasons. Industry and OMB argued that the rule disproportionately affected country elevators. Between 80 and 100 percent of export terminals and inland elevators were thought to be in compliance with most of the OSHA requirements (other than housekeeping). No more than 15 percent of country elevators were. Large facilities generally had dust-control programs; many country elevators did not. As a result, the costs of the proposal fell much more on country elevators than on other facilities. Yet, as OMB argued, the risks were more significant in larger facilities.[57] OMB took the position that "big" facilities should be covered and "small country elevators" should not. OSHA did not want to exclude any facilities. As an OSHA official testified, "When workers are hurt or killed [we] don't particularly care about the size of the facility." Both positions were less than reasonable. OMB wanted to exempt all "country" elevators, even though some were, by any measure, as large as inland terminals and export facilities. But OSHA's position indicated complete disregard for *marginal* costs and benefits. The cost of bringing the smallest facilities into compliance would be far out of proportion to the losses likely to occur in those facilities.

A political dispute of surprising dimensions took shape. Both the vice president of the United States and the president of the AFL-CIO got involved when OMB held up the rule for months longer than the normal sixty-day review period. The housekeeping provision was the major bone of contention. In a compromise that pleased practically no one, the proposed rule was released for publication when OSHA, at OMB's insistence, added two alternative proposals for housekeeping: sweeping once per shift or installing pneumatic dust control.[58] It was no secret that OSHA still favored the action-level alternative.

The added alternatives did not cool the political debate. The NGFA organized an impressive campaign to flood OSHA with "worksheets" from elevator operators opposed to all three alternatives.[59] A few congressmen held hearings to allow elevator operators in their home districts to complain that "the people who wrote these standards have never been to a country elevator."[60] OSHA continued to take heat from all sides, with the exception of labor. In what was termed an "unusual alliance," the AFL-CIO supported the proposed rule even though it would have preferred an action level stricter than one-eighth of an inch.[61]

The OSHA Standard Prevails (with Minor Improvements)

The stalemate between OMB and OSHA lasted until there were two more serious explosions. In July 1987, following a fatal explosion in

Burlington, Iowa, Senator Tom Harkin (D-Iowa) complained to the OMB director about delays in releasing the rule. He complained again four months later, following another explosion. The rule was published on the last day of 1987.[62]

The rule contains a major change, but not an actual softening, in OSHA's position on housekeeping. The standard retains the action level of one-eight of an inch for housekeeping—eliminating the ineffective "once-a-shift sweeping" option. OSHA modified the provision, however, by limiting its application to three "priority areas."[63] This seems much more reasonable than the earlier version, which applied to *any* 200-square-foot area in the facility. It may even help reduce frivolous or unreasonable enforcement actions. But it does little to alter the basic housekeeping tasks required by the rule, since many of the steps used to minimize grain dust in "critical" areas will also minimize it elsewhere. OSHA also moderated the rule slightly to favor country elevators. Some country elevators are exempt from the requirements for alignment and motion detection devices.[64] But none are exempt from the action-level requirement. Country elevators were given three extra years to come into compliance, however. The symbolism of these changes, all conciliatory, far exceeds their actual substantive impact.

The most substantial change in the final standard concerned feed mills, and again the adjustment was in the direction of leniency. In response to arguments that risks are lower in feed mills, OSHA exempted these facilities from the most powerful provisions in the standard: the housekeeping and bucket elevator requirements. OSHA defended this decision, calculating that "the risk of an employee death or injury resulting from an explosion is almost five times greater in grain elevators than in mills."[65] OSHA rejected this line of argument in the case of country elevators, however, justifying the apparent discrepancy on the grounds that "the available data are not sufficient to permit an accurate estimate of the relative risks in large and small elevators."[66] Although nobody was entirely pleased with the final standard, it certainly was reasonable in many respects. An editorial in the trade journal *Feedstuffs*, often an outspoken critic of OSHA, allowed that "grain elevators and feed mills can be much safer places to work merely as a result of OSHA's attention. . . . The rules on bin and entry, housekeeping plans, work permits, etc., are needed. A federal edict appears to be the best way to implement such rules."[67] But industry was incensed at the housekeeping requirements and immediately challenged them in court. Labor countered, challenging the exemption for feed mills. The

Fifth Circuit Court of Appeals upheld all but the housekeeping provisions, remanding that issue for "reconsideration of the economic feasibility of the standard."[68]

Summary Evaluation

The OSHA standard is a classic example of the time-consuming adversary process often attributed to government regulation. Ten years elapsed between the 1977 explosions and the final OSHA rule. The most controversial issue, housekeeping, remains unresolved after a court challenge, even though OSHA spent at least half a million dollars on consulting firms. Hearings held around the country produced volumes of testimony, mostly to the ill will of industry toward OSHA. The standard was loosened somewhat during this arduous administrative process. Whether these changes were a victory for business or a calculated bargaining strategy by OSHA depends on whom you ask. Whatever the reason, OSHA exempted small facilities from some requirements and extended the deadline for compliance with others. OSHA also restricted the final standard to bulk grain-handling facilities, exempting feed mills and other processing facilities included in the original proposal. Most important, OSHA concentrated the housekeeping provisions in three "critical" areas. These changes all made the standard more reasonable.

OSHA's final standard has fewer requirements but packs more punch than NFPA 61B. OSHA stood firm on the action-level approach to housekeeping, resisting strong political pressure to weaken the provision by allowing sweeping once per shift. The agency adopted an action level identical to that used in several proprietary standards, which, if anything, is too lenient (the NAS suggested a more stringent level). The standard is strict enough to cover the worst facilities, however. (These "bad apples" are estimated to constitute 10 to 30 percent of the facilities.) OSHA's housekeeping requirements also have the advantage of being performance-based, allowing firms to determine the most efficient method of compliance. The overall cost of compliance is difficult to estimate, but the range of estimated costs is lower than the range of estimated benefits.

In contrast, the NFPA standard bears out the common conception that private regulation is weaker than its public counterpart. To NFPA's credit, its committee meetings are not plagued by adversity or delays. Committee members are knowledgeable, bringing an array of practical experience to the task. They meet regularly and adopt revisions in relatively short order. But the outcome (at least in the case of grain elevators) leaves much to be desired. NFPA 61B is relatively spineless. Many important topics, including housekeeping, are glossed over with empty generalities. This situation is due in part to concerns about liability. Seeking to avoid a standard that can be used against business in any post-explosion lawsuits, the Agricultural Dusts committee relegates many issues to the appendix, while making others intentionally vague. The committee also shares the sense that certain "management" issues should not be subject to industrywide regulation. A representative of the Grain Elevator and Processors Society disavows "any kind of declarative 'thou shalt do so-and-so'" standard.[69]

Not all aspects of the NFPA standard are as flimsy as the housekeeping provisions: 61B is fairly strong on basic design issues. Because of the retroactivity clause, however, these provisions apply to fewer facilities every time the standard is upgraded. This technique minimizes political opposition and helps explain why upgrading is possible. Some provisions of general application are also strict, a few to the point of being unreasonable. Provisions such as the UL specifications for equipment used in hazardous locations are far more demanding than is warranted by the circumstances. These provisions require expensive electrical devices where normal equipment would pose no real hazard. Other requirements, aimed at reducing fire hazards more than explosion hazards, may actually be counterproductive—reducing the former at the expense of increasing the latter.

These unexpected tendencies are not major aspects of 61B; they are noteworthy because they are evidence of a "technical" decisionmaking realm characterized by influences and behavior not normally attributed to the private sector. These "technical" decisions reflect the professional norms of engineers. This engineering ethic is conservative in some respects and stringent in others. Engineers are loathe to get involved with political issues, including matters of management prerogative, but they are zealous advocates of safety on occasion. OSHA has no quarrel with the fire safety provisions in NFPA 61B. The extent to which private standards-setters are influenced by regulatory philosophy and professional ethics is explored in detail in chapter 7.

FOUR

Standards for Aviation Fire Safety

Unlike grain elevator safety, aviation safety is an entire *field* of regulation. While the major hazards in a grain elevator can be addressed in a single standard, there are clusters of standards around each of the major aviation hazards. Navigation, aircraft integrity, equipment maintenance, and fire safety each accounts for a myriad of standards, both public and private. Perhaps the most accessible standards, given their familiarity on the ground, are those for fire safety. Even here, the array of regulatory issues is overwhelming. There are at least four facets of fire safety—prevention, detection, suppression, and evacuation—and each accounts for a multiplicity of standards. Suppression, for example, involves standards for fire extinguishers as well as flammability requirements for seat cushions and building materials. The regulatory territory can also be divided by location in the aircraft. The galley, the cabin, the lavatories, and the baggage compartment all pose special conditions that occasionally merit separate standards.

Out of this complicated maze of potential topics for regulation, public standards tend to emerge from specific accidents. The "Airplane Cabin Protection Rule" examined in this chapter stems directly from the Air Canada fire in 1983. The standard covers fire extinguishers and smoke detectors. On the private side, standards evolve quite differently. The number and scope of those developed by the National Fire Protection Association is controlled by the organization's Standards Council in conjunction with the Correlating Committee on Aviation. NFPA does not have a standard for aviation smoke detectors; but it does have a standard for aviation fire extinguishers. That standard is compared to the FAA regulation in this chapter.

Many of the propositions borne out by the standards for grain elevator safety are contradicted by the standards for aviation fire safety. In some respects, the NFPA standard is better than the FAA's. It is rooted in a technical understanding of fire detection and suppression, and it avoids some of the pitfalls of the FAA regulation. Surprisingly, the NFPA standard requires more fire extinguishers than its public counterpart. That does not necessarily make it better. It is doubtful whether the benefits of this standard exceed the costs. Most remarkable, given the common perception that concerns about cost dominate private standards-setting, is the absence of any arguments to this effect by NFPA committee members.

Compounding the curious juxtaposition of this demanding private standard and the lenient one for grain elevators is their common origin: both were written under the auspices of the National Fire Protection Association. Apparently, NFPA is capable of producing standards ranging from almost spineless to possibly too stringent. The NFPA standard examined in this chapter also changed dramatically over time. It was stringent when first adopted in 1956, languished and became outdated some twenty years later, but was revitalized in 1980 to its stringent, possibly unreasonable, form. These differences across NFPA standards and over time suggest the importance of influences beyond institutional design and administrative procedure. Three influences are identified through this case: (1) the professionalism of fire safety engineers, (2) the tangled web linking this standard and UL's generic standard for fire extinguishers, and (3) the peculiar political culture of aviation safety.

On the public side, the standard described in this chapter shatters the popular image of federal "notice and comment" rulemaking as burdensome and time-consuming. The FAA adopted it less than a year after it was proposed. There were no lengthy hearings, no subsequent judicial appeals. Although the FAA standard suffers from failure to take certain technical realities into account, it is unquestionably strict, like many aviation standards, and arguably unreasonable. These unexpected outcomes, both public and private, suggest that regulatory behavior can be quite issue-sensitive. Cultural attitudes about the risks of flying are, to say the least, peculiar. Apparently *no* risk is acceptable so long as regulation holds out the promise of improving safety. As elaborated below, this results in decisionmaking dynamics, both public and private, unlike those attributed to other agencies charged with regulating health and safety.

Fire Extinguishers, Smoke Detectors, and the FAA

The FAA has an expansive regulatory mandate—to certify the airworthiness of new aircraft, to control the nationwide air traffic control system, to regulate pilot certification, and to police airline operations and maintenance. The agency functions by leaving much to the discretionary judgment of the airlines and airframe manufacturers. Aviation technology is so complicated that the FAA realized years ago it did not have the resources or expertise to pass judgment independently on all new airframe designs. Instead, "designated engineering representatives," engineers employed by the airframe manufacturers, certify new airplanes for the agency. Matters of operation and maintenance are almost as complicated as aircraft design, involving highly technical systems and countless potential subjects for regulation. Airframe manufacturers employ hundreds of safety engineers and continually issue bulletins and warnings to their customers, the airlines. Airlines adopt their own safety routines and maintenance procedures as well. Confronted with the complexities of aviation safety, the FAA proceeds with a mixture of deference, prodding, and formal regulation. All three strategies are reflected in the evolution of the FAA's regulation of fire extinguishers and smoke detectors on commercial airlines.[1]

Prodding takes the form of advisory circulars and general notices, both of which are "non-binding" but carry significant weight with the airlines. Smaller airlines with limited engineering capacity to develop their own standards are likely to adopt these recommendations. Larger carriers do their own evaluation, cognizant of the cost of ignoring government recommendations should something go wrong.[2] Formal regulation usually follows from the most serious accidents and those that result in National Transportation Safety Board (NTSB) recommendations that have been made before. How these stages take shape depends on the seriousness of the accident and the nature of any prior experiences.

In the case of fire extinguishers and smoke detectors, the formal standard was largely influenced by two tragic accidents: the Varig fire in 1973 and the Air Canada fire a decade later. Before these tragedies, however, the FAA long took a deferential approach toward fire extinguishers, mandating simply that "the type and quantity of extinguishing agent must be suitable for the kinds of fires likely to occur in the compartment where the extinguisher is intended to be used."[3] The airlines and airframe manufacturers were left to determine what was "suitable." The agency provided additional guidance with the advisory circular in 1965 that recommended up to three fire extinguishers per airplane and sanctioned the use of carbon dioxide extinguishers.[4] It contained no actual product specifications such as capacity, discharge time, or nozzle type. Nor did it speak to the placement of extinguishers or the training of personnel in their use.

Cabin fire safety attracted intense attention in 1973 when a terrible in-flight fire killed 124 people on a Varig Airlines Boeing 707 en route to Paris from Rio de Janiero. The fire, attributed to a discarded cigarette in a lavatory wastepaper disposal unit, broke out shortly before landing. Thick black smoke soon filled the cabin and cockpit. The pilots literally stuck their heads out the window in order to make a forced landing a few miles from the airport. Of the 135 people on board, only eleven survived; the remainder died of asphyxiation or from toxic gas. The NTSB focused on facilitating earlier detection and more effective suppression through smoke alarms and smoke masks for flight attendants respectively. The NTSB made numerous recommendations, including requirements for "a means of early detection of lavatory fires . . . such as smoke detectors or operating procedures for the frequent inspection of lavatories by cabin attendants."[5] The FAA opted for more "No Smoking" signs, an appeal to the airlines for better monitoring by the crew, and a promise that the "FAA has begun a preregulatory study of the feasibility and justification for a requirement for smoke detectors in lavatories."[6]

The advisory circular on fire extinguishers was completely out of date by the late 1970s, failing to take into account changes in airplane size and extinguishant technology. New jumbo jets with a seating capacity in excess of three hundred require many more extinguishers than the old planes. Virtually all airlines carried more extinguishers than suggested in the circular. Some also used the new Halon extinguishant, a liquid gas that extinguishes fire by chemically interrupting the combustion chain reaction (rather than by physically smothering it). Halon is a derivative of halgonated hydrocarbon. It is suitable for use in cold weather, leaves behind no chemical residue to contaminate or corrode aircraft parts, and can be three times more effective than carbon dioxide extinguishers of equal weight.

Boeing provided it on all new airplanes after 1979, but Halon still was not mentioned in the FAA advisory circular until a series of "volatile liquid hijackings" raised concerns about the capability of current extinguishers. (The hijackers in these cases carried jars of gasoline, threatening to set the plane on fire.) The FAA's Office of Civil Aviation Security sponsored a study of hand-held fire extinguishers by the Factory Mutual Research Corporation. The FAA quickly revised the advisory circular on fire extinguishers to explain the advantages of Halon.[7] The circular did not require Halon, however, and it provided no additional product specifications. The agency stepped up the pressure after tests at the FAA Technical Center revealed that Halon was better than carbon dioxide or dry chemicals at extinguishing volatile liquid fires. The agency's strategy, something between unsolicited advice and formal regulation, was to issue a general notice. G-NOTs, as they are known in the agency, are formal requests for "voluntary" compliance with a suggestion. They are the FAA's way of putting the airlines on the spot—requesting a specific safety improvement and requiring a formal response concerning the airlines' intentions. The agency accordingly issued a general notice on November 29, 1980, requesting all airlines to carry at least two Halon extinguishers.[8]

About half of the carriers indicated that they had complied or would do so. A few expressed mild resentment at the FAA's refusal to take responsibility for the issue. If Halon was desirable, argued the vice president for engineering and quality control at Frontier Airlines, "there are regulatory means of requiring it rather than encouraging such devices be installed without providing sufficient justification."[9] Several carriers worried about the possible toxic effects of Halon extinguishers. Some of this concern was prompted by warning labels. ("Use in an enclosed place may be fatal," warns the label on a Kidde hand-held Halon extinguisher.) But the evidence about the toxic effects of Halon in aviation use was limited and mixed. Boeing conducted live fire tests and endorsed the use of Halon, although the engineers refused to release their test data.[10] American Airlines also conducted tests, and declined to use Halon because it left behind "a strong bromine smell that caused burning eyes and coughing."

The FAA relied on mild coercion until June 2, 1983, when an in-flight fire killed twenty-three people on an Air Canada flight near Cincinnati. The FAA was backed into a regulatory stance toward fire extinguishers and smoke detectors. As a rulemaking staff member put it, the agency gets "one free bite" in adopting regulatory strategies; that is, it has the most discretion in deciding how to address issues being raised for the first time. But the FAA had already had one bite at these issues. The agency had tried gentle and coercive "advice" on fire extinguishers, and the NTSB had already recommended smoke detectors. New regulations would certainly follow. Their genesis is so clearly in the Air Canada disaster, however, that it is necessary to recount some details of that tragedy.

The Air Canada Fire

Stories from the survivors of the fire, which eventually killed twenty-three people, were sensational, frightening, and widely publicized. A fire broke out in the lavatory of the DC-9, and, as in the Varig fire, thick acrid smoke soon filled the plane. During its emergency descent to the Greater Cincinnati Airport, described by one passenger as "like an elevator ride," the pilot's chair was literally on fire.[11] His vision was totally obscured by the time he landed the plane, tires exploding on impact. Flames burned through the roof of the fuselage, and scenes of firefighters combating the blaze with foam and water topped the national news.

The complete story, pieced together from separate reports by the National Transportation Safety Board and a special investigative unit of NFPA, is much less dramatic than the emergency landing and rescue effort.[12] It all began with an electrical short in a lavatory pump. Three circuit breakers tripped in the cockpit, and a crew member tried without success to reset them. Eleven minutes later, a flight attendant detected smoke emanating from the lavatory. An attendant entered the lavatory, saw smoke coming from the wall liner, and discharged a carbon dioxide fire extinguisher in the general vicinity. Minutes later a second extinguisher was also discharged, and the smoke appeared to clear; but a flight attendant checking on the situation soon thereafter found the lavatory door so hot it was considered unsafe to open. The smoke reappeared and got worse. A master caution light in the cockpit signaled an electrical system failure. The pilot decided to make an emergency landing. It took ten minutes to land the plane. Visibility approached zero as the plane filled with smoke. Only those passengers who reached the emergency exits within about one minute of landing got out of the plane safely. The rest apparently succumbed to carbon monoxide poisoning.

Aviation accidents are almost never attributed to a single cause. Usually a combination of mechanical and human factors are involved.

With fires, the direct "cause" of any particular incident is obviously the ignition source. In that sense, a short circuit in the lavatory flushing pump *caused* the Air Canada fire. The *consequences* of ignition, however, depend on the combustibility of surrounding materials, the quality of fire detection and suppression, and various elements of the emergency response. Accordingly, the extensive damage from the Air Canada fire—the consequences of ignition—can be attributed to the delay before the crew detected and responded to the fire, the ineffective use of the fire extinguishers, the toxicity of the seat covers, and the difficulties encountered in evacuation.[13]

Accident investigators tend to take an expansive approach when determining the "cause" of an accident. Aware that regulations are influenced by accident reports, investigators often seek to effect the greatest possible change. "It's better if you don't find the exact cause because then only one thing will get fixed," according to an NTSB investigator. Instead, for every serious accident the NTSB recommends a laundry list of changes in FAA regulations.

The Air Canada incident was no exception. Many culprits were identified. The NTSB was particularly critical of the crew for the delay between detecting the fire and deciding to land. A few independent experts consider this criticism unfair but concur that the crew was ineffective in its use of fire extinguishers. The NFPA report emphasized the problems of smoke and toxic gas, suggesting the need for more research on flammable materials, particularly seat covers. The NTSB wanted several things "fixed" as a result of the fire. It immediately recommended that the FAA inspect lavatory flushing pumps and establish a procedure for verifying whether the circuitry had been damaged over time. Three months later it recommended, among other things, the installation of smoke detectors and the use of Halon fire extinguishers.[14]

Political Pressure and a Prompt Proposal

Every fatal airplane accident generates extensive media attention and strong political pressures. Congressional committees have an almost limitless inclination to investigate airplane accidents. In his study of policy analysis in the FAA, Steven Rhoads notes that "it would be difficult to overestimate the seriousness with which Congress views commercial air crashes." Within two months of the accident, three separate congressional committees held hearings on the Air Canada fire.[15] Accused of "footdragging" and indifference bordering on callousness, the FAA soon became Congress's scapegoat for the incident. Congressman Dan Burton (R-Ind.) made the exaggerated claim that "had [Halon extinguishers] been on-board Air Canada nobody would have died."[16] Several congressmen introduced bills to mandate the NTSB's proposals on smoke detectors and Halon fire extinguishers.[17] Congress was unlikely to regulate the matter by statute, however, since it had neither the inclination nor the resources to address such technical questions. (In any case, as one congressman put it, "I would not want to fly in a plane designed by Congressional committee.")[18] Instead Congress strengthened the oversight process. One committee required the FAA to file monthly progress reports on the implementation of various NTSB recommendations. The pressure to adopt new regulations, including ones concerning fire extinguishers and smoke detectors, was intense.

The FAA knew it had to respond to the Air Canada fire with a regulation and was prepared to do so quickly. In short order the agency drew on its previous experience and drafted a simple standard. First, smoke detectors would be required in airplane lavatories and galleys. No effort was made to define the technical specifications for these devices. Second, a built-in fire extinguisher would be required in the towel disposal receptacle of each lavatory. (This had been suggested by the NTSB after both the Varig and Air Canada fires.) Finally, the number of fire extinguishers required would be increased, and at least two Halon 1211 extinguishers would be required on every plane. The choice of Halon 1211, and the exclusion of Halon 1301, was apparently based on the general notice sent out after the gasoline hijackings. The increase in the number of extinguishers required was simply an incremental guess. "We took a look at the wide bodies," a rulemaking staff member stated, "and said 'we need another extinguisher for every one hundred people.'" Otherwise, to a large extent, the NTSB essentially drafted the regulation.

Objections to the proposal were meek. The American Transport Association, which represents most major airlines and is considered by many to be a powerful lobbying organization, did not oppose "the basic thrust" of the proposal, only the requirement for smoke detectors in galley areas. The few other objections to the rule were technical. Some engineers argued that the standard should permit Halon 1301 as well as Halon 1211 (the numbers denote differences in chemical structure). Others alleged that household smoke detectors would not necessarily be reliable in airplanes. The effects of vibration were cited by Underwriters

Laboratories as one of several possibly significant aspects of aviation use that might impede performance. Unusual air currents might also be important, particularly in airplane lavatories, where the air moves down and out through the toilet bowl.

These claims might have been self-serving—UL was basically advocating that the FAA require laboratory certification of smoke detectors for aviation use—but they were also well founded. Devices designed specifically to endure the rigors of the aviation environment are far more sophisticated than a standard household detector. Detectors for airplane cargo holds, produced in accordance with an FAA Technical Standards Order, cost $800 to $1,300 each.[19] When the Regulatory Analysis Division in the FAA first analyzed the proposed rule, they used cost estimates based on these devices and arrived at a benefit-cost ratio of less than one. The critical but unanswered question is to what extent accuracy and reliability are sacrificed by allowing the basic dime store model instead of the sophisticated aviation model. Household detectors are not particularly sturdy either. Given the rigors of aviation use, they might not work in time of need. (Liability concerns of this nature prompted at least one major manufacturer to decline an airline's recent order for 1,500 detectors.) Missing batteries, a problem noted by carriers that experimented with smoke detectors, could also incapacitate the smoke detector. Petty theft would not be the only motive. Sabotage by smokers breaking what is widely thought to be one of the most ignored FAA prohibitions—against smoking in the lavatory—is another possibility.

Another possible consequence, argued an official of the British Civil Aviation Authority, is false alarms, which would "soon give rise to a loss of faith in the detection system." Household detectors are sensitive to changes in air flows, something that occurs regularly in flight but seldom at home. Smoke is also common in galley areas, partly as a by-product of food preparation. Several airlines feared that the panic caused by an activated alarm might be worse than the possibility of a fire going undetected without a smoke detector.

Technical Objections and a Final Rule

The other technical objections to the proposed FAA standard concerned either the fire extinguishant or the nozzle configuration. Several manufacturers argued that Halon 1301 should be permitted in addition to

Halon 1211.[20] Halon 1211 discharges in a more liquid state than Halon 1301 and has better range and direction in use. But Halon 1301 is considerably less toxic than 1211, so it may be advantageous in small areas such as the cockpit. The use of Halon 1301 in hand-held fire extinguishers is relatively recent. There were no hand-held Halon 1301 extinguishers when the FAA issued its general notice in 1980. Three years later, Metalcraft, Inc., received Factory Mutual Research Corporation's first approval for such a product. UL still did not list any. So there was limited information about the merits of this technical question.

The FAA balked and refused to consider the Halon 1301 alternative because, according to an FAA rulemaking staff member, "1301 is not rated for a Class A fire." The reference is to the UL method for rating fire extinguishers by type of fire and extinguisher capacity.[21] But the reasoning is flawed because UL's Class A fire is simply too big. "Halon is effective on an 'A' fire," notes a fire protection engineer, "but the smallest 'A' fire [that UL builds] takes about nine pounds of agent." Hand-held extinguishers usually have three to five pounds. There may be technical reasons for restricting the use of Halon 1301, particularly in large cabin spaces, where it might be less effective than Halon 1211, but the reason offered by the FAA indicates no understanding of these issues.

A few commenters suggested that the FAA require flexible discharge hoses on all fire extinguishers. This would be particularly helpful in battling fires in concealed spaces, overhead, or under the seats. Fixed nozzles, which are supposed to be operated in an upright position, are difficult to operate under such circumstances. Tests conducted by one airline suggested that flexible nozzles increased effectiveness by an incredible magnitude of ten. The FAA showed little interest in this issue. The rule was published in final form less than four months after the comment period closed. There was only one significant change: smoke detectors would not be required in the galley. This eliminated the airlines' strongest objection without compromising on anything the staff considered critical. The safety record with galley fires was far more reassuring than the record for lavatories. There has never been a catastrophic in-flight fire, domestic or foreign, that originated in the galley. While this requirement was easily dropped, addressing the other objections raised in the comment period was not so easy. They called for changes in specific requirements and would require additional analysis. The FAA had no patience for these arguments. The agency wanted to placate Congress and get the rule published. The rulemaking staff had no intention of letting public comments delay the process. The candid explanation of a staff member about comments concerning the value of requiring a flexible hose on Halon extinguishers illustrates the attitude: "There probably is a lot of benefit in a flexible hose. But we have a certain practical limitation here: we can't just go ahead in the middle of a rule action and change our minds and say that when the rule comes out we want twenty-five hundred airplanes to be equipped with flexible hoses. That throws everything into a cocked hat. . . . We had to make a decision and we made it." The rule was finalized in record time. It was promulgated on March 29, 1985, less than ten months after it was first proposed. Three years later, the FAA banned smoking on all domestic flights of under two hours. This may be the most cost-effective move the FAA could take toward reducing the risk of a cabin fire. The ban was adopted for health reasons, however, not for reasons of fire safety.

Evaluating the FAA Standard

Whether the FAA's new regulation would have prevented the Air Canada disaster or, more important, another catastrophe in the future is difficult to determine, partly because serious accidents are so rare. There were no deaths on U.S. commercial aircraft in 1980, for example, and only four in both 1981 and 1984. Even 1985, considered by many "the worst year ever" for aviation safety, was remarkably safe by comparison to other modes of transportation (particularly if deaths due to terrorist acts are subtracted from the total).[22] Accidents are so rare, according to an actuary at Metropolitan Life, that "it is almost pure chance as to which [major commercial airline] has a total loss" in any given year.[23] The chances of a serious in-flight fire are even more remote. Most aviation injuries and fatalities are caused by impact, not fire. As an airline safety engineer put it, the fatal in-flight fire is "a rare animal of a rare breed." The first recorded fatalities from an in-flight cabin fire in the United States were in the Air Canada calamity.

The almost random nature of accidents creates the first paradox of developing (or analyzing) aviation safety regulations. Accidents precipitate strong political pressures for regulatory change, but they provide little factual basis for making meaningful improvements. Preventing random events is practically an impossible task. Instead of trying to anticipate the unknown, attention tends to get focused on preventing any repetition of what has already happened, regardless of the likelihood that it will happen again.

The politics of aviation safety also conflict with broader political trends concerning government regulation. Many members of Congress openly challenge the notion that aviation safety regulations should be undertaken only if benefits are at least commensurate with costs. Testifying before a House committee about several recent proposals for upgrading cabin safety, the chairman of the NTSB said he "would hate to see [their] implementation delayed for a cost-benefit analysis."[24] Nevertheless, the FAA is bound by the same executive orders that require all agencies to conduct an economic analysis of proposed regulations.[25]

This raises the second dilemma of aviation regulation: the FAA must justify in economic terms regulations that sometimes can only be justified on other grounds. This is not to say that the FAA's Regulatory Analysis Group engages in trickery or deception. The agency has refined the use of economic analysis over the years through its capital improvement projects for airport facilities. A detailed FAA manual spells out the procedures and many specific values (including the always controversial value of a life) to use in cost-benefit analysis.[26] This simplifies and standardizes the agency's analysis. Nevertheless, this case demonstrates how the use of favorable assumptions can make a regulation of questionable economic benefit look economically desirable.

The FAA's Regulatory Analysis Group wrote a forty-three-page cost-benefit analysis of the proposal for smoke detectors and fire extinguishers. The analysis is systematic, comprehensive, and prominently featured in the *Federal Register* notice. The bottom line, according to the analysis, is that "total expected benefits equal $42.8 million and total costs equal $13.8 million, resulting in a total expected benefit-cost ratio of 3.1 and a total expected net benefit of $29.0 million."[27] There is much to take issue with in this analysis. For example, smoke detectors, assumed to cost $50 each, will very likely cost much more if airlines choose even a few of the features justified by the aviation environment (for example, tamper-proof battery packs, better vibration tolerance).

More important, there are several reasons to call into question not only the *magnitude* of estimated benefits but whether they actually exceed expected costs. One problem concerns predicting catastrophic in-flight fires. Recognizing the difficulty in predicting the distribution of essentially random numbers, the FAA staff utilized an elegant statistical solution: the Poisson distribution.[28] The elegance of the solution masks the significance of one critical underlying assumption: the "expected mean value" of two catastrophic cabin fires in the next ten years. This figure is purportedly based on "historical data." The Varig fire occurred in July 1973 and the Air Canada fire in June 1983. But the Varig fire was neither on a domestic carrier nor a domestic accident. The Air Canada fire caused the first fatalities in the United States from an in-flight cabin fire. To expect two similar fires every ten years seems overly gloomy, especially since there have been improvements in aviation fire safety since the Varig incident. After that fire, several airlines installed heat-sensitive fire extinguishers in trash receptacles. Moreover, there is nothing magic about a ten-year period. Thomas Hopkins, an economist at the University of Maryland's School of Public Affairs, notes in connection with the FAA's analysis of Floor Proximity Emergency Lighting—another proposal linked to the Air Canada fire—that "if the past five years are considered more representative of what lies ahead, there were no pertinent fatalities and so no plausible benefits."[29] One problem with the agency's cost-benefit analysis, then, is that it does not test the sensitivity of this important assumption. Assuming a mean of one catastrophic fire (instead of two) every ten years could cut the potential benefits of the rule in half.

Other assumptions of vital importance to the analysis include the estimated "coefficients of effectiveness" for smoke detectors and fire extinguishers. Here the analysis purports to incorporate "conservative" estimates. These estimates are not as unambiguously "conservative" as the FAA staff suggests. One assumption is that a smoke detector could avert 50 percent of catastrophic lavatory fires. The staff provides no basis for this estimate or for labeling it "conservative." Stated another way, the coefficient is based on two assumptions: first, that in 50 percent of the lavatory fires that become catastrophic, quicker detection would prevent the catastrophe; and second, that off-the-shelf smoke detectors would actually provide quicker detection. Both assumptions are doubtful. Speed of detection certainly was not the problem in the Air Canada fire. The short-circuit alarm probably alerted the pilots faster than a smoke alarm would have. Delays and uncertainty in responding to the alarm—something as likely to occur with smoke detectors as with circuit breakers—were the main problems. Second, the detection capability of household smoke detectors in an aviation environment, as already mentioned, is quite uncertain. False alarms are likely to be a problem; some fires may go undetected. Combining these considerations, it appears that 25 percent, or maybe even 10 percent, is as reasonable an estimate as 50 percent. Similar arguments apply to the coefficients used for calculating the benefits of trash receptacle extinguishers.

A third problem with the economic analysis is that it overstates the benefits by failing to take into account existing "compliance" with the proposed rule. At least half of the commercial carriers voluntarily complied with the FAA's 1980 request to carry Halon extinguishers (a few even installed smoke detectors without any FAA advice). The benefits attributable to the proposed rule should reflect only the *incremental benefit* of adding Halon extinguishers to the remaining carriers. Instead, the FAA adjusted the cost figure to reflect the marginal cost of Halon extinguishers but not the marginal benefits.[30]

The cost-benefit analysis also did not take into account the special training necessary to use a Halon extinguisher effectively. This means either overstated benefits or understated costs, depending on whether the airlines voluntarily improve existing training programs. Most airline employees receive cursory instruction in fire fighting. Only two airlines provide actual "hands on" training with fire extinguishers.[31] "Hands on" training is particularly important with Halon extinguishers, which discharge in a liquid stream that must be carefully applied because it lasts less than ten seconds. Those not properly trained in the use of these sophisticated extinguishers may actually be less effective than with other extinguishers. Even with less-sophisticated extinguishers, untrained operators are generally able to extinguish only about half as big a fire as those with training.[32] The carbon dioxide extinguishers aboard the Air Canada jet were discharged without effect in the early stage of that disaster. As an engineer with Factory Mutual Research Corporation put it, "It wouldn't have made any difference if you had given them another thirty extinguishers." The cost-benefit analysis never considered this issue. In fact, the provision for Halon extinguishers was given only superficial treatment. The staff considered these extinguishers "clearly cost-beneficial" because they are lighter than older extinguishers, so "fuel savings alone are expected to pay for this proposal." In short, they were assumed to be more effective. The projected $2.9 million in "pure safety benefit" might be more than outweighed, however, by the cost of training flight attendants adequately to ensure effective use.

Finally, even if the FAA were predisposed to write its own standard, the rulemaking staff should have been aware that the private standard NFPA 408 existed. At least one FAA employee has been on the NFPA's Aircraft Rescue and Firefighting Committee, charged with standards for aviation fire extinguishers, since NFPA 408 was first adopted in 1956. Two FAA representatives were on the committee when the standard was revised in 1980 and later when the FAA decided to draft and adopt its own standard.[33] One reason the rulemaking staff was unaware of NFPA 408 is organizational. Neither of the FAA employees were from the Airworthiness Division—the division that wrote the FAA's standard for fire extinguishers—and neither took a particular interest in NFPA 408. They were more interested in other aircraft rescue and firefighting standards.[34] Beyond these peculiar circumstances, however, the fact that the rulemaking staff did not think to check for the existence of an NFPA standard is evidence of the low profile that currently characterizes these standards.

None of these issues was raised by those commenting on the proposed rule or, surprisingly, by the Office of Management and Budget in its review of the cost-benefit analysis. Politics, it seems, loomed larger than economics. "This was a motherhood issue," explains an FAA rulemaking staff member. "Who is going to argue about fire extinguishers in airplanes?" Indeed, the FAA received hundreds of handwritten letters and postcards from individual citizens in favor of the proposed rule.

A Little-known and Surprisingly Strict Private Standard: NFPA 408

One of the comments the FAA never formally responded to was a suggestion that the agency adopt a private standard for hand-held aircraft fire extinguishers, NFPA 408. That the FAA did not do so is not surprising—government regulators often look on private standards with disfavor. What seems unusual is that the FAA (at least the staff member in charge of drafting the standard on fire extinguishers) was unaware of the existence of NFPA 408 until the agency received the suggestion (which, incidentally, came from NFPA). Ignorance in this instance was a function of poor communication within the FAA and, more broadly, of the waning influence of private, industrywide aviation safety standards.

As with several other areas of regulation, aviation safety used to be addressed entirely by the private sector. When NFPA first got involved in the subject, government regulation was minimal, and the future of private aviation regulation looked promising. Responding to requests from the National Aircraft Underwriters' Association, UL formed an Aviation Department in 1920, and two years later it started offering a service that the FAA would later take over: certifying the airworthiness of aircraft. Insurance groups, interested in standards to use in making underwriting decisions, asked the NFPA to develop various aviation standards.

NFPA is a membership organization similar to the American Society for Testing and Materials. "Volunteer" committees write the 260 NFPA codes and standards, and the membership at large votes on various standards at semiannual meetings. NFPA has over thirty-two thousand members, including architects, engineers, firemen, and representatives of manufacturers, insurance interests, labor, and government.

One of the standards NFPA developed in the aviation area was NFPA 408,[35] which contained recommendations concerning the "type, capacity, location and quantity of aircraft hand fire extinguishers and accessory equipment provided essentially for the protection of aircraft compartments occupied by passengers and crew."[36] It was drafted between 1947 and 1955 by a technical subcommittee of NFPA's Aircraft Rescue and Firefighting Committee. The group had twenty-four members, including seven from government agencies in the United States and Canada, six from commercial airlines, two from academia, and one each from UL and UL of Canada. NFPA 408, with appendices, was less than six pages long. It provided information on the two most prevalent types of extinguishers (dry chemical and water) and mandated that airlines carry one small extinguisher in the cockpit and, depending on occupancy, between one and three in the passenger compartment. The standard also set forth a suggested training outline on the use of fire extinguishers. Unfortunately, NFPA has no record of how these specific provisions were developed. (Only in recent years have comments and committee minutes routinely been retained.)

Over time, interest in private, industrywide aviation safety standards diminished—at least in this country. The Civil Aeronautics Board, predecessor to the FAA, displaced UL's entire Aviation Department. Insurers began using compliance with the FAA's airworthiness standards as a condition of insurance. As technology became more complicated, airframe manufacturers (for example, Boeing, Lockheed, McDonnell-Douglas) assumed much of the responsibility earlier undertaken by commercial carriers. Currently, "most carriers will accept what the airframe manufacturer offers," according to the fire protection engineer at the only major airline to employ one.[37]

This apathy affected NFPA 408. Although reissued in 1965, 1970, and 1973, the standard was largely unchanged from its original version. The main reason, suspects a current member of the Aircraft Rescue and Firefighting Committee, is expressed by the adage about letting sleeping dogs lie: "There had never been a demonstrated problem warranting attention." There also was little interest in such standards among domestic airlines and airframe manufacturers. The in-house standards at Boeing were more important than NFPA 408. The primary interest in NFPA 408, and in many of NFPA's other aviation safety standards, was from foreign countries. As one committee member put it, "There is no FAA in Greece." Many foreign governments thus look to these standards for guidance. But the foreign contingent on the committee did not attend meetings regularly, and many lacked sufficient technical background to suggest improvements. Moreover, given the limited demand for the standard, NFPA 408 generated almost no income for NFPA. (The sale of publications accounts for two-thirds of NFPA's income.) But NFPA 408 is one of many NFPA standards offered more as a public service than as a money-making proposition, and at times these standards suffer from lack of attention.

NFPA 408 languished in the late 1970s when changes in technology rendered it out of date (it did not take into account the new jumbo jets, which could hold over three hundred passengers). The relevant provision in the 1973 version (for occupancies "over 61 passengers") called for three fire extinguishers. "An airframe manufacturer would never provide so few extinguishers [for a jumbo jet]," notes an NFPA committee member. Halogenated extinguishing agents also came into use in the 1970s, but NFPA 408 made only a passing reference to them.[38] The 1973 version still allowed carbon dioxide extinguishers, which had long since fallen out of favor with most fire protection engineers because of the damage they can do to electrical equipment.

The 1980 Revival of NFPA 408

The Standards Council, the general oversight group within NFPA, recognized the problem in 1980, when nine aviation safety standards, including NFPA 408, were overdue for revision and reissue. The chairman of the Technical Committee on Aircraft Rescue and Firefighting considered 408 so inadequate that he proposed that NFPA withdraw it and start over from scratch. Withdrawing the standard as outdated was not in the interest of the Standards Council, however, which seeks to protect NFPA's reputation and is aware that the organization obtains its income largely from the sale of standards.[39] Even though the income from this standard is minimal, it is in NFPA's general interest to keep its standards available. The Standards Council instructed the committee to expedite the process of bringing the standard up to date. A technical subcommittee met several times in the following year and drafted a new version. The new standard included changes in the number of extinguishers required, the type of extinguishers, and the nature of employee training. All of these changes were in the direction of being more stringent, although a few were left as suggestions rather than stated as requirements. Most significant, however, the basic requirements of NFPA 408 were more demanding than what the FAA eventually required.

The most significant and costly provision in NFPA 408 specifies the number of extinguishers required. The revised version requires more than twice the number specified in the old version—and more if necessary, to ensure that there is an extinguisher within thirty feet of any passenger.[40] How did the subcommittee choose these numbers? By doing for aviation safety what the 61B committee would not do for grain elevator safety: a combination of guesswork and fire protection rules of thumb. "If you are asking whether it is like Newton's law, where we can categorically support the conclusion, the answer is no," explained an engineer on the committee. There was surprisingly little disagreement among committee members, however, concerning the specific numbers chosen. Most members, even those representing the airlines, took the general view that the standard should err on the side of safety. In this respect, NFPA 408 reflects the professional norms of aviation safety engineers, who frequently rely on significant margins of safety. The margin of safety in the revised version is more than adequate. This standard is unlikely to produce benefits in excess of costs, however. A candid NFPA staff member admitted that this is probably true of all NFPA aviation safety standards.

The revised version of NFPA 408 also takes into account recent changes in extinguishant technology. The standard prohibits carbon dioxide extinguishers. (The FAA still allows them.) NFPA 408 also specifically requires, for the first time, the use of Halon 1211 extinguishers. Several key committee members knew that Halon 1211 is an extremely effective extinguishant. The toxicity question, raised by several airlines in response to the FAA's general notice, was not a sticking point. Most members consider these concerns exaggerated and inappropriate. "You have to put out the fire before you start worrying about toxicity," explained one member. There was minor disagreement about which Halon agent to require, but the idea of Halon was endorsed largely on the recommendation of the committee's engineers. Representatives of companies that manufacture such extinguishers naturally supported the idea as well, but those firms make all types of extinguishers and have no particular stake in Halon.

Flexible Nozzles and Special Training

The Technical Committee on Aircraft Rescue and Firefighting considered two other issues to be important—flexible nozzles for extinguishers and special training for the use of Halon—but they acted in a markedly less decisive manner on both. On flexible nozzles, the fire protection engineer from a major airline made a convincing case that extinguishers would be much more effective with this design change. He conducted tests that indicated that models with a flexible hose could be almost ten times more effective than current models in aviation use. The committee was largely unmoved, however, and simply changed the standard to *permit* flexible hoses but not require them. An appendix section advises that "for access to underseat, overhead, and other difficult to reach locations consideration should be given to using extinguishers with a discharge hose."[41]

This seemingly timid approach is a product of the tangled web between installation standards (such as NFPA 408) and product standards (such as UL's). NFPA does not write product standards per se. It does, however, specify some performance characteristics for products. This creates an awkward relationship with the product standards written by such organizations as UL. Sometimes performance characteristics are closely linked to basic product specifications. For example, requiring high enough temperature tolerances for a chimney necessitates that it be made of metal, not masonry. In some instances, NFPA's requirements seem to drive UL's standards; in others, the UL standard appears to control the NFPA standard. The situation is often compared to the proverbial chicken-and-egg problem. In the case of fire extinguishers, however, it is clear which came first: UL did.

Realistically, NFPA can require something different from UL only when it is sure that UL will change accordingly. This is practically assured when the NFPA standard affects a substantial share of the certification market.[42] But in the case of aircraft fire extinguishers, the NFPA standard affects a minuscule portion of the market regulated by UL. Not only does UL feel little pressure to change its fire extinguisher standard to satisfy the special concerns of aviation use; it foresees a limited reward for the effort as well. The market for aviation fire extinguishers is too small.

The generic UL standard for fire extinguishers continues to take precedence over any NFPA requirements in 408. UL tests extinguishers under specific conditions and certifies them with different ratings.[43] NFPA 408 depends on these standards to define the capabilities of the fire extinguishers required by NFPA standards. What UL requires is not necessarily what NFPA would choose for aviation use. UL does not require a flexible hose on small hand-held extinguishers, for example. Nor does it require a discharge time of more than eight seconds for the typical small Halon extinguisher. A United Airlines engineer thinks that twelve to fourteen seconds would be much more desirable. And flexible nozzles are clearly a major improvement over fixed nozzles for aviation use.

The other technical issue considered, but skirted, by NFPA involved the training requirements for using Halon extinguishers. The committee settled on a vague requirement that "training shall provide classroom instruction and manipulative skills training." The appendix removes the teeth from this provision, however, by adding that "it is highly recommended that live fire training on representative aircraft fires be conducted . . . [but this is] not required by this standard."[44]

The mild-mannered approach to this provision also stands in contrast to the other more stringent provisions of 408. It reflects in part NFPA's reluctance to specify training requirements and in part the resistance of the airlines to a significant and recurring expense. The representative of Factory Mutual, who had recently conducted a study of hand-held fire extinguishers under contract to the FAA, recalls that the importance of training costs was repeatedly mentioned by those he surveyed. Fire safety experts agreed that training in realistic test situations would be costly. NFPA has a general position against addressing training or other seemingly managerial tasks. The Aircraft Rescue and Firefighting Committee managed to include more specific statements about the nature of recommended training procedures than are contained in most NFPA standards. But even that language is weak.

The committee members approved the proposed changes in May 1983, a full year before the FAA proposed its own rule. A public comment period followed release of the document to the NFPA membership, and when the committee met the following November it was faced with a total of fourteen comments from only four individuals. UL submitted the most detailed comments, most of them definitional, demonstrating a better understanding of fire extinguishers than the committee as a whole. There was a minor spat about whether a competing Halon agent—lower in toxicity, but also less effective—should be permitted. The committee rejected those proposals on the grounds that they were not supported by accompanying technical data.[45] NFPA 408 was approved without comment or question by the general membership at the organization's 1984 annual meeting. It became effective on July 5, 1984, a little more than two years after the Standards Council instructed the committee to expedite the revision process.

Summary Evaluation

Deciding whether either the FAA or the NFPA standard is desirable depends on the choice one makes between the economic and political views of aviation safety. In economic terms, it is unlikely that either standard produces benefits in excess of costs. Aviation safety experts in both sectors confirm that almost no recent proposals for improved aviation safety can be justified on economic grounds. This does not render these standards unpopular, however. The political culture of aviation safety is characterized by an extreme "no-risk" perspective that apparently cuts across public and private boundaries.[46] Congressman Norman Mineta (D-Calif.) recently allowed that "no rational risk analysis or cost-benefit analysis would conclude that the next increment of safety improvements needed in this country is in aviation." He went on to argue for precisely such expenditures.[47] A similar view prevails at NFPA. Apparently, all that matters in either sector is whether new regulations might make the skies safer—how much safer and at what cost are of little interest.

"Safe enough," notes an NTSB official, sounding a popular chord, "means safer every year." In those terms, both the FAA and NFPA standards are probably desirable. That is, they would contribute, however minimally, to improvements in aviation safety. But even that conclusion is unsure, particularly for the FAA standard. One aviation safety expert considers the FAA's response to the Air Canada fire purely "cosmetic." While virtually everyone connected with the smoke detector business had serious doubts about putting household detectors in airplane lavatories, the FAA was unconcerned. A rulemaking staff member demurred that the UL standard for household detectors "is a very impressive document," implying that it provides sufficient requirements for aviation use. UL disagreed, detailing in a letter to the FAA's public docket numerous reasons why household detectors are inappropriate for aviation use. The height of FAA hubris is summed up in a staff member's conclusion that, although there might be operational difficulties, "we say in the rule that [the airlines] are expected to keep [the smoke detectors] working."

A lack of technical understanding, similar to that expressed by OSHA in the grain elevator proceedings, was evident in how the FAA dealt with fire extinguishers. The rulemaking staff did not appreciate the possible significance of flexible nozzles. Nor did they apparently understand the need for special training in the use of Halon extinguishers. These points were called to the FAA's attention, however, and the failure of the agency to respond demonstrates the extent to which FAA rulemaking is driven by political pressures. After the Air Canada fire, the FAA was painfully aware that Congress wanted the agency to enact a rule, any rule. And that is precisely what the FAA did—placate an impatient Congress with a quick, but half-baked, safety standard.

In sum, the FAA displayed a surprising range of regulatory behavior over time. The agency relied on quiet advice for years, deferring largely to private decisions. That tactic is more effective than it is often portrayed. The airframe manufacturers probably do more to advance aviation safety than the FAA does. But the FAA is quick to regulate when it is subject to strong congressional pressure, usually triggered by the NTSB recommendations that follow every calamity. The FAA's response to the Air Canada fire demonstrates that public standards-setting need not get bogged down in procedural requirements. This encouraging note is tempered, however, by the realization that important technical issues were overlooked in the rush to regulate.

The private sector, on the other hand, was slower and more sensitive to technical issues. Expressing the kind of technical knowledge also present in the grain elevator proceedings, the NFPA committee recognized the benefits of flexible nozzles and proper training. Showing the same regulatory philosophy present in the grain elevator proceedings, the committee declined to adopt specific requirements in areas deemed "managerial." The committee made "non-binding" recommendations instead. But the NFPA standard is actually more demanding than the FAA's in its requirements for fire extinguishers. That is probably because professional fire safety engineers played a central role in the development of NFPA 408. These engineers do not profess to balance costs and benefits in the pursuit of fire safety. Rather, there is a powerful professional tendency, even in the private sector, to "favor fire protection for the sake of fire protection."

The NFPA standard does not address smoke detectors; they are not within the formal jurisdiction of the Aircraft Rescue and Firefighting Committee. While this lapse is not necessarily bad, it suggests a possible shortcoming of private standards-setting. The specialization of committees threatens to overlook broader regulatory issues and ignore some of the connections between standards. To address these problems, there is a proposal within NFPA to create a "Cabin Fire Protection" committee. An active participant in NFPA 408 calls the proposal controversial and political. "It would require much broader expertise than anyone has. But everyone would want to be on that committee."

The tangled connection between so-called installation standards (such as NFPA 408) and product standards (such as UL's standards for fire extinguishers) also affected the quality of NFPA 408. The standard relies on UL's generic standards for fire extinguishers. But the UL standard is not geared to the aviation environment. Technological changes that would be appropriate to aviation standards—such as flexible nozzles, longer discharge time, or a Class A rating for five-pound extinguishers—are therefore not incorporated into NFPA 408. Unfortunately, the cause and possible cure of this disjuncture between installation standards and product standards is not clear from this case alone. This chicken-and-egg problem confounds various cases of overlapping private regulation.

There was also a marked change in private behavior over time, but for reasons unrelated to the Air Canada fire. NFPA 408 languished in the 1970s, when, as an NFPA officer quaintly explains, there was "an attendance problem." The Standards Council intervened in 1980, and the standard was revitalized shortly before the Air Canada fire in 1983. The changing fortunes of NFPA 408 reflect the importance of the demand for private standards. Standards are demanded for a host of reasons: for example, to provide technical information, to lend credibility, and to minimize exposure to liability. The first two of these influences waned as airframe manufacturers seized the initiative for most safety issues. These manufacturers obviously have the technical capability, and they apparently have attained the political credibility to engage effectively in self-regulation. (Liability law does not appear to be an important influence in aviation standards, since the law assesses liability practically without regard to fault.) As the demand for NFPA 408 waned, so did attendance at the Rescue and Firefighting Committee. Some foreign air carriers still sought regulatory information, but the domestic demand was minimal. The correspondingly low revenue generated by this standard probably helps explain NFPA's acquiescence in this lapse. The evolution of NFPA 408 suggests that minimal demand can beget minimal standards. Attempting to reverse this trend, the NFPA Standards Council pushed its aviation committees to update their standards in 1980. This restored the standard to the substantive status it had enjoyed before falling into disuse. But the demand is artificial. There is no evidence that air carriers or airframe manufacturers actually use this standard. It seems likely, therefore, that it will languish again, NFPA's gallant efforts to sell more standards notwithstanding.

FIVE

Safety Standards and Labeling Requirements for Woodstoves

In the first two case studies, the public and private standards were developed largely in isolation from each other: by choice with grain elevators, through ignorance in aviation fire safety. These standards were essentially independent. They were not aimed at each other, so they are conducive to being analyzed alone. The final two case studies are more complicated. Both involve the Consumer Product Safety Commission, an agency that has packed considerable experience with private standards into its short history. The CPSC was born of controversy about the desirability of private standards and has since experimented with various strategies for interacting with the private sector, including the ill-fated offeror process.[1] Currently, the agency is required by statute to consider the desirability of private standards before proposing any government regulation. This relationship—where instead of being isolated, standards are deliberately intertwined—raises important questions about the *interaction* between public and private standards. Both of the remaining paired cases suggest that the secondary effects of safety standards—that is, how they affect each other—is as important as how they regulate behavior directly.

In the case of woodstoves, the effects of the CPSC regulation on the private standard are perhaps the only saving grace of an otherwise disappointing regulatory effort. As with so much government regulation, the process of developing the woodstove rule was long-drawn-out. The final CPSC standard addresses the labeling issue but avoids the more serious problem of creosote fires. The prospect of judicial "second-guessing" has apparently intimidated the CPSC in much the same way that liability law is thought to stifle innovation in the private sector. Fortunately, the private standard improved significantly while the CPSC standard was being developed.

This case also highlights some important and unexpected differences in the patterns of compliance with public and private standards. The private sector achieved much better compliance with its standard than did the CPSC. Apparently, the force of law behind "mandatory" public standards is not necessarily stronger than the forces that induce compliance with "voluntary" private ones. Although the CPSC refuses to recognize it, the institutional arrangements attendant to UL's standards—a function of being in the business of product testing—are sometimes superior to command and control regulation in attaining high levels of compliance.

In addition to dispelling the notion that private standards are "voluntary," the UL standard for woodstoves partially contradicts the idea that private standards are lax. The standard can be faulted for avoiding certain hazards (particularly creosote fires) but several of its requirements are rather stringent. As with the private standards already examined, this standard was developed long before the threat of government regulation arose. Many of its provisions are not supported by specific scientific evidence; rather, they are the product of engineering judgment and educated guesses. These judgments apparently command respect, and there have been minimal objections to the UL standard. This suggests that UL has greater credibility or, perhaps, greater clout than the CPSC. A strong demand for compliance with private standards, emanating in this case from building codes and product liability insurers, may bolster the effectiveness of private standards-setting.

An Overview of Woodstove Safety

Americans rediscovered the woodstove in the 1970s, almost 250 years after Benjamin Franklin designed the first model intended primarily for heating rather than cooking. Sales of woodstoves tripled between 1974 and 1978. With increased popularity came improvements in technology. Franklin's design was altered first by the addition of doors—the Franklin stove was simply a firebox with an open front—and more recently by airtight construction that makes stoves burn hotter and more efficiently.

Woodstove-related fires also became common in the 1970s. Woodstoves were mentioned frequently in fire incident data analyzed by the Center for Fire Research at the National Bureau of Standards. Whether these hazards should be addressed through safety standards is disputed. It is widely agreed, however, that woodstoves are potentially dangerous. "Making wood heat an effective alternative to conventional heating requires the ultimate in careful planning," warns a popular consumer magazine.[2] In the absence of proper precautions, woodstoves pose four general hazards: creosote fires, ignition of nearby combustibles by radiant heat, escaping sparks or fire, and surface burns.

The Creosote Problem

Creosote fires account for approximately 60 percent of woodstove-related fires. Creosote is formed when the moisture expelled from burning wood combines with unburnt combustible gases in the flue. A tarry substance builds up on the flue lining, eventually becoming brittle and highly flammable. If the chimney is not cleaned in time, high temperatures will start a fire that can spread to the surrounding structure through radiant heat or, if the fire is hot enough, by burning through the chimney.

The process of burning wood inevitably produces creosote. The amount depends on the type of wood, its moisture content, and, most important, the temperature of the fire. Greener wood creates more creosote. So do low burning temperatures, such as those obtained when the stove damper is adjusted for overnight burning. Product design also affects creosote production. New high-efficiency stoves burn hotter and create less creosote than most traditional models. Catalytic combustors, an even newer technology, reduce creosote production through a complex chemical interaction between wood smoke and noble metals such as platinum that enables the smoke to release more heat before going up the chimney.

Nearby Combustibles and Other Hazards

Woodstoves radiate heat that is deceptive in its capacity for igniting nearby walls or furniture. As a rule of thumb, stoves should be installed at least thirty-six inches from the wall and surrounding furniture. This varies both by stove and by building material, but installing a stove even a foot too close to a wall can eventually result in a fire. There is a similar problem with chimney connectors and other piping, which require about an eighteen-inch clearance from the wall and ceiling but are often installed closer, particularly when passing through a wall or ceiling (see figure 2). Approximately 20 percent of woodstove-related fires are thought to be caused by insufficient clearance to combustibles. Some experts consider the connection to the chimney—rather than the distance from the wall—to be the most dangerous aspect of woodstove installation.

The third hazard, least significant in occurrence, is that fire will escape from the stove. This includes fires caused when (1) sparks escape from the air inlets, (2) coals or flames escape through the stove door (often because it is open), and (3) the fire actually burns through the firebox.

The final hazard associated with woodstoves is the most common, the least severe, and is almost impossible to control through regulation. It is surface burns caused by contact with a hot stove.

Are Woodstoves a Serious Problem?

Woodstoves appear to pose a sizable safety problem. They are second only to careless smoking as the leading cause of residential fires. The CPSC estimates that solid-fuel heating equipment was involved in 140,000 fires in 1985, causing approximately 280 deaths and over $300 million in property damage.[3] There are several reasons to discount the significance of these numbers, however. First, they stem from dubious extrapolation techniques.[4] The CPSC's sample is limited and nonrandom. The data do not distinguish between woodstoves and fireplace inserts. They are both lumped together under "solid-fuel appliances," leaving it unclear how much of the problem is actually attributable to woodstoves. Moreover, reports compiled by local fire departments are usually sketchy and sometimes inaccurate in assessing causes.[5]

Second, these national estimates conceal the fact that most woodstove-related fires are minor. According to the National Bureau of Standards, "of the 11,534 residential solid fuel related fire incidents reported in the [eleven-state] data base . . . the loss was under $1,000 in seventy-two percent of the fires."[6] Finally, and most important, it is not clear whether any of these hazards, whatever their frequency, can be reduced by product standards. There is a report in the CPSC files, for example, of an injury caused when an adult tried to retrieve an aerosol can from his woodstove. Obviously, no product standard could prevent

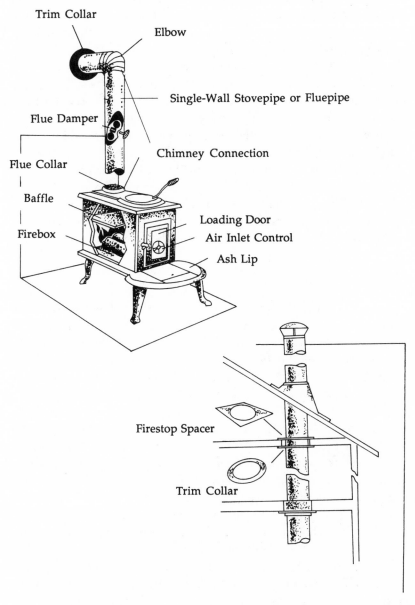

Trim Collar

Elbow

Single-Wall Stovepipe or Fluepipe

Flue Damper

Flue Collar

Chimney Connection

Baffle

Firebox

Loading Door

Air Inlet Control

Ash Lip

Firestop Spacer

Trim Collar

Figure 2. Woodstove and Wall Pass-through System

this kind of injury. This is not necessarily true of all, or even most, fires commonly attributed to the consumer. "Injuries," as one independent consultant put it, "are often caused by an unfortunate combination of design, installation, and use." The number of fires directly attributable to the product itself is probably very small.[7]

Even with all these uncertainties, both a public and a private organization chose to write standards for woodstoves. UL officially proposed a draft standard for woodstove safety in January 1978—seven months after the CPSC received a petition requesting that the government regulate woodstoves. But forestalling government regulation was not, as it might appear to have been, UL's motive. The UL standard (in "unpublished form," as explained later) actually predates the petition to the CPSC by several decades. Moreover, there is minimal overlap between the CPSC's standard and the UL standard. The former addresses only labeling; the latter aims to be comprehensive and includes performance tests and design requirements as well as labeling requirements.

Underwriters Laboratories

UL is the premier product testing lab in the country. Building codes and other use and installation codes inevitably require that various products be certified by a "nationally recognized testing laboratory such as Underwriters Labs." In fact, there is no other organization quite like it. This has led to charges that UL is a monopoly—a charge that UL officials privately admit is true in many product areas. It is not true, however, in the case of woodstoves.

Founded in 1894, the year after the Palace of Electricity astonished visitors at the great Chicago Exposition, UL was established by an electrical investigator hired earlier by the Chicago Board of Fire Underwriters to assist exposition officials. Aware of the burgeoning market for electrical equipment and the lack of available safety standards, William Merrill started a business with the still-popular UL motto: Testing for Public Safety. The original idea was to provide information to insurance companies on the fire risks attendant to various electrical equipment. The organization (known then as Underwriters Electrical Bureau) soon became affiliated with the National Board of Fire Underwriters. Incorporated as Underwriters Laboratories in 1901, UL began offering its testing services directly to manufacturers. A manufacturer would submit its product to UL for testing, pay a testing fee, and receive permission to display the UL label (also for a fee) if the product was approved. This third-party certification service, as it is often called, was soon expanded to include a "follow-up service," now a major part of UL's function. Currently, the "listing" of a product is contingent upon the use of UL's follow-up service, whereby representatives of UL make periodic inspections of the products at the factory and possibly from the open market to determine compliance with UL requirements. This comprehensive inspection system is a form of quality control, meant to assure that proper tolerances are kept in the manufacturing process. Subscribers to UL's listing service are visited approximately four times per year.

UL has always prided itself on its independence from manufacturers' interests. Although originally affiliated with the insurance industry, UL became legally independent in 1936, when it incorporated as a non-profit corporation in Delaware. The Internal Revenue Service challenged the tax exemption, however, and a federal court eventually agreed that UL "may be good business, but it is not charity."[8] The tax exemption was restored by Congress, and UL continues to be viewed as the most independent of the private standards-setters. UL's reputation is excellent. It has been remarkably free of scandals or horror stories. Staff members at the Federal Trade Commission, which proposed to regulate private standards and certification in 1977, concur that UL is usually above reproach.

UL has branched out considerably over the years from its best-known area, electrical devices. There are over three thousand employees (a third of whom are engineers) and six major departments—burglary protection, casualty and chemical, fire protection, heating and refrigeration, marine, and electrical—handling literally thousands of product categories. In 1984 over 2.5 billion labels bearing the UL mark were used at 35,381 manufacturing sites in sixty-four countries.[9] Other testing labs compete with UL, but only in a limited sense. The competition often uses UL's standards. Some labs provide certification at a lower cost than UL, in part because they do not have to bear the expense of developing standards. They also do not have to assume the same risk of being held liable in a product liability suit, since they bear no responsibility for the content of the standards. These labs are not always considered "nationally recognized" for the purposes of regulation, however, and some insurance companies charge higher premiums for product liability insurance when the manufacturer uses a testing lab other than UL.

UL 1482: Room Heaters, Solid-Fuel Type

At first blush, UL's standard for coal and wood-burning stoves appears complicated and highly technical. The current version, incorporating minor changes made four years after the first edition was published in 1979, is sixty-one pages long and covers both the construction and performance of stoves. Some provisions specify design requirements. For example, cast-iron stoves must not be thinner than 3.17mm (one-eighth of an inch).[10] Other provisions involve mechanical tests. The "strength test" for chimney connectors calls for a twenty-pound sand-bag to be swung on a pendulum against the chimney connector.[11] The stove itself is subject to various stability tests, including a "drop test" in which the stove is dropped ten times from a height of one inch. Other provisions are more general and subjective, such as the prohibition against "edges, corners, or projections that present a risk of a cut or puncture-type injury to persons."[12] Twenty-six pages of UL 1482 are devoted to electrical blowers, an optional item not included on many stoves, which help circulate heat throughout the room. Given UL's orientation toward electrical devices, this section is extremely detailed and refers to many other UL standards for motors, wire, switches, and component parts.

But the fire tests are the guts of UL 1482. They subject the stove to both intense "flash fire" conditions and more stable, long-term burning conditions. The temperature at designated points on the stove's surface and surrounding walls must stay within specified tolerances during three separate tests. The manufacturer specifies the distance the stove should be from the wall during testing. If the stove passes, the subsequent label indicates the precise certified clearance (or "distance to combustibles").

From Proposal to Publication

There are two versions of the making of UL 1482: official and unofficial. Like textbook descriptions of the legislative process, the official version misses most of the important subtleties. But it describes the framework within which the standard was written and is necessary to understanding the unofficial story that follows, which is based more on interviews than on official documents.

The official story begins in January 1978, when UL "proposed" the standard to its Fire Council and to manufacturers of wood-burning appliances, circulating the standard for written comments. Five engineering councils composed of outside safety experts provide input to UL engineers in standards development. Council members may not have any formal relationship with manufacturers or distributors. Councils meet only every other year, however, so most business is conducted by letter ballot. The standard was revised and circulated for comments in August. Three months later, UL hosted a two-day meeting for stove manufacturers and trade association representatives to discuss the proposed standard with UL's engineers. Based on comments received at those meetings, another revised version of the standard was circulated for comments in January 1979. By this time, the wording of the warning label was the only provision at issue. A revised warning label proposed by UL in April 1979 received sufficient support from industry for UL to consider the standard acceptable and publish it.

Successive drafts of the proposed standard indicate how it changed during this process. Unfortunately, this paper trail reveals little about the motivation for these changes. And UL employees are reluctant to discuss the deliberations that go into a standard.[13] Even the so-called rationale statements recently added to UL standards are often brief and general, providing little insight into the trade-offs and underlying issues.

In the case of UL 1482, most of the changes involved the finer points of test methods. For example, the proposed standard described the charcoal briquettes to be used in testing by reference to the product manufactured by the Kingsford Chemical Company. The revised version adopted a more generic approach, specifying the size, weight, and moisture content of acceptable briquettes.[14] The aspects of the standard that were changed most significantly during this process and appear to have generated the most disagreement were the warning labels and installation instructions. As originally proposed, UL 1482 required limited installation instructions and a warning label—or "caution mark," in UL terminology—on the stove.[15] The Wood Energy Institute took strong objection to the warning label and convinced UL of Canada,[16] but not UL, to drop the requirement. UL revised the labeling requirement, however, in response to this opposition. The minimum letter size for the warning label was reduced and, for stoves with glass doors, the label did not have to appear on the front of the stove.[17] The requirements concerning installation instructions were less controversial. They were expanded during the revision process without substantial opposition.

Canvassing for Consensus

Once satisfied that industry representatives had no major objections to the standard, UL began a separate process to obtain acceptance from the American National Standards Institute that UL 1482 was a "nationally recognized consensus standard." ANSI aims to be a central clearinghouse and general overseer of nongovernment standards-writers. However, the organization has limited resources, no technical staff, and no information collection system. It depends on the voluntary cooperation of standards-writers. Although UL routinely submits its published standards to ANSI for such approval, the gesture is largely a matter of courtesy without any practical significance for the recognition or use of UL standards.[18]

There are three separate procedures for gaining ANSI approval. UL uses the one subject to the most criticism: the canvass process.[19] Under this procedure, UL developed (and ANSI reviewed and approved) a "canvass list" of parties thought to be interested in reviewing the wood-stove standard. A professor at Auburn University who had conducted research on woodstoves for the CPSC was the only individual on a list of twenty-six. The rest represented organizations ranging from the Alliance of American Insurers to UL's Consumer Advisory Council and the National Safety Council. The standard was distributed to those on the list with a request for comments and an affirmative or negative vote. ANSI also solicited "public review comments" through a notice in its newsletter, *Standards Action*.

Under ANSI's canvass method, public comments and a compilation of canvass votes are submitted to ANSI's Board of Standards Review (BSR), whose job is to certify "consensus." They do so mainly by examining any "unresolved negatives" that emerge from the process. In the terminology of the BSR, UL 1482 was a "clean case." It was submitted to ANSI with no "unresolved negatives." No comments were received from the general public during ANSI's own comment period. On the basis of that information, the BSR approved UL 1482 without discussion on January 28, 1981.

What appeared to be a "clean case" to the BSR was not nearly so straightforward for UL. The canvass process took UL over twenty months—longer than it took from official proposal to publication of the standard—and it generated numerous negative comments along the way. Negative ballots were cast (at least initially) by members of five organizations on the canvass list, including NFPA, the National Bureau of Standards, the International Conference of Building Officials (ICBO), and the American Society of Heating, Refrigeration and Air-Conditioning Engineers (ASHRAE). Others voted affirmatively but registered negative comments.

The objections were to the scope and severity of the standard. Representatives from NFPA and NBS objected to the lack of any provisions concerning the tendency of stoves to produce creosote.[20] Representatives from ICBO and ASHRAE objected to the stringency of various test methods. The former considered an aspect of the fire tests too weak, while the latter argued that the impact test for glazing was unreasonably stringent.[21]

UL responded to each party that cast a negative vote, seeking to elicit a vote in favor. The Standards Department at UL is charged with this task. The department, with almost fifty employees, acts as an intermediary between commenters and UL engineers. The department aims to defuse opposition and gain acceptance for UL's standards by informing commenters of the reasons for the provision in question and, if this fails, by trying to convince them that improvements can be made in the future. Commenters often agree to vote in favor of a standard on the assurance of the Standards Department that the issue will be addressed in the future. This tactic changed all of the votes against UL 1482 but that of the International Conference of Building Officials. UL had to request a six-month extension from ANSI in order to bring ICBO around.

Several of the objections to UL 1482 were dismissed by UL in a rather perfunctory fashion. Those who objected to the lack of provisions governing creosote formation were told that ongoing research in the scientific community was expected to provide a data base upon which a future test method might be developed. This response appears less than forthright given the events preceding the canvass. There, in response to questions about how (and whether) to deal with creosote formation in chimneys, the matter was dropped because, according to UL's report of the meeting with industry representatives, "the discussion indicated that it was primarily an installation consideration and not a product construction or performance requirement for inclusion within the body of UL 1482." An internal UL memo dated March 19, 1985, indicates that UL is still "not in a position to include any creosote tests."[22] And a UL engineer confirms that without a request and financial support from industry, there are no plans to develop such a test.

Other objections to UL 1482 were also "resolved" in an unresponsive manner. A building code official objected that the glazing impact test would "increase the cost of glass doors without producing a safer product." UL's response: the test was intended "to provide the assembly with impact conditions under various modes." UL offered no evidence that the product would actually be safer as a result.

The Unofficial Story and UL's Unpublished Standards

Missing from the official version of the adoption of UL 1482 are any details of what turns out to be the most critical step in the process: developing the "proposed" standard. Although the proposed standard was modified through UL's review and comment process, the changes were not significantly related to the safety implications of the standard. The most important provisions in UL 1482, at least from the point of view of safety, came from the original proposal and were not affected by the formal process that followed. The official story, then, picks up where the unofficial story ends—with the "proposed first edition" of UL 1482.

It is misleading to describe the standard circulated by UL in January 1978 as a "proposal." It was, in fact, both a proposal and a working (but unpublished) standard. UL had actually been certifying wood-stoves for over twenty-five years when it circulated as a "proposal" the requirements it had been using. These provisions were contained in an unpublished UL standard (also referred to as a "desk standard"). Unpublished standards, the foundation of all UL standards, are not well known or understood. When the CPSC first began investigating wood-stove safety, it operated for several months under the mistaken impression that there was no UL standard. In fact, there was an unpublished standard, just not a published one.

Unpublished standards and their method of development are one of the only blemishes on UL's otherwise excellent reputation. These standards are written entirely in-house by UL engineers and, true to their name, are not generally available to outsiders. Those who evaluate standards-writing by the extent to which the procedures are public and accessible are most critical of UL's unpublished standards.[23] Leaving the merits of that debate aside until later, the fact is that unpublished standards are an integral part of UL and its standard for woodstoves. Relevant to the present discussion is how these standards take shape.

The Importance of Precedents

The process begins when a manufacturer of a product for which there is no UL standard asks UL to test and certify the product's safety. Lacking a standard with which to test the product, UL creates a rough draft (an unpublished standard), which is refined through use. Then, if there is sufficient demand, a formal "proposal" and publication follow.

Precedent is a guiding principle at UL, and it explains the direct origin of most provisions in UL 1482. The test method for the three fire tests, for example, came from UL's standard for fireplace stoves, UL 737. (Fireplace stoves are basically woodstoves without doors, and many of the provisions in UL 737 provided the basis for UL 1482.) Similarly, the provisions concerning metal thickness came from UL's standard for oil-burning appliances, according to a UL engineer in the Fire Department. That standard was also cited by UL as a precedent for the warning label eventually included in UL 1482.[24]

Precedent says something about the source, but not the underlying rationale, of these provisions. The same question lurks behind each precedent: Where did the original provision come from? Take, for example, UL 737, which accounts for many provisions in UL 1482. Where did the provisions for UL 737 come from? Unfortunately, UL's own records do not document the complicated regulatory genealogy that covers ninety years, hundreds of published standards, and active testing in thousands of product categories. Even if it did, the original question would still remain: How does UL formulate requirements when there is no UL precedent? The answer seems to vary by type of requirement. Design requirements, performance standards, and labeling provisions seem to evolve differently. Like all UL standards, UL 1482 contains all three types of requirements. Deciding the appropriate combination of these approaches turns out to have safety implications as significant as the eventual content of each type of requirement.

Design Standards and Delegation

Design standards are disfavored by economists and standards purists, but not by UL engineers. Many of the requirements in UL 1482, and other UL standards, specify design parameters, such as the minimum metal thickness for cast-iron stoves. Economists favor performance standards—for example, a "burn through" test instead of a specific metal thickness—because such standards are less likely to constrain technological innovation.[25] However, all of UL's design standards are qualified by an "equivalency statement" that, in theory, allows for technological innovation. This reads:

> A product employing materials or having forms of construction differing from those detailed in the requirements of this Standard may be examined and tested in accordance with the intent of these requirements and, if found to be substantially equivalent, may be judged to comply with the Standard.

This clause is invoked "at least once a week," according to a UL attorney, who would not disclose any details about whether or when it has been applied to woodstoves (or any other specific product).

UL uses design standards for two reasons that are often overlooked in the discussion of performance and design standards. First, design standards are much cheaper from the point of view of testing. The thickness of cast iron can easily be measured. A performance test intended to simulate "burn through" would be much more complicated and expensive. Second, design standards—at least the way in which they are used by UL—allow certain matters to be "delegated" to the manufacturer. This is particularly helpful when field data or relevant research do not provide an adequate basis for a performance standard.

Many of UL's design standards are actually codifications of generally accepted business practice. The requirements for minimum metal thicknesses do not constrain woodstove manufacturers; they choose them in the first place. Design standards of this origin appear to contradict the notion that UL's standards are an "independent" test of safety. In UL's defense, reliance on industry practice, if done critically and selectively, helps keep down the cost of testing, while ensuring that products beneath the accepted minimum are not certified.

Performance Requirements and Educated Guesses

The design requirements in UL 1482 are not the most important from the point of view of safety; the performance requirements are. The fire tests, for example, specify that during testing the stove must not cause temperatures on exposed walls to rise more than 117° F above ambient temperature. Similarly, "a chimney connector furnished as part of the assembly shall not break, disassemble, or become damaged to the extent that it is unacceptable for further use after being subjected to a longitudinal force of 100 pounds."[26] Unlike design specifications, which often leave the decisionmaking to industry, performance requirements are created entirely by UL's engineers. UL decides which aspects of performance to test and how to go about doing so.

On the first score, UL 1482 is quite comprehensive. It tests several aspects of normal stove operation as well as performance following various mishaps (for example, a heavy impact to the chimney connector). On the other hand, 1482 is far from scientific. According to UL, "sound engineering principles, research, records of tests and field experience . . . [and] information obtained from manufacturers, users, and others having special experience" form the basis for its standard.[27] Most test methods in UL 1482 reflect two factors not included in this list: educated guesses and concessions to the practicalities of product testing.

Guesswork abounds in UL's standards, although it is usually disguised by the exactitudes of scientific language. For woodstoves with glass doors, for example, the impact test for glazing calls for a steel sphere of 1.18 pounds mass and 50.8mm diameter to be dropped against the glass from a pendulum arc with a height of 16.25 inches.[28] Research results certainly do not form the basis for this test. The explanation provided by a UL engineer is that a two-inch ball bearing—the steel sphere described more "scientifically" above—swung from around 45 degrees "seemed about right." The idea, according to this engineer, was to simulate an accidental jab against the glass with a fireplace poker. A larger ball would, of course, simulate a more serious jab. But absent any information on real-world experience with jabs and related mishaps, this educated guess lives up mainly to the second half of its name. A representative of a major glass manufacturer takes exception to UL's explanation. "We could never get [UL] to tell us why [the falling ball test] has these specific requirements." This engineer believes that the requirements came from some other UL standards. In fact, rather than simulating a specific hazard for woodstoves, the two-inch ball bearing test would more accurately be described as UL's generic impact test. It appears in similar form in a host of product standards, including the standard for portable video recording systems.[29]

Even the most basic requirement of the three fire tests—that the temperature not rise more than 117° F on exposed surfaces and 90° F on unexposed ones[30]—is largely guesswork. "There is some evidence to support these temperatures," observes a widely respected woodstove expert, but "they are still doubtful. Lots of different temperatures are plausible." A challenge to the rationale for these specific temperature tolerances was raised in the canvass process, but UL was unable to provide a specific response.[31]

The practical necessities attendant to laboratory product testing help explain why guesswork often takes the place of science. In writing performance requirements, UL's engineers are sensitive to the cost of the endeavor. UL will not undertake costly scientific experiments where guesswork seems satisfactory. The engineers also try to keep the cost of the test itself within reasonable limits. For example, in UL 1482 a photoelectric method for measuring wisps of smoke was abandoned in favor of less accurate visual observation tests because the former was considered too costly. Similarly, since walls and ceilings are made of a variety of materials, the most realistic test method would include separate tests for each material. Striking a balance that favors economy over realism, the tests are done with only one building material.

Product Certification and the Real World

The business of product testing also requires that test methods be reproducible. For example, myriad factors other than the woodstove itself affect the extent to which temperatures on surrounding walls will increase when the stove is used at a specified distance. The type of fuel, the type of chimney, the insulation in the room, not to mention the finer points of product testing (for example, type and placement of thermocouples), are all significant. A test method must control these influences sufficiently to ensure that the same test will yield similar results over time. Unfortunately, the more "controlled" the test, the less likely it is to bear a relationship to reality.

This is a recurring problem in product testing. The more inexpensive and reproducible the test, the more tenuous its relationship to what happens to the product in the real world. Performance standards require that numerous assumptions be made about how the product will be used in the real world. These assumptions can take many forms. Different sections of UL 1482 appear to be based on different notions of the relationship between test methods and reality. In some sections, UL takes its lead from the NFPA standards for chimneys and venting. The stove is tested, in other words, on the assumption that it will be installed in the method recommended by the NFPA. This assumption is on the utopian side of optimistic. An NBS engineer recounts that when the Bureau contracted to have a regulation NFPA 211 masonry chimney built for testing purposes, the mason exclaimed that the chimney was unusually sturdy. "We never build them like this," he told the engineer.

A particularly difficult question for UL is to what extent it should "test for" consumer misuse. Or, as a UL engineer puts it, "How forgiving should products be?" The answer implicit in UL 1482 is mixed. Several of the tests for structural integrity in 1482 simulate what might be considered average mishaps (for example, bumping the stove door or chimney connector). Other portions come much closer to simulating "worst case" conditions. The flash fire test, for example, is supposed to simulate the kind of overfiring that would occur if, say, a Christmas tree or cardboard box were burned in the stove. The fire used in this test burns unusually hot and much longer than in a typical overfiring situation. Chimney height affects, among other things, the tendency of the stove to emit sparks into the room. The chimney used in all fire tests simulates a kind of worst condition. According to an NBS engineer, the chimney specified by UL has an unusual propensity to emit sparks. (This is not necessarily why UL chose the chimney, however, and neither is this particular chimney required if the manufacturer specifies otherwise.)

The portions of UL 1482 that are most controversial are those in which real-world experience diverges most from testing conditions. UL generally assumes that consumers are literate, obedient, and only occasionally clumsy. Most of the test methods in UL 1482 presume that the user will follow the manufacturer's instructions. Therefore, if the manufacturer's instructions say that a grate should not be placed inside the stove, UL tests without a grate. Since the use of grates is widespread and results in higher burning temperatures, an engineer with the International Conference of Building Officials thinks that "if a conventional grate [can] be placed in a heater, then it should be tested with one."[32] UL disagrees.

This difference in testing philosophy explains why Consumer's Union (CU), publisher of *Consumer Reports,* graded down a stove that UL considered acceptable.[33] CU considered the stove dangerous because of its tendency to emit sparks through the air inlets. UL, which tests stoves in accordance with NFPA's installation instructions—including, among other things, use of a floor protector—does not recognize the problem as a legitimate testing concern. That stove poses no danger—assuming it is used with a floor protector.

Evaluating UL 1482

Assessing the quality of UL 1482 as a safety standard is difficult because information about actual fires is limited and there may be significant variations in how the standard is applied.[34] How test results are evaluated may also vary by laboratory. UL 1482 leaves many decisions to the discretion of the testing laboratory.[35] Differences in test methods might allow a woodstove to pass the fire test at, say, twenty-eight inches at one lab and thirty-six inches at another. But since the UL standard itself is based on a combination of educated guesses, an agreed-upon margin of safety, and limited test data, it is likely that stoves certified for thirty-six inches would actually be safe at closer distances. In other product areas, test data have frequently revealed that UL standards contain large, some say too large, margins of safety. Moreover, manufacturers often build in a margin of safety (actually, a margin of error) when they have their stoves tested. On the basis of stove design alone, engineers cannot calculate the distance at which the stove will pass the UL tests. Therefore, the manufacturer, who specifies the distance at which the stove is to be tested, must *estimate* the clearance, knowing that an overly optimistic estimate will result in expensive retesting. Accordingly, a stove certified for thirty-six inches might pass the test at a closer distance. In short, differences in product testing might lead to inconsistent applications of UL 1482, but the inconsistencies do not seem very important. As an NBS engineer put it, "The standard could be tightened up a great deal, but I don't think that it would make much difference in safety."

Several government studies of fire incident data have attempted, with mixed success, to quantify the nature and extent of fire damage related to woodstoves. All of these studies support the proposition that the consumer is responsible in one way or another—usually by improper installation or maintenance—for almost all such fires. A UL spokesman cites this as evidence that the standard is effective. While the conventional wisdom appears to hold true in a numerical sense—most studies blame the woodstove itself for only a few percent of all woodstove-related fires—it is not necessarily true in a policy sense. Even if the universe of injuries preventable by product improvements is small, it might still be easier to eliminate some of those injuries than to achieve a similar reduction in fires caused by consumer behavior. Moreover, some of the injuries "caused" by consumers could nevertheless be prevented by changes in the product.

Unfortunately, it is impossible to ascertain from recent studies of fire incident data whether certified stoves are actually any safer than uncertified ones. The data are both too general and unreliable. According to an NBS engineer, "Fire incident reports are *sometimes* detailed enough to indicate whether the fire originated in the appliance or the chimney, but they almost never indicate the appliance type or how far it was from the wall." None of the existing data bases even differentiates certified from uncertified stoves.

The Nagging Creosote Problem

UL 1482 enjoys wide support. Unlike UL's standards for fireplace inserts and metal chimneys, it has not been controversial within UL.[36]

Insurance companies and various independent consultants endorse the standard without qualification. Even the CPSC concluded, at least unofficially, that the standard is adequate in all respects save some minor labeling provisions. A few manufacturers have voiced opposition to UL 1482, but their complaint, contrary to what might be expected, is that the standard is too lax. Anticompetitive motives apparently explain the opposition in one case.[37] More typical of those who do not actively endorse UL 1482 is the view of a woodstove consultant who thinks that "listing under 1482 has little or nothing to do with safety." This is not an indictment of UL's standard so much as an expression that standards per se have little effect on woodstove safety.

While that may be true in general, one of the only substantial complaints about UL 1482 is that it should cover a problem it largely ignores: creosote. The standard has no provisions for evaluating the tendency of a woodstove to create creosote. In fact, the existing test procedures intentionally "control for" the two major causes of creosote formation: low burning temperatures and high-moisture wood. All of the fire tests are conducted when the stove is burning its hottest, and the "test wood" is much drier than seasoned firewood, often with a moisture content approaching zero. It has been argued that these performance tests may actually encourage greater creosote formation in stoves, at least when they are used under normal conditions. In other words, design changes that might help bring a stove into compliance with UL's temperature limits can, according to several woodstove consultants, also increase the stove's tendency to produce creosote in the real world.[38] Whether the standard has actually prompted such design changes is not known.

UL claims that it cannot test for creosote. "We would test for [it] if there was a way to do it," according to a UL engineer familiar with the myriad factors affecting creosote formation. To be sure, just switching to wood with normal moisture content would pose big problems. It is much harder to standardize wood at a moisture content of, say, 20 percent than at percentages approaching zero. Creosote formation is also a slow process, raising the specter of long and involved test procedures. Tests for compliance with UL 1482 can be accomplished in a few days. The NBS spent several months of constant firing for its measurements of creosote formation.

Although these difficulties are not trivial, neither are they insurmountable or of a nature very different from the problems attendant to most product testing. There *is* a way to test for creosote formation. One independent laboratory already conducts such tests (not for certification purposes, but as a consultative service). Similarly, there is an established test procedure for measuring woodstove efficiency—a factor directly related to creosote formation. The test uses high-moisture wood and is being performed without difficulty by the same lab.

So why doesn't UL do it? The short answer is that there is insufficient demand. Inside UL there is a feeling that creosote formation is a user problem, not a product problem. UL argues that the tendency to create creosote is irrelevant if the user avoids wet wood, monitors burning temperatures, and has the chimney cleaned whenever indicated through regular inspections. This philosophical position is reinforced by practical considerations. Including creosote tests in the standard might invite product liability suits. There have been very few woodstove product liability suits, and UL has never been named in one. However, given that creosote is the second leading cause of woodstove-related fires, that situation would likely change if UL 1482 treated creosote as a product problem. Setting an acceptable limit on creosote would also be difficult to justify, but no more difficult than the educated guesses behind many provisions in UL standards. Unlike other provisions, however, it would arouse strong opposition from some manufacturers. A UL engineer, implicitly acknowledging that these considerations outweigh any technical concerns, allowed that UL would test for creosote "if industry came to us and asked for a test and would pay for it." But that hasn't happened and isn't likely to.

The certification business for woodstoves, at least in 1979, when UL 1482 was formally adopted, was neither comprehensive nor consistent. The market for third-party certification was unusual in several respects. On the demand side, UL is often thought to have leverage over industry because the demand for its services is inelastic. In countless product areas, such as microwave ovens and television sets, everything on the market is UL-listed. Firms often need UL approval to meet requirements incorporated into law or contract. This puts UL in a position to demand various safety measures. However, in the mid 1970s there were only scattered local requirements that woodstoves be listed "by a nationally recognized testing laboratory," and the demand for certification was correspondingly weak. No more than 10 to 25 percent of the woodstoves were certified by independent labs.

On the supply side, UL is often in a monopoly position. This allows UL to invest in standards-related research without the concern that other labs will capitalize on the effort. With woodstoves, however, there has always been considerable competition from small testing labs. A CPSC survey conducted in 1981 concluded that UL had only 28 percent of the market. The competitors use UL 1482 as the standard for certification, but, as mentioned earlier, studies by the National Bureau of Standards confirm that actual test methods vary and some labs are far less demanding than others in judging woodstoves.[39]

The government played no role regulating woodstoves; that is, until a man in Midland, Michigan, wrote a letter to his congressman.

The CPSC Labeling Rule

Adam Paul Banner, a retired chemist turned woodstove salesman, thought the labeling on most woodstoves sold in 1976 and 1977 was inadequate. Of particular concern to Mr. Banner were stoves that did not specify "minimum clearance to combustibles and type of chimney required." Mr. Banner put his concerns on paper. Familiar with the world of private standards through an earlier association with the American Society of Chemical Engineers, he sent copies of his letter to the NFPA, the National Bureau of Standards, the CPSC, his congressman, and the governor of Michigan. The CPSC took the letter seriously, classifying it as a "petition" and assigning the staff to analyze it. (NFPA and NBS took no formal action.)

Under statutory provisions that have subsequently been amended, the CPSC was supposed to rule on the petition within ninety days.[40] That meant gathering all information currently available, analyzing it, and presenting a recommendation to the commission. An informal ground rule provided that the staff would not attempt to generate new information in handling petitions. Experience proved the ninety-day period unrealistic. According to one program manager, "Four to six months is more realistic." In the case of the Banner petition, the process took almost two years.

Staff members attribute the delay to the "low priority" status of the petition. Unlike unvented gas-fired space heaters, for example, woodstove safety had not been singled out by the CPSC for special attention. Ignorance compounded indifference as the staff discovered how little it (or the commission) knew (or could easily find out) about woodstoves. The commission was briefed three times in the two years after the petition was received. Each time the commissioners requested more information from the staff. By the third occasion the staff voiced annoyance at the commission's seeming inability to make a decision.

Part of the problem was turnover on the commission. Three of the five commissioners were new when the staff conducted its March 1979 briefing, twenty-one months after receiving the petition. One commissioner asked what "overfire" means. (It means what it sounds like, firing the stove beyond its capacity, as, for example, in burning a dry Christmas tree.) Another dwelled on questions about the toxicity of artificial logs—something irrelevant to woodstoves, but apparently the subject of a *Washington Post* article. The scarcity of helpful data available to the staff further hindered the commission. The staff was unable to find out, for example, what percentage of woodstoves were installed by consumers versus professionals. (They eventually turned to the *Washington Post* for this as well, citing an estimate from a then-recent article.) The staff was also unable to determine the percentage of fires related to installation. "I don't have any quantitative feel," a staff member eventually told the commission, "but installation is mentioned a lot in the in-depth investigations."

The situation changed when the commission learned in May 1979 that the National Bureau of Standards had been studying woodstoves for almost two years under contract with the Department of Energy. Before receiving the NBS report, the commission expressed confidence that it would provide an authoritative basis for CPSC action. The report did not actually answer the previously unanswered questions, but it confirmed that installation was a major culprit in woodstove fires.[41] The commission apparently agreed with a staff memo arguing that "we cannot state the specific reason for the fires" but "common sense indicates that there is a problem."[42] With draft copies of the NBS report in hand, the commission granted the petition with little discussion on June 7, 1979.

Several reasons explain why the commission got involved in an issue it knew little about and that many people considered trivial. First, woodstoves were a trendy topic. The Department of Energy was studying them, and the issue tied the CPSC into a topic of national importance: energy use. Second, there was a virtual vacuum of private interests to oppose a CPSC regulation. Three separate trade associations claimed jurisdiction over woodstoves, and were barely more effective than no association at all.[43] The commission sensed a natural (and easy) area for regulation. Finally, the idea of a labeling rule, as opposed to a full-fledged product standard, was attractive to the commission and the staff. It seemed simple and likely to keep the agency out of the kind of complex technical arguments that bogged down the CPSC's lawn mower and chain saw proceedings.[44]

The Staff Drafts a Rule

Following a directive from the commission, the staff set out to develop a labeling rule. The desirability and effectiveness of mandating information disclosure was not considered during this process; it was taken for granted. Since the commission had already endorsed the notion of requiring information on minimum clearances, the staff concentrated on two other questions. First, what problems other than the "safe distance to combustibles" should be addressed by the labeling rule? Second, in relation to each problem, what specific information should the rule require?

The staff took an expansive approach in determining the scope of the labeling rule. Almost every hazard scenario that might be associated with woodstoves was considered an appropriate subject for the warning label. Many proposed warnings addressing the obvious—cautioning, for example, that stove surfaces are "hot during operation" and that hot ashes should not be placed in cardboard boxes. Others seemed more practical, such as disclosing the conditions that signal overfiring and stating how often a chimney should be cleaned and inspected. Deciding on the scope of the labeling requirements was easier for the staff than determining what specific information should be required on the label. In the case of information about clearances to combustibles, the staff had to confront the same intricacies of test methods faced by UL. The safest minimum clearance between a woodstove and a combustible wall—the information considered most important by the commission—is neither readily apparent nor easily measured. It is akin to the gas consumption of an automobile. Just as "your mileage may vary" with different driving conditions, the safest minimum clearance for woodstoves varies by such factors as fuel type, chimney size, and, most of all, by type of wall materials.

The staff recognized the problem and attempted to sidestep it. They knew that the commission did not want to get into the business of testing stoves. The CPSC had neither the budget nor the necessary technical skills. Part of the attraction of the woodstove labeling rule was its seemingly low cost and simplicity—the agency could accomplish *something* without facing difficult, technical issues. The commissioners also wanted to avoid the kind of criticism EPA had received over automobile mileage standards, so the development of a CPSC test method was out of the question.

Instead, the staff sought to put the burden on industry, reasoning that "because the staff cannot know all the conditions for which manufacturers may recommend or promote their appliances, the determination of the appropriate information is the responsibility of the manufacturer."[45] How the "appropriateness" of test methods would be reviewed and the extent to which different methods would be comparable were questions left unanswered, at least in the first draft of the regulation.

The staff took the same approach with other provisions. Instead of trying to figure out how often a chimney should be cleaned, they put the burden on the manufacturer to specify how often. Similarly, the staff proposed that labels "indicate the conditions which signal overfiring" rather than setting forth an accepted statement. Stated in terms most favorable to the staff, the rule was a paragon of flexibility; in a less favorable light, this flexibility disguised the inability of the staff to write its own standard.

Analysis or Post Hoc Rationalization?

Several of the CPSC directorates—functional divisions within the agency—analyzed the proposed rule. The Epidemiology Directorate revised its national injury estimates and conducted in-depth investigations of specific incidents. The Economics Directorate used this information in a preliminary and final "economic impact statement." The significance of this analysis, later cited in the *Federal Register* as justification for the rule, is questionable, because the concept of a labeling rule was endorsed by the commission before these analyses were done.

The Epidemiology Directorate analyzed the hazards associated with woodstoves with two goals in mind: estimating the total national losses (death, injury, property damage) related to woodstoves, and determining the most common hazard scenarios. CPSC's national injury estimates have long been subject to criticism. They are based on a reporting system from seventy-one hospital emergency rooms. These estimates are practically blind to cause, and they pick up only certain kinds of injuries. The injury data for woodstoves suffer from both problems. On the one hand, the estimates indicate a dramatic increase in injuries associated with woodstoves (546 percent from 1974 to 1978) without revealing that almost all of these injuries were caused by touching or falling against the stove—something that could not possibly be eliminated by regulatory action.[46] On the other hand, these estimates do not reflect incidents involving property damage, however significant, but not injuries requiring emergency treatment—the case with most residential fires.

In order to better understand the scenarios in which woodstoves resulted in injuries, CPSC field representatives conducted "in-depth investigations," following up on incidents reported by consumers or collected from hospitals or the CPSC's newspaper clipping service. Approximately 150 in-depth investigations were conducted on wood-stove-related incidents in 1980–81. These reports verified the hazard scenarios that the staff had in mind when considering the scope of the rule. Unfortunately, most of the "in-depth investigations" do not provide information that would be particularly helpful in evaluating the rule. For example, few indicate whether the stove was certified or whether the owner read or followed the instruction manual. Some of these omissions were due to the limited training these investigators had in fire incidents. In other cases, the investigators faced uncooperative or hostile subjects.

Minimal Costs, Doubtful Benefits

Armed with these assorted injury data, the Economics Directorate attempted to analyze the costs and benefits of the proposed rule. As is so often the case, the costs of the rule were easier to estimate than the benefits. The staff concluded that the rule would cost approximately $2.80 per stove, or $3.6 million annually. The estimate is probably low. It was based on several optimistic, but questionable, assumptions.[47] Although a higher estimate of costs would have been more realistic, the CPSC's estimates were not unreasonable. The same cannot be said about the estimated benefits.

CPSC's economic analysis did not seriously consider whether the benefits of the rule were likely to exceed the costs. Instead, the costs were presented alongside the national injury estimates with the assertion that "any reduction in these injuries and deaths would result in significant benefits to consumers."[48] When the rule was published, the *Federal Register* notice included the statement that "the Commission is unable to estimate the degree to which the rule may reduce fire incidents, [but] a reduction of seven percent (or possibly less) . . . would offset the total yearly cost of the rule."[49] The likelihood of this happening was never discussed, and although it would be very costly to conduct tests to ascertain the probable effects, there are two reasons to think that a reduction of 7 percent is extremely unlikely.

First, consumer information and education campaigns are notoriously unsuccessful. A former CPSC commissioner argues in a recent analysis of three such efforts that they frequently fail.[50] A CPSC staff member in the Human Factors Directorate agrees that measured results "around 2 percent are about all you can expect." Second, the estimated impact must be adjusted to reflect the percentage of stoves already labeled. Since over 70 percent of the stoves on the market already bore labels substantially equivalent to those proposed by the CPSC, the marginal benefit of the CPSC rule would, at best, constitute 30 percent of the estimated potential of labeling. (As explained later, this figure is optimistic, since the CPSC has not even matched the performance of the private sector in achieving compliance.) Moreover, by the CPSC's own estimates, injuries did not decrease at all during the years in which product certification, and hence product labeling, increased significantly.[51]

Comments, Some Changes, and a Deferred Decision

The woodstove labeling rule was "kind of a small potatoes rule," according to a CPSC economist. "It was very low visibility." It drew few comments from the public and generated little controversy. Seventy-six comments were received after the rule was published in the *Federal Register:* thirty-seven favored the rule, twenty-four were against it, and fifteen stated no position. Only seven people took the opportunity to testify before the commissioners at a hearing in Washington, D.C. Dissatisfaction, to the extent that it was expressed, mainly concerned issues peripheral to the content of the labeling rule. A consumer group complained that the rule should also cover fireplace inserts.[52] Manufacturers complained that the proposed rule would take effect before they had an adequate opportunity to adapt and sell off existing inventories.

The relationship between the proposed government standard and the existing UL standard ended up being the most difficult issue for the CPSC to put to rest. Testing labs, aware of the intricacies and importance of test methods, pointed out that mandating the disclosure of clearance information would have little meaning without specifying what constitutes "appropriate" test methods. Lacking the resources, and possibly the knowledge, to develop test methods or criteria for evaluating them, the CPSC was forced to defer to the testing labs. The proposed rule was changed to indicate that UL 1482 was an "appropriate" method.

More troublesome to the adoption of the CPSC's labeling rule, particularly given the agency's practical endorsement of the test methods in UL 1482, were increases in private product testing. The percentage of stoves tested to the UL standard rose significantly in the two years after the CPSC received the Banner petition. By some estimates, 80 percent of the new stoves on the market were certified to UL 1482 when the CPSC finally published the proposed rule in November 1980. (In 1978, it was approximately 10 percent.) The UL standard also changed while the CPSC analyzed the Banner petition. In direct response to concerns expressed by the CPSC, UL changed its labeling requirements to conform, in all but a few minor respects, to the proposed CPSC standard.[53]

Manufacturers argued that a federal rule was unnecessary and possibly counterproductive. With compliance levels near 80 percent, the rationale for a federal rule was limited to whatever benefits the government could generate by affecting the remaining 20 percent. Unfortunately, the CPSC staff did not acknowledge the concept of marginal benefit. None of its analyses pointed out that most of the benefits of labeling, if indeed there were any, were already captured by the UL standard. Moreover, as discussed below, there was little reason, then or now, to believe that a federal rule could achieve *any* additional benefit.

A more difficult question for the CPSC was whether a federal rule would have an adverse effect on the laboratory certification business. The testing labs argued that the existence of a mandatory federal rule would decrease the use of independent testing and, by implication, compliance with their standards. In other words, manufacturers, content in the knowledge that they satisfy all federal requirements, might stop meeting the "voluntary" requirements, which cover much more than just labeling. Since woodstoves generated approximately $350,000 in income for UL alone in 1982, the economic implications of a drop in business were at least as significant as the possible safety implications. These two concerns were so troubling to the commission that adoption of the proposed rule was deferred in order to address these issues.

In a May 1981 briefing paper, the staff informed the commission that an estimated 70 to 85 percent of new stoves were certified to UL 1482. It was not known how many of the remainder were nevertheless built in conformance with the standard. In light of this new private sector initiative, the staff was hard pressed to recommend adopting the proposed rule. Neither did they want to abandon it, particularly in the absence of total compliance by the private sector.

The commission opted to delay its decision so that a market survey could confirm the extent of third-party certification.[54] The survey confirmed that approximately 80 percent of new stoves were certified to UL 1482; however, some of the laboratories competing with UL apparently were not as demanding in applying the labeling requirements.[55] This compounded the staff's already considerable skepticism about voluntary compliance. The generally high levels of voluntary compliance confirmed in the market survey did not lessen the reluctance of the staff to abandon the proposed rule.

The commission agreed and adopted the rule, using as the main justification the differences between the informational requirements in UL 1482 and the proposed rule. The differences were slight. The CPSC rule demanded more detailed instructions on installing chimney connectors and cleaning the chimney.[56] Whether the type of detail envisioned by the standard would be forthcoming depended on the process of implementation; the requirements themselves were not specific. On the other hand, a staff memo (not mentioned in the *Federal Register* notice) identified several respects in which the UL standard was "stricter" than the CPSC rule.[57]

The arguments advanced by the CPSC in the *Federal Register* rang hollow. Information disclosure is generally considered capable of affecting only a few percent of all product injuries, if wildly successful. And the commission was fiddling with the difference between using the word "furniture" as opposed to "combustibles" on the warning label. The real reason for the CPSC rule was that levels of compliance with the UL standard—estimated at 70 to 85 percent—were considered too low. Whether or not such levels of compliance should be considered acceptable, the important, but unstated, premise behind the CPSC rule was that a government standard would result in higher levels of compliance.

Presumed Benefits, Implementation Problems

The CPSC's experience has not been as rosy as the staff's expectations. Stated in terms most favorable to the agency, approximately 70 percent of the woodstoves on the market comply with the CPSC standard— less than the percentage in compliance with the UL standard. Using assumptions least favorable to the agency, compliance may be well below 50 percent.[58]

One reason for this relatively poor performance is that the agency has had trouble reaching many of the small, family-sized businesses that manufacture woodstoves. A more important reason is the loose wording of the CPSC rule. Flexible requirements, while desirable in theory, can be difficult to enforce in reality. Most of the woodstove labeling requirements are purposely open-ended. The commission wanted to appear flexible, and the staff had no desire to decide (and later defend) such matters as the minimum size for lettering on labels or the best way to describe how to pass a flue pipe through a combustible wall. The CPSC had already lost a similar battle in court over proposed warnings for swimming pool slides.[59]

Some firms, in the view of the Enforcement Directorate, are subverting the rule by taking advantage of its vagueness. The rule mandates, for example, that a warning label must be "legible," "conspicuous," and "readily visible."[60] To the CPSC this means understandable; to many manufacturers it means capable of being understood. The difference, something not addressed in the rule, entails how *well* the information is conveyed. A few firms stamp the warning label into an aluminum plate, for example. The practice does not clearly violate the rule, but, as a staff member in the Enforcement Directorate put it, "I defy anyone to read it." Print size poses a similar problem. The lettering on many labels is small and difficult to read. It is not, however, illegible.

A more widespread problem, at least in relation to the installation manual mandated by the rule, is that firms do not understand what the rule requires. Vagueness can be confusing. Manufacturers are supposed to provide "step-by-step installation instructions." The rule says nothing about how detailed these instructions should be. Practically no firms are providing all of the details deemed appropriate by the Enforcement Directorate. The agency's response provides an ironic conclusion to the tale of its involvement in woodstove safety regulation: after justifying its entry into woodstove safety regulation on the grounds that independent laboratories were not doing an adequate job, the CPSC is now turning to the same labs for assistance in correcting the problems with the agency's rule. The Enforcement Directorate is trying to persuade these labs to ensure a level of detail in installation manuals beyond that specified by the CPSC rule.[61]

Summary Evaluation

"A smidgen of good and no harm" is how a former CPSC commissioner describes the effects of the woodstove labeling rule. That assessment might be apt for UL 1482, but for the CPSC rule it is overstated. Given the modest scope of the rule and the low level of compliance with it, there is little doubt that the rule cost more than it is worth. It is not a very burdensome rule, however, so the loss itself might be only a smidgen. But adopting the standard did not demonstrate good judgment on the part of the commission. The performance of the staff was equally disappointing, as they were unable to provide the commission with answers to many of the questions that arose during the proceedings. They shied away from technical issues at all possible junctures. Although the CPSC regulation apparently did little to improve safety directly, it may have done so indirectly. The CPSC's proposal certainly prompted UL to modify its own labeling requirements, and those changes might have produced minor benefits. The CPSC's action may also have contributed to the dramatic increase in the percentage of stoves certified to UL 1482 in the years after the Banner petition was received.

The major fault with the CPSC rule is not what it covers, but in what it does not. By writing only a labeling rule, the agency missed the opportunity to regulate a problem not covered by the UL standard: creosote production. CPSC staff members defend the decision on the grounds that the agency was responding solely to the Banner petition. This excuse is disingenuous in light of the broad reading given to other petitions. Mr. Banner's general concern was woodstove safety, and the agency certainly would not have exceeded its statutory authority by adopting a more comprehensive rule. Why, then, did the CPSC ignore the creosote problem? Two explanations are most likely. First, the agency misperceived the problem. It thought that most fires were caused by poor installation, when the data suggest that creosote in chimneys is in fact a much larger problem. Second, the staff sought to avoid technical issues. They realized that a product standard would be complicated and difficult to support in court. The agency had lost legal challenges to several earlier rules and, of late, had also lost substantial funding from Congress. A labeling rule seemed easier to defend in court and would be much less resource intensive for the agency. In short, the CPSC staff did not address creosote because they were looking for simple issues susceptible to simple solutions. A labeling rule fit the bill much better than a full-blown product standard, even though the latter might have had much more effect on safety.

UL's performance is harder to evaluate. UL 1482 has prompted some manufacturers to make design changes, while it codifies the existing design of others. Some of the changes dictated by the standard have improved the safety of the product; many have made little difference.

This suggests an element of unreasonableness in the standard. Although some firms express displeasure with UL 1482 for this reason, the sentiment is not widely held. The woodstove manufacturers' trade association endorses the standard almost without qualification. The main benefit of UL 1482 is the fire tests, which provide helpful, standardized information on clearances to combustibles. There are legitimate questions about the assumptions built into the test methods, and there are only limited data to support the specific performance criteria, but no one familiar with UL 1482 considers it to be grossly inappropriate. The standard appears to do a good job of determining safe clearances—something the CPSC knew it could not accomplish.

To the extent that labeling matters, UL can be faulted for allowing limited warnings and installation instructions for so many years. These provisions were upgraded when the standard was formally published, probably in response to the CPSC. The UL standard also avoids the creosote problem. It does not test for creosote production and, contrary to UL's assurances to canvass participants, the organization has no intention of addressing the issue. This appears to reflect a philosophical position that UL has against addressing problems caused by consumer misuse or neglect. The causes and implications of this philosophy are explored in chapter 7.

SIX

Safety Standards for Unvented Gas-Fired Space Heaters

The final paired case study is the most interactive. The CPSC essentially made an "optional" provision of a private standard mandatory (and then later revoked the standard). The CPSC standard has been considered favorable even by some of the agency's strongest critics. The obvious question is why the private sector was unwilling to upgrade its standard sufficiently to fend off government regulation. The mystery deepens with the realization that the private standard, written by the American Gas Association Laboratory, was otherwise strict and had been upgraded significantly over the past few years. The answer reveals much about regulatory philosophy. This case strikes at the core of some fundamental differences between public and private approaches to safety regulation. The inexpensive oxygen depletion sensor (ODS)—required by the CPSC, but made "optional" in the private standard—became a lightning rod for concerns about paternalistic regulation, liability law, and antitrust law. The case highlights significant differences between the regulatory environment in the public and private sectors.

The CPSC may have been given more credit than it deserves. The rule was slow and painful in coming. Only reluctantly did the CPSC drop its original idea of banning space heaters entirely. Moreover, the agency's information is so poor that it is impossible to be sure whether the standard has generated the hypothesized benefits. Finally, in a bizarre twist that emphasizes the importance of federalism issues, the CPSC rescinded the rule after it was deluged with petitions for exemption from preemption. In the final analysis, the case demonstrates several shortcomings of CPSC standards-setting in specific and federal regulation in general.

By contrast, the performance of the private sector was surprisingly good. The standard for unvented gas space heaters, developed decades before the CPSC was created, provided an ample degree of safety for basic operations. Moreover, the standard was strengthened over time. But AGA Labs refused to require the ODS before the CPSC made it mandatory. This position demonstrates both the significant role of regulatory philosophy and the subtle influences of product liability law. Those factors are elaborated below following an introduction to the unvented heater.

The Unvented Gas Space Heater

Space heaters are inexpensive, convenient, and popular with energy-conscious consumers. They are also illegal in many jurisdictions—at least certain types are. Unvented space heaters fueled by gas or kerosene are the most controversial because, unlike electric heaters and various vented heaters (including woodstoves), they discharge their combustants indoors. The long-term effects of these pollutants are unknown. The acute effects—carbon monoxide poisoning—are better understood and, under the worst circumstances, can be fatal. Owing to the differences in fuel, gas-fired heaters pose a more serious threat of carbon monoxide poisoning than those fueled by kerosene. An unvented gas-fired space heater, along with the controversial oxygen depletion sensor (discussed later in this chapter), is pictured in figure 3. In the interest of brevity, this product will be referred to as the "unvented heater" for the remainder of this chapter.

The unvented heater is a primary heating source for poor families in southern states, where many homes do not have central heating. With installation and operating costs considerably lower than those of other space heaters, and fuel efficiency of nearly 100 percent, these appliances are popular with cost- and energy-conscious consumers. They are disfavored in northern states, however, where homes tend to have central heating and better insulation. Three major producers currently account for almost all of the 180,000 units sold annually in the United States. (There were thirteen manufacturers and much higher sales before the CPSC proposed a ban on space heaters in 1975.)

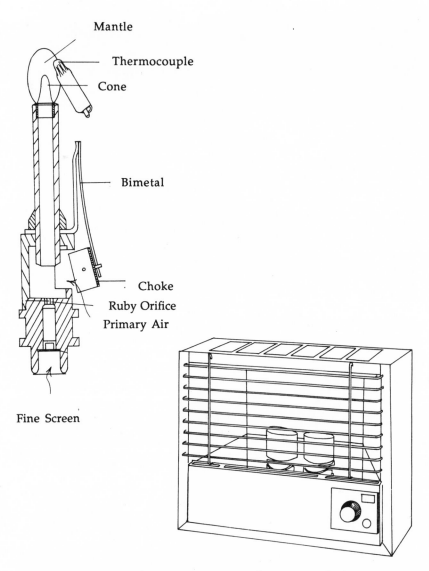

Figure 3. Unvented Gas Space Heater and Oxygen Depletion Sensor

Two acute safety problems are posed by the gas space heater. The first, fire and burn hazards, is common to all heating equipment but is somewhat more serious with gas or liquid fuel sources. The primary fire and burn hazards are contact burns and clothing ignition. The burn hazard is easily mistaken for the hot radiator problem. In fact, temperatures on certain parts of the unvented heater can exceed 500° F, so the resulting injury can be extremely serious. Lesser problems include the clearance between the heater and combustible materials, and gas explosions—less serious because they are so rare.[1]

The Invisible Hazard: Carbon Monoxide Poisoning

The second acute hazard—carbon monoxide poisoning—is the most significant. This hazard is not common to all heating equipment. It is unique to unvented (or improperly vented) space heaters fueled by gas (or, to a lesser extent, kerosene). Carbon monoxide poisoning can occur if the heater's burner is maladjusted or if the heater is used without adequate ventilation. The hazard is particularly ominous because carbon monoxide is odorless and colorless—you can be poisoned without knowing it, especially if you are asleep. Most deaths appear to be caused by inadequate ventilation, and apparently most of those are in bedrooms. It seems counterproductive to many consumers to open a window while heating a room, but ventilation is required to ensure safe use.[2]

The carbon monoxide hazard is well recognized but poorly documented. Industry trade associations do not collect injury data in any systematic way. Representatives on the relevant AGA committees are aware of the common hazard scenarios, sometimes as a result of newspaper clippings sent to the committee.[3] But the problem is not widely discussed, and anecdotes are not freely exchanged during the standards-setting process.

The CPSC is the only organization that has attempted to quantify these hazards, relying on files of death certificates, reports from hospital emergency rooms, and its own in-depth investigations. The CPSC placed the unvented heater fifteenth on a list of over 350 hazardous consumer products. Except for possible publicity value, however, this designation is of dubious assistance to the agency's regulatory effort.[4] More pertinent than the total number of injuries is the character and seriousness of various components of the injury problem. How many cases of carbon monoxide poisoning occur? What are the causes and possible solutions?

Epidemiologists at CPSC have reached two relevant conclusions. The first is widely accepted: contact burns are the most common hazard associated with the unvented heater. Four-fifths of reported injuries are contact burns; the majority of these are children and elderly people who fall against the heater.[5] The second conclusion is more controversial:

unvented heaters are responsible for some seventy carbon monoxide deaths per year. This number has appeared repeatedly in briefing papers and newspaper articles over the past ten years, although its origin and accuracy are unclear.[6] Still, the number emerged with what Max Singer has dubbed "the vitality of mythical numbers."[7]

AGA Labs: The UL of Gas Appliances

AGA Labs is the premier certifier of gas appliances in the country. Best known for its Blue Star Certification Seal—which appears on furnaces, ranges, and virtually all other types of gas appliances—AGA Labs tests these products for compliance with so-called voluntary safety standards. These standards are not actually voluntary, since many jurisdictions require compliance with them through building or related installation codes.[8] AGA certification is also required by many utility companies as a condition of providing service. As a practical matter, then, it would be almost impossible to market a gas appliance in this country, at least one requiring professional installation, without complying with the "voluntary" AGA standard.

Other labs test gas appliances for compliance with the same standards as AGA Labs, but AGA plays a unique role in this private regulatory scheme. It is both the oldest and the best-recognized organization in the field. Some people refer to it as the "UL of gas appliances." The description accurately conveys AGA's stature, but not its mission or method for writing standards. AGA Labs is devoted solely to testing gas appliances, while UL's interests have branched out considerably, and somewhat controversially, over time.[9] As the creation of a trade association, AGA Labs is also looked upon with more suspicion than UL by those concerned about anticompetitive motives. The "trade association mentality," as a government attorney describes it, fosters in organizations such as AGA Labs a "bias toward protecting members of the trade" that does not, in his view, characterize "the purists, like UL."

AGA Labs stresses that it does not actually write the standards it uses to test products. "Our job at the Labs is policeman, not judge," explains the Labs' director for product certification. The safety standards that AGA Labs uses to test gas appliances, including the unvented heater, are the product of the Z21 committee of the American National Standards Institute. The unvented gas-fired space heater is a distinct species in the American Gas Association's taxonomy of gas appliances. It has its own safety standard, numbered Z21.11.2—the "Z21" denotes gas appliances, the "11" is for room heaters, and the "2" signifies unvented equipment. The Z21 committee, with approximately thirty-five members, is "balanced" in accordance with ANSI requirements. Nine members represent AGA, nine represent the Gas Appliance Manufacturers Association (GAMA), and one or two members come from each of eighteen additional organizations, including the American Insurance Association, Consumers Union, the National Safety Council, the Southern Building Code Conference, UL, the General Services Administration, and the CPSC. The Z21 committee meets annually and has jurisdiction over the forty-seven standards. Some of these standards cover gas appliances; others, component parts.

AGA Labs is an unusual policeman; it is directly involved in writing the "law" it enforces. AGA Labs is the official "secretariat" of the ANSI Z21 committee. The arrangement is confusing, particularly to those who know that AGA wrote these standards before the American Standards Association (predecessor to ANSI) was formed in 1930. As recently as 1969, the year ANSI was formed, AGA Labs was recognized as the author of these standards. Many existing Z21 standards, including the unvented heater standard, were first developed under the old system. Since the power of precedent carries significant weight in most standards-writing schemes, the trade association of old may really be the co-author of any long-standing AGA standards.

Parties disagree about the extent to which standards are influenced by AGA Labs under the current ANSI system. Officially, AGA prepares meeting agendas and minutes, circulates draft standards for comments, and occasionally provides "technical input" to the subcommittees. These subcommittees, consisting primarily of utility representatives and appliance manufacturers, are responsible for proposing the actual standards and any revisions to the parent committee, Z21. There is a technical subcommittee for every standard.

The Standards Department at AGA Labs provides the secretary for each subcommittee. Other lab personnel attend subcommittee meetings to provide "technical input" and, in some instances, to draft language or proposals. Lab personnel, however, are not voting members of these subcommittees. The only decisions made explicitly by lab personnel concern the date when a standard will take effect. Decisions about content are made in the first instance by the subcommittees. Those decisions must be ratified by the Z21 committee. "If somebody wants to grumble," as an engineer at AGA Labs puts it, "they can go to the Z21 committee." Evidence of conformance to ANSI's procedural criteria is subsequently reviewed by the ANSI Board of Standards Review in the same cursory fashion as most UL and NFPA standards.[10]

The ANSI Z21 committee is not a meddlesome parent. The subcommittees normally send what one AGA staff member termed "very polished documents" to the parent committee for "rubber stamping." The Z21 committee almost never overrules subcommittee actions. Most of the Z21 committee decisions are made by letter ballot. When the committee meets in person, very few people come to grumble. Occasionally the Z21 committee raises concerns or requests "further consideration" by a subcommittee. Like many parental pleas, however, these requests are often discounted, if not entirely disregarded.

The Z21 standards differ from other ANSI standards in one important respect: AGA, as secretariat, has its own elaborate procedural requirements for approving standards at the subcommittee level. These requirements are similar to ANSI's public review process.[11] Actually, they steal the show. AGA circulates "review and comment texts" of all proposed changes in standards to a diverse group of manufacturers, gas companies, and state and local officials, as well as to interested federal agency representatives. This process generates far more interest and participation than when it is publicized later by ANSI. In March 1982, for example, AGA Labs sent draft revisions of Z21.11.2 to 7 gas appliance manufacturers, 4 manufacturers of decorative appliances, 185 gas companies, and 220 state and local officials and other miscellaneous organizations. Numerous comments were sent back to AGA. When ANSI repeated the process, notification was through *Standards Action,* and only one party responded.

AGA Labs maintains that these gas appliance standards are ANSI standards, not AGA standards. The organization frequently asserts its "independence" from the standards-writing process.[12] This position is weakened by admissions that AGA provides financial support for the standards-writing activity. (The official line is that standards-writing is financed solely by fees for service.) Critics go much further, charging that Z21 standards are simply the product of two large trade associations—AGA and GAMA, organizations that were one and the same before an antitrust decision in 1935.

Neither "independence" nor "collusion" seems an appropriate characterization in the case of the unvented space heater. The AGA and GAMA did not agree, let alone collude, on the content of the standard. The AGA at large was split over the issue, and there were disagreements within AGA Labs.

ANSI Z21.11.2

The first standards for gas space heaters were adopted more than sixty years ago by gas utilities concerned about the safety of gas appliances. The Pacific Coast Gas Association published a standard for gas space heaters (vented and unvented) in 1924. The newly created AGA Labs followed suit two years later. In 1930 the AGA "Approval Requirements Committee" became "Sectional Committee Z21" of the American Standards Association, predecessor to ANSI. A technical subcommittee oversaw fourteen editions of the standard for gas-fired room heaters in the next thirty years. Records from this time are not readily available, but in all likelihood the standard was changed in only minor respects during these years. There were no major controversies, according to a recently retired committee member. "Things rolled along fairly smoothly for many years."

The Z21 subcommittees for gas heating appliances were reorganized in 1959, and separate committees were given jurisdiction over vented and unvented room heaters. The first standard specifically for unvented gas heaters—American Standards Association Z21.11.2—was published in 1962. It was sixteen pages long and contained both construction and performance requirements. Many of these provisions are still in effect today. Some of the construction requirements were design standards. For example, "Sheet metal air shutters shall be of a thickness not less than 0.0304 inch."[13] Others were performance-based. "Orifice spuds and orifice spud holders shall be made of metal melting at not less than 1000 F."[14] Many of the construction requirements were of a more subjective nature, however. "Burners shall be easily removable for repair and cleaning."[15] "Gas valves shall be located or constructed so that they will not be subject to accidental change of setting."[16] The performance requirements included a host of tests covering burner and pilot operation, wall and surface temperatures, valves, thermostats, combustion, and safety guards.

The standard assured that certain basic elements of safety were achieved. In other words, a heater certified to Z21.11.2 could safely be connected to a gas line and, under the right conditions, be used without incident. The standard could be faulted, however, for being less than forthcoming with warnings about the dangers that still existed. These early versions of the standard did not require any information about the need to ventilate the room in order to prevent carbon monoxide poisoning. The prevailing attitude of many manufacturers about disclosing

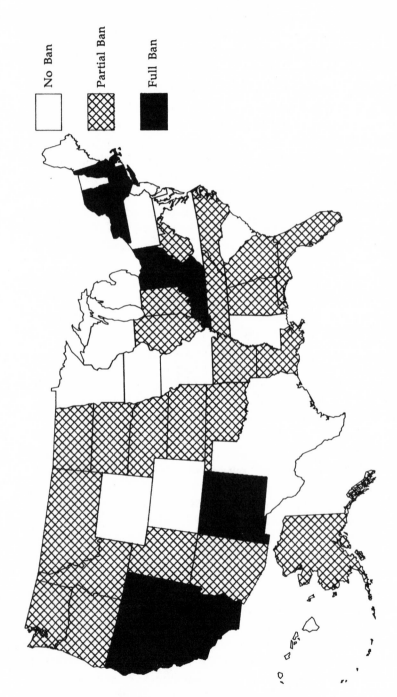

Map 1. Statewide Distribution of Unvented Gas Residential Space Heaters and Bans

No Ban

Partial Ban

Full Ban

information seems callous by today's standards. Warning labels and instructions were generally disfavored. The space heater standard required, for example, that "instructions provided with the heater shall include information to adequately cover cleaning of the heater." But a manufacturer took the position in 1964 that it did not have to include such instructions because the requirement was optional—in other words, the provision applied only if the manufacturer *chose* to provide instructions. The subcommittee agreed.[17]

The fire and burn hazards associated with the gas space heater also received short shrift in the early versions of Z21.11.2. A performance test was supposed to ensure that clothing "could not readily come in contact with flames or with parts of the heater which would easily cause ignition or charring." The test method involved exposing a piece of twenty-pound bond paper to the front of the heater for ten seconds.[18] For reasons explained later, this test bears little relationship to reality and, surprisingly, is not very effective in detecting the tendency of a heater to ignite clothing. The subcommittee did not take this hazard very seriously. The problem was periodically raised and routinely referred to a working group of some sort, where the issue languished until the cycle began anew. The triggering event tended to come from outside the committee. In 1962, for example, the NFPA forwarded a newspaper clipping concerning accidents resulting from contact with open-front heaters. AGA appointed a working group that concluded further study was necessary![19] The same conclusion had been reached by AGA working groups in 1953 and 1955. In 1970 the secretary of commerce sent the committee details of six clothing ignition cases. Another working group got its marching orders. No changes were made in the standard.

This early version of Z21.11.2 also did little to address the problem of carbon monoxide poisoning. The combustion tests included a threshold limit for carbon monoxide, but under conditions in which there is seldom a problem—when the heater is properly cleaned and adjusted. Thus, while the standard assured that the appliance was capable of safe use, it made no provision for the possibility of unsafe conditions such as poor ventilation. This is not to say that the subcommittee was unaware of the problem. The gas space heater had long been a controversial product, and there are oblique references to the carbon monoxide problem in the minutes of various meetings. The controversy predates Ralph Nader, the expansion of the tort law, and the Presidential Commission on Product Safety. The danger of carbon monoxide poisoning, particularly in northern states, prompted many utilities to oppose the product in the 1960s. Gas space heaters were banned in Columbus, Ohio, in 1958. Several states later banned them, many others have partial bans (see map 1). Federal "minimum property standards," applicable to 15 percent of new housing in this country (but recently revoked by HUD), also prohibit the unvented heater.[20] A Philadelphia utility company argued recently that it is "immoral" to allow use of the unvented heater.[21]

Whither the Unvented Heater?

The Z21.11.2 subcommittee could not ignore these developments. More than once, the subcommittee addressed the same existential question: Should Z21.11.2 exist? The answer was not necessarily a foregone conclusion. Within the AGA, sentiment at large was (and still is) divided over the unvented heater. AGA represents the distributors of gas. These companies have different interests because some are "gas-only," while others sell gas and electricity. Some do a great deal of marketing; others do not. Their interest in protecting a product such as the unvented heater varies accordingly.

Privately, some manufacturers were also less than enthusiastic about the appliance, leading one CPSC commissioner to conclude that the industry "didn't really care" about whether the heaters were banned. Some of the engineers at the AGA Labs even supported the notion of a ban. Not surprisingly, however, the committee's position has always been in favor of the gas space heater.

The stated reasons have been less than compelling. The standard should exist, the subcommittee has stated on several occasions, because without it space heaters will continue to be sold, but not necessarily with the safety levels maintained by Z21.11.2. In other words, economically speaking, the standard creates a marginal benefit. This benefit is real, however, *only* if the product would still be marketed without AGA approval. This is a critical and dubious assumption. AGA approval is practically a prerequisite to marketing a gas appliance. There are strong reasons to believe that the lack of an AGA standard would eliminate the product from the market, and that if it did not, manufacturers would continue to satisfy the requirements in the current standard.

The forces that motivate AGA certification would not disappear with the enactment of a limited government standard. There is no reason to think that utilities who refuse to install or service appliances without AGA certification would change their behavior in light of a federal requirement that does not even address some of their most serious concerns (explosions, fire hazards). Moreover, pressures created by product liability law would remain unchanged. A manufacturer who chose to forgo AGA certification would run serious liability risks in relation to those hazards covered only by the AGA standard.

Relying on the distinction between product standards and installation standards, AGA Labs took the position that the existential question should be answered by someone else. Accordingly, the preface to Z21.11.2 warns: "Safe operation of a gas-fired unvented room heater depends to a great extent upon its proper installation, and it should be installed in accordance with the National Fuel Gas Code, ANSI Z223.1, manufacturers' installation instructions, and local municipal building codes."[22] In short, AGA Labs took the same position UL often does with respect to "banning" a product: it claimed to defer to use and installation codes. If NFPA will not allow an appliance, then AGA will not list it. This is the case with a cousin of the gas space heater, the so-called cabinet heater. Cabinet heaters are unvented heaters without a gas line connection. They use a gas cylinder instead. These heaters are not permitted under NFPA 58, so AGA Labs does not list them.

With the space heater, however, the most important installation code—the National Fuel Gas Code—is written by AGA Labs, further complicating the symbiotic relationship between installation codes and product standards.[23] The Fuel Gas Code recognizes the seriousness of the hazards connected with the space heater but takes the ineffectual position of "prohibiting" the appliance in sleeping quarters, sanitariums, and certain other institutions. Although an unqualified prohibition would probably keep the product off the market, the use restriction leaves enforcement largely in the hands of the consumer, who has probably never heard of the National Fuel Gas Code. The code notwithstanding, most carbon monoxide deaths apparently occur in sleeping quarters.

In reality, the existential question caused the subcommittee no existential distress. They were committed to the unvented heater. This assured certification business for AGA Labs and an imprimatur for manufacturers. As an AGA engineer remarked in response to suggestions that space heaters be redesigned to lower surface temperatures: "There is no point in pricing them out of the market if your intent is to keep them in the market." Utility representatives did not object to this unofficial intention, because even if the heaters were on the market, they could keep them out of specific gas distribution networks by refusing to hook them up and service them. Those who objected to the gas space heater politely abstained from the discussion. A representative from Peoples Natural Gas Company, for example, responded to a proposed change in Z21.11.2 by commenting: "Peoples does not approve the installation or use of unvented heaters by our customers. I am sure that you will understand that the decision to abstain [on these revisions] was dictated by these factors and does not reflect on the fine work of the Subcommittee."[24]

The Overhaul of Z21.11.2

Z21.11.2 may never have been in danger of being scrapped, but a major revision was inevitable. Space heaters were getting a bad name, and worse yet, the federal government, for the first time ever, was considering regulating a gas appliance. The results were significant. Between 1960 and 1980 the committee added requirements for an automatic ignition system, a pilot regulator, lower surface temperatures, and improved shielding. The average retail price of the appliances more than tripled as a result, from around $50 to approximately $180. How beneficial were these requirements? Opinions vary, and the data are inconclusive.

Surface temperatures have come down slightly over the years, reducing the burn hazard to some extent. Organizations such as Consumers Union argue for further reductions. This would not prevent accidents, of course, but it would provide a longer response time before a burn injury becomes serious.[25] How that would translate into the real world of product injuries is impossible to say. There are no good estimates of the number of injuries involving surface burns, let alone how changes in surface temperature might affect them. Significantly lower surface temperatures probably cannot be obtained, however, without substantial changes in heater design. The cost and feasibility of this task cannot be estimated without research and development work. If, as manufacturers argue, surface temperatures cannot be reduced without dramatic changes in design, then it is likely that the cost would not justify the fractional change in response time to accidents. Similar uncertainty confounds any analysis of the other performance tests in Z21.11.2. The clothing ignition test, long criticized for using twenty-pound paper, was revised to incorporate the use of terry cloth. This makes the test more realistic,[26] but the real-world significance of the revised test method is impossible to ascertain given existing data. And without access to confidential certification records, it is impossible to determine whether the new test resulted in actual product changes.

Perhaps the most dramatic result of these changes was elimination of a model of small bathroom heaters known to be connected with many injuries.[27] This "drop-out ban," as a trade association representative dubbed it, apparently did not improve the image of the unvented heater enough to forestall government intervention. But the industry claims that the overhaul of Z21.11.2 improved the safety of the product sufficiently to eliminate almost all carbon monoxide deaths. The CPSC disputes this claim.

The CPSC and the ODS

The CPSC first got involved with space heaters in 1974 when it received a petition from the Missouri Public Interest Research Group to ban *all* "space heaters." The request was apparently prompted by a tragic fire, ignited by an electric space heater, that claimed the lives of several children in Missouri. At the time, the commission did not understand the differences between the various types of space heaters (that is, electric, gas-fired, kerosene, and wood-fueled), let alone differences in styles and models. Choosing not to read the petition narrowly, and with a predisposition to grant it, the commission approved the petition "in substance" and directed the staff to figure out which space heaters should be banned.[28]

It took the CPSC several years to become familiar with the world of heating appliances. The education process was terribly frustrating for AGA Labs and GAMA. "They just didn't understand the equipment," complains a GAMA staff member who tried, with mixed success, to point out the difference between vented and unvented gas space heaters.[29] The agency's uncertainty stemmed largely from ignorance, but it was also indicative of a larger problem. Gas appliances, like most consumer products, are diverse and difficult to analyze with specificity. The CPSC's injury surveillance reporting system did not have a product code for unvented gas space heaters. Few of the newspaper reports collected through the Injury Surveillance Desk specified whether or not the appliance was vented. Even the CPSC's own "in-depth investigations," intended to compensate for data problems elsewhere, were sketchy and sometimes of questionable accuracy. Thus, even when they tried to find out specifically about unvented heaters, the staff had trouble obtaining helpful information.[30]

Eventually the CPSC singled out the unvented gas space heater, deciding that it should be banned and that vented gas heaters and other types of space heaters need not be regulated at all.[31] The overriding concern about the unvented gas space heater was carbon monoxide poisoning. "The thing that motivated the commission most over the years," according to a former commissioner, "was the actual experience of consumers as manifest by death and injury statistics." In this case, people were dying in their sleep—as many as seventy a year, according to the widely cited CPSC estimate. Industry representatives took issue with the figure. In addition to echoing familiar criticisms of the CPSC's information system, they argued that changes in the product had rendered it much safer in recent years. A representative of the Gas Appliance Manufacturers Association boldly claimed that there had been no carbon monoxide deaths involving heaters built after 1978. There is no way to prove or disprove this allegation with existing data.

Criticisms of the government's injury estimates masked a larger complaint about its motives. The unvented heater was a "politically targeted product," charged one industry representative.[32] "It isn't nearly as bad as the kerosene heater," charged another, who manufactures only gas equipment. In fact, political forces favoring regulation of the gas space heater were in motion long before the commission received the petition from Missouri. The unvented gas space heater was investigated by the FDA in the early 1970s, and by the Public Health Service before that. It was also mentioned by the Presidential Commission on Product Safety, precursor to the CPSC.

If the unvented heater was politically targeted, the CPSC missed the mark—sort of. The agency was set to ban the product when word arrived of a technological answer to carbon monoxide poisoning. The ideal solution, a carbon monoxide sensor, had always been considered far too expensive to be practical, but a second-best solution—an oxygen depletion sensor (ODS)—was touted by a European manufacturer, Sourdillion, at the CPSC hearings in 1978. Similar to a pilot flame, the ODS consists of a Bunsen burner that utilizes a synthetic ruby orifice and other precision parts to achieve uniform control of aeration and flame characteristics (see figure 3). The ODS is a delicate device; it relies on an unstable flame, also known as a metastable flame. It is stable with normal levels of oxygen but less stable as oxygen levels decrease, to a point where the flame literally lifts off and shuts down the heater.[33]

Since the CPSC was prohibited by statute from banning products for which there was a viable private standard, Sourdillion's presence at the hearings demanded attention. Even those commissioners who person-ally favored a ban felt obligated to examine the ODS option. The CPSC's in-house engineers examined the device, and the agency con-tracted with NBS for additional research.

The most startling thing about the CPSC's analysis of the ODS is how late it occurred in the discussion of unvented heater safety. The device was introduced in 1961 in Europe. In 1972 the Z21 committee appointed a subcommittee to "follow the development of such devices and, if warranted, to develop revisions" for existing standards.[34] (They had not yet done so when the CPSC first got involved in the issue.) Remarkably, it was not until 1978, four years after receiving the peti-tion to ban space heaters, that the CPSC acknowledged the existence of these devices. Even then, in a January 1978 briefing package, the staff informed the commission that although the device "might be technically feasible [it is] economically impractical."[35]

The European manufacturer, which boasted worldwide sales of thirty million units since 1961, begged to differ. But the success of the ODS in Europe must be put in context. European fuel gases differ from those widely available in this country, so technology that works in Europe will not necessarily work in the United States. To Sourdillion, however, adapting the ODS to this country did not pose anything more than a good engineering challenge. Still, there were two important re-spects in which the reliability of the ODS was called into question. First, the device does not measure carbon monoxide; it measures oxygen. Whether the relationship between oxygen and carbon monoxide was sufficiently predictable for the ODS to provide reliable protection against specified levels of carbon monoxide was a legitimate concern. Second, the metastable flame can be inhibited by dirt and lint. The dirtier the pilot, the more stable the flame and the less reliable the shutoff. How reliably the shutoff device would work in the field was a serious concern. (It was not an equivalent concern with European equipment, which requires the pilot light to be lit with each use, min-imizing the amount of dirt and lint.)

Optional Equipment: AGA's Uneasy Solution

These concerns had been raised years earlier when a manufacturer re-quested AGA certification for a heater with an ODS device. The existing standard did not address these devices, so the engineers on the testing floor had no guidance. AGA was on the spot. Its engineers did not know enough about the ODS to assess its reliability, let alone its desirability. The device had no track record in this country. On that basis, they decided to make the ODS an "optional requirement." For the short run, this sounds reasonable (even if oxymoronic). The solution was an uneasy one, though, because "optional requirements" appear to contradict two cornerstones of AGA/ANSI standards-writing: uniform requirements and open participation.

The certification process, both at AGA and UL, is built on a binary approach to safety regulations. Either a product receives the AGA label or it does not. AGA Labs does not want to get into the business of rating degrees of safety, putting asterisks on labels, or otherwise differentiating between products. First, the manufacturers—the lab's clients—would object.[36] Second, it might diminish the use of AGA standards. The influence of "voluntary" standards, and hence the demand for certification, is due at least in part to their ease of use. The certification process simplifies the job of building officials. No label, no approval. If asterisks are placed on labels, putting conditions or qualifications on the meaning of approval, or if safety features are labeled "optional," then the standard becomes harder to use. It cannot be applied without additional judgments about the desirability of the optional equipment or the significance of the asterisk. Once this occurs, deference to the remaining portions of the standard may also diminish. Why rely on AGA's judgment about the need for, say, automatic ignition when you are already making your own judgments about the ODS device?

Optional requirements also contradict the procedural premises of standards-writing under ANSI's committee method. AGA constantly maintains that it does not write standards, the Z21 subcommittees do. The ODS, as an optional requirement, is a clear exception. The Labs drafted the "AGA requirement" for the ODS. Such provisions are akin to UL's "desk standards." They are written by staff and not reviewed by the public. In time "AGA requirements" are usually submitted as formal revisions to standards, thereby subjecting them to the normal process of public review. This did not happen very quickly, however, with the ODS. The manufacturer who originally requested approval of the ODS device never actually marketed it. The reasons are disputed: some claim that there was no interest among manufacturers, others say that the device was not adequately proven. In either case, the ODS issue remained a theoretical one for the AGA Labs.

The CPSC Investigates the ODS

Sourdillion's presence at a Washington, D.C., hearing put tangible pressure on the CPSC. The firm apparently considered a mandatory standard the best way to create an American market for its product. The commission, committed to banning space heaters, was forced to reverse its position and examine the ODS (about which it knew practically nothing). The obvious technological question was whether the device would operate reliably under U.S. conditions. There were secondary technological questions as well. The cost of such technology was of prime concern to industry, but apparently less so to government.

To answer the basic technological question, the CPSC contracted with the National Bureau of Standards. Simple questions do not always elicit simple answers, however, particularly when a regulatory agency is asking and NBS is answering. In this instance, NBS gave a more complicated answer than the CPSC wanted. Yes, the ODS works, it concluded, but the shutoff level in the "optional AGA requirement"—an 18 percent oxygen level—might not be appropriate.[37] A higher shutoff level, such as that used in the French standard, would be more protective, since the corresponding levels of carbon monoxide would be lower. The problem is that higher shutoff levels are also more likely to cause "nuisance shutoffs" (where the heater shuts off accidentally because the cutoff point is so close to normal levels of oxygen).

The origin of the 18 percent level remains something of a mystery. Minutes of the Z21 subcommittee meetings at which the ODS was first discussed do not reflect any discussion of the adequacy of the 18 percent level. An NBS engineer who analyzed these documents for the CPSC concluded that the figure most likely came from the American Conference of Government Industrial Hygienists, a nongovernment standards-writing organization (contrary to its name).[38] Since the relevant health concern is carbon monoxide, however, and not oxygen, it would be strange indeed if the shutoff level for the ODS was selected without considering the estimated corresponding levels of carbon monoxide. More likely, members of the Z21 committee had a rough idea of the relationship between oxygen and carbon monoxide and made their decision without explicitly discussing the details. According to one frequent guest at the subcommittee meetings, "We knew what the curves would look like."

Whatever its origins, 18 percent appears to provide substantial margins of safety. The NBS tests revealed that ODS devices set for 18 percent actually shut down at higher oxygen levels (18.2 to 20.4 percent). The corresponding carbon monoxide levels in those conditions ranged from 7 to 90 ppm, with a mean concentration of 37 ppm. A 1971 OSHA standard permits normal concentrations in the workplace of up to 50 ppm. At four times that level, the expected medical response, according to the CPSC's Directorate for Epidemiology, is a "possible mild frontal headache in two to three hours." Another twofold increase, and nausea is likely; twice again higher, unconsciousness.[39]

The CPSC staff divided on the question of whether the shutoff level in the AGA standard was adequate. The Directorate for Engineering, sensitive to the "nuisance shutoff" problem concluded that 18 percent was "adequate" and that higher levels were probably "overly conservative." The Directorate for Epidemiology disagreed, urging reconsideration of the 18 percent level because it "appears to be based largely on technical feasibility rather than on possible health effects."[40]

Whether the ODS device was commercially feasible was not a question that much interested the Program Management staff. A negative answer would have been humiliating. The proposed ban had already been tabled because of the ODS. Frustration grew as NBS engineers questioned the appropriateness of the 18 percent cutoff and industry raised the specter of nuisance shutoffs at higher levels. "We had to get a consistent story," explains one staff member. "First we said ban them, then we said no. We had to get our story straight." The story, then, was that the ODS *was* technically feasible and would work well with an 18 percent shutoff.

The issue never reached the commission. "Staff assured us that 18 percent was all right," recalls one commissioner. Actually, the staff was more pragmatic than it was satisfied. "Nineteen percent would have meant a five-year fight," recalls a staff member who favored the stricter level but was even more concerned about keeping things as simple and uncontroversial as possible. Eighteen percent had history on its side.

Playing Poker with the Private Sector

Once the CPSC was convinced that the ODS technology was sufficiently feasible to favor a product standard over the proposed ban, the obvious question was whether the private standard could do the job. AGA was not about to ban the space heater, but it might regulate it to the extent deemed necessary by the CPSC. The AGA standard already had an "optional requirement" for the ODS, along with provisions covering many other hazards. If the Z21 committee would simply require the ODS device, the "voluntary" standard could eliminate the need for a government one.

The matter was not so simple from the perspective of the AGA. Industry was largely opposed to the ODS device for reasons that were never stated explicitly. Some of the resistance no doubt was based on the cost of the device. Others objected to requiring a device that was only available from one supplier—and a foreign one at that. Whatever the reason, an AGA vice president wrote the commission in the summer of 1978 that a "strong statement from the Commission as to the value of the ODS and experience with it would be needed" in order to prompt revisions in the voluntary standard.[41] There was not enough support for the idea in the private sector, even given the specter of government regulation. Changing a voluntary standard generally takes more than a year, but, warned the AGA, it takes "much longer when there is any controversy." There was in this case. To the surprise of several commissioners, the AGA seemed to be suggesting government regulation.

Assured that the device was desirable and technically feasible, the CPSC drafted a proposed mandatory standard. The action did not push the private sector too far; but the AGA made one apparently significant change. The Z21 committee added the "optional AGA requirement" to the standard at large. In other words, the ODS was now a "mandatory" part of the so-called voluntary standard. But there was a catch: the "mandatory" requirement would take effect only when AGA determined that a "suitable and certifiable device [was] available."[42]

In the eyes of the CPSC staff, it would take an additional push to make this happen. "As long as unvented heaters without ODS devices can be sold for an indefinite period," the CPSC staff argued in a memo, "the industry is not compelled to develop and test the device in a short time." Therefore, the CPSC went ahead with its proposed rule duplicating almost exactly the provisions in the AGA standard, with the addition of a specific effective date—December 30, 1980.[43] "We called their bluff," boasts one CPSC staff member.

The staff could press for an early effective date without worrying that inability to meet it would mean a de facto ban. That was what staff wanted in the first place! "Fortunately or unfortunately," as a CPSC program manager put it, "we were working with a product that was not absolutely needed by the public." In other words, the staff did not care whether the requirement would result in a short-term ban. Apparently blind to the commercial interests of space heater manufacturers, the Economics Directorate concluded that an interruption in production would cause "no serious economic impacts."[44]

Aware that concerns about meeting the deadline would not get a sympathetic hearing within the CPSC, private interests argued against the CPSC proposal on the grounds that a government standard would displace the nongovernment one, worsening safety in areas regulated only by the private standard. These areas were significant. The AGA standard addressed surface temperatures, sharp edges, clothing ignition, and a host of other hazards unrelated to carbon monoxide. The proposed CPSC standard covered only the ODS and related labeling. But the argument against CPSC involvement depended on whether manufacturers would actually change their behavior in the event of a federal standard and forgo AGA certification on items not required by the government. That was highly unlikely, since the forces for complying with the AGA standard were unaffected by the existence of a CPSC standard. The argument was really about turf, not safety. AGA's concern was that the CPSC was embarking on a venture that might, if extended, cut into its business. And industry's concern was more about the implications for the future than about the implications of a single requirement.

There was one potential hazard that neither the CPSC nor AGA Labs addressed: chronic health effects. The issue came up during the CPSC proceedings, but the staff had no idea which elements of combustion, if any, posed potential long-term health problems. "It would have created a furor to try to address chronic hazards," recalls a former CPSC program manager. Subsequent research at the Lawrence Berkeley Laboratory, under contract to the CPSC, suggests that one of the six tested pollutants—nitrogen dioxide—might pose a serious long-term health hazard. The CPSC has called for further studies. For now, AGA Labs is deferring to the government. "We don't have the expertise or experience to address long-term health effects," notes an AGA Labs engineer. Neither does the CPSC for that matter, ensuring that the unvented heater story is not over.

Petitions and Confusion Follow the CPSC Rule

The CPSC was determined to go ahead with the standard even though AGA Labs had all but required the ODS device. Some staff members earnestly argued that a federal standard was desirable because the CPSC had a better warning label than AGA. But the differences were, by any measure, trivial.[45] Others felt that without a federal rule, the ODS would never be commercially adopted. One of the commissioners was determined to get back at an industry that had dared to start producing its product immediately after the CPSC lifted its proposed ban. This distrust was shared by many CPSC staff members. The commission eventually approved the rule but extended the effective date in a gesture of accommodation.

The gesture was lost on industry. Less than two weeks after the CPSC published a *Federal Register* notice adopting the space heater rule, GAMA petitioned the agency to revoke it. This was only the first of a plethora of petitions and other postadoption posturing that confused the commission and, years later, resulted in revocation of the ODS rule. The GAMA petition was a foregone conclusion, dependent more on the CPSC's presence than on its program. This was the federal government's first foray into regulating gas appliances. Although the rule was one that GAMA now agrees that "industry could live with," some segments of the industry could not live with the idea of government regulation. An association spokesman says that it was inconceivable that the commission could have written a rule that GAMA would not have petitioned to revoke.

Petitioning so soon after the rule was adopted was probably a tactical error on GAMA's part. To grant the petition, the CPSC would have to admit that it had made a mistake—not enough time had elapsed to argue that circumstances had changed. Positions had also hardened as a result of the just-completed rulemaking process. It was doubtful whether the CPSC would take a hard look at the petition. In fact, the staff responded to the petition with a brief memo prepared in a matter of weeks, instead of with the conventional briefing package prepared over a course of months.

The petition brought forth unexpected disagreements within the commission and within industry. The CPSC Office of Program Management could not reach a consensus. Representatives from the Engineering Directorate favored granting the petition, those in Epidemiology and Compliance opposed it, and the economists said that it would make little difference either way. Industry was similarly divided. GAMA did not want the federal government to regulate gas appliances, but some major retailers saw an advantage in federal regulation. The "carrot of preemption," as CPSC staff members often refer to it, holds out the promise of preempting state and local regulations. For the space heater this means preempting bans in many jurisdictions, opening up a possible national market. (That is, unless the states and localities petition for an exemption from preemption—something that GAMA predicted, and that soon came to pass.)

Unwilling to revoke what it had just enacted, the commission rejected the GAMA petition. Petitions for exemption from preemption soon followed. Officials at AGA Labs who questioned the desirability of the unvented space heater persuaded the president of AGA, without the approval or knowledge of those departments concerned with marketing, to provide information to jurisdictions interested in reinstituting their bans by obtaining an exemption from preemption. Petitions poured in from cities such as Victorville, California, which argued that a ban "provides a significantly higher degree of protection from the risk of carbon monoxide than does the Commission's standard."[46]

The legal issues concerning exemption were cloudy.[47] And the practical implications of these petitions were formidable—the CPSC apparently had to rule on each petition individually. By mid 1983 there were more than two dozen petitions. On October 5, 1983, the commission proposed what looked like an easy way out: revoke the rule. Sufficient time had passed since enactment of the rule to argue that circumstances had changed. The private sector had achieved important gains; by now, the ODS was standard equipment on all space heaters. To GAMA, it was a wish come true. To some of GAMA's members, however, it meant losing the carrot. Both Atlanta Stove Works and Birmingham Stove and Range Company opposed revocation as an unfair impediment to market expansion plans undertaken after the rule was first adopted.[48]

The issue was emotionally charged within the commission, but the reasons seemed symbolic, not substantive. Since the AGA/ANSI standard required the ODS, the only practical effect of revocation was that many states and localities would reinstitute bans that might have been granted anyway through the exemption process. There were no arguable detrimental effects on safety. Still, two of the five commissioners voted against revocation. One wrote a twenty-nine-page dissent that castigated the commission for taking "such an extreme and unparalleled action."[49] The same commissioner objected so strongly to wording in the proposed revocation notice that intimated CPSC endorsement of the voluntary standard that the notice was eventually reworded. The

CPSC had (finally) deferred to the private sector, but it was unwilling to say so directly.

Summary Evaluation

Even among CPSC critics, of whom there are many, the ODS rule is widely considered to have been a desirable government action.[50] The adverse effects of the rule predicted by some did not come to pass. The ODS has become standard equipment on unvented gas space heaters, and a trade association representative confirms that there has not been a significant problem with nuisance shutoffs or consumer tampering. Moreover, there was no decrease in AGA certification after the CPSC rule went into effect. In short, there is good reason to believe that as a result of the ODS device required by the CPSC, fewer people are dying in their sleep. That is sufficient reason for the CPSC staff to conclude that the standard was beneficial. Unfortunately, there is not enough information to determine whether the averted harm is small, as industry maintained all along, or whether it is substantial (that is, as many as seventy fatalities per year), as maintained by the CPSC.

In general, the CPSC's performance was mixed. Many of the issues, such as the appropriate shutoff level, were highly technical, and the agency was not well equipped to analyze them. Delay gave way to deferral, and the technical content of the CPSC standard was eventually borrowed almost entirely from the private sector. The CPSC staff changed only the warning label and effective date of the requirement. On the former, the CPSC was insensitive to industry's concerns—product liability and adverse consumer reaction to shrill warnings—and petty in its insistence that the wording itself was an important safety issue.

The CPSC was most controversial and probably most effective in setting the date for the regulation to take effect. The staff thinks that setting an early date was a bold move that forced industry to make the ODS commercially feasible. Some industry representatives still maintain that universal use of the ODS would have been forthcoming without government intervention. That may be true, but it certainly would not have happened as quickly. Moreover, several AGA staff members speculate privately that the ODS would never have been required by AGA Labs but for the CPSC.

Outcomes aside, the process leading up to the CPSC standard was not commendable. Early in that process, the CPSC relied on political instincts instead of information to make its decisions; and its instincts were not very good. Granting "in substance" a petition to ban *all* space heaters was ill informed and needlessly antagonistic. Although the CPSC did not end up banning any kind of space heater, it expended considerable goodwill in the process of reaching that decision. Beyond insensitivity, there was a streak of anti-business sentiment among the commissioners throughout the space heater proceedings. That sentiment was most evident when the commission decided to revoke its standard in favor of the private one. Publication of the revocation notice was delayed while two commissioners argued for changes in wording that would erase any affirmative statement that the CPSC endorsed the AGA standard (even though it obviously did so by implication).

On the private side, the performance of AGA Labs and ANSI was also mixed. Z21.11.2 long provided an ample degree of safety for basic operations. It also got stricter over time. Surface temperatures were reduced, and the small bathroom heater was eliminated. But before the CPSC intervened, the standard did little about the carbon monoxide problem. For years the subcommittee maintained that the ODS device should not be required because it was "not a proven technology" and had "no track record" in this country. That explanation was reasonable in 1971 when the issue first arose. Eight years later, the same explanation looked more like a lame excuse. The explanations suggested in private interviews are more convincing than those found in committee minutes. Several segments of the private sector never really believed that carbon monoxide poisoning was a product problem. Since it only occurred through misuse of some sort, they considered it a "consumer problem." Some utility company representatives and AGA Lab employees disagreed, but they respectfully kept their view outside of the standards-setting process. But the standard did address some misuse problems," including surface burns and clothing ignition, so there must have been other reasons for eschewing the ODS device. The most likely reason is product liability law. According to a representative from a gas control manufacturer, "nobody wanted to be put in the position of selling a safety device that was a safety device when you sold it but didn't necessarily stay that way." Translation: if the ODS device failed, the manufacturer would get sued. Without the device, carbon monoxide poisonings would probably be considered the consumer's fault—a rare event in the world of product safety law.[51] The perverse result, in the eyes of manufacturers, was that adding the device would *increase* exposure to product liability even though it would *decrease* product-related hazards. This view may not hold in a court of law, but it certainly prevailed in the Z21 subcommittee.[52] Only the desire to keep the federal government from regulating gas appliance safety was strong enough to overcome the opposition of manufacturers who were unsympathetic to "the problem" and afraid of "the solution."

PART THREE

Analysis

SEVEN

Public and Private
Conceptions of Safety

In the abstract, public and private standards-setting are easily equated. Both ostensibly involve similar objectives and entail similar tasks, although differences in political dynamics obviously slant outcomes accordingly. In this respect, standards-setting boils down to a question of strictness or, in more economic terms, what balance to strike between probable costs and benefits. The case studies suggest, however, that regulatory philosophy circumscribes the range of possible outcomes in both sectors and that different conceptions of safety regulation prevail in the public and private sectors. Estimating the costs and benefits of possible action is practically the last step in setting safety standards. Several important tasks precede the consideration of any specific proposals. First, the organization must define "the problem" or problems to be addressed. Then it must conceptualize a range of possible solutions.

The case studies indicate that decisionmakers in the public and private sectors view the same "problems" quite differently. The difference is not just in what should be done about a problem, but whether anything should be done at all. Taking a paternalistic view of safety regulation, the public sector is much more likely to favor standards to protect people against their own folly or mistakes. Even when public and private organizations address the same or similar "problems," the range of acceptable solutions can vary considerably. Some solutions, never seriously considered by one sector, are routinely favored by the other. These conceptual preferences are not arrived at in a deliberative fashion. In fact, they are almost never openly discussed. Rather, these working assumptions are reflections of a shared *regulatory philosophy*. This chapter describes several manifestations of regulatory philosophy and analyzes how the professional ethics of engineers and lawyers influence the framework for setting standards in the two sectors.

Paternalism and Problem Definition

The first step in writing a safety standard is determining the scope of "the problem" to be addressed. As Charles Lindblom and David Cohen point out, "we do not discover a problem 'out there'; we make a choice about how we want to formulate a problem."[1] That choice reflects certain values and in turn constrains the realm of possible solutions. Ideally, those defining public "problems" base their analysis on "feelings of distress, or discontent, or annoyance, or unhappiness of some subset of the citizenry."[2] But the more technical or obscure the issue, the weaker the links to democratic problem definition. Professionalism appears to fill the gap.

Defining "the problem" is a more complicated matter than is often imagined. Deciding, for example, to address safety concerns in grain elevators is only the starting point in defining "the problem." Usually there are many hazards related to a single process or product, only some of which are considered appropriate topics for regulation. In the grain elevator case, OSHA considered housekeeping a much more significant problem than NFPA. With aviation safety, both sectors had similar concerns about fire extinguishers, but only the FAA worried about smoke detectors. Of course, there is a danger that any observations from the case studies are colored by the interaction unique to "paired" cases. In other words, OSHA's definition of the problem might be contingent on NFPA's. As it turns out, OSHA and the FAA acted almost independently of NFPA; but the CPSC acted in response to UL and AGA Labs. (The special issues attendant to standards aimed at complementing or supplementing standards in the other sector are taken up in the next chapter. As explained below, however, these interactive cases seem to accent, rather than distort, the differences in public and private regulatory philosophy.)

Paternalism is one of the distinguishing tenets of the CPSC's regulatory philosophy. Most injuries related to the woodstove and gas space heater should be blamed on the user, not the product. Properly installed woodstoves pose very little risk; so do space heaters that are operated properly. But protecting people against their own mistakes is part of the mission of the CPSC staff. Private standards-setters, by contrast, are loath to recognize such safety "problems." They are also loath to discuss the topic of which hazards are appropriate for regulation. It would be inopportune for UL to state baldly that a significant hazard scenario is "the consumer's fault." As a result, some of the arguments about paternalism are cast in technical terms. GAMA's stated opposition to the CPSC's gas space heater standard concentrated on alleged technical problems with the oxygen detection sensor. None of these problems materialized in the four years after the rule was adopted, suggesting that nontechnical concerns were probably the underlying motivation.

Although a UL engineer allows that "there are occasional arguments within the organization about how forgiving products should be," the answer is almost always less forgiving than what the CPSC would require. Why should a metal chimney have to tolerate a creosote fire, UL wonders, when the consumer can prevent such an occurrence by cleaning the chimney at proper intervals? Similarly, why should kerosene heaters be tested for "flare up," when the problem stems from the use of improper fuel mixtures?[3] Surface temperatures are another case in point. The CPSC has long worried about the surface temperatures of products such as gas space heaters, kerosene heaters, furnaces, stoves, and small kitchen appliances (such as toasters). Reluctantly, UL has toughened some of its surface temperature requirements in response to CPSC pressure. In the case of kerosene heaters, however, where the effort would require substantial reengineering, a UL representative candidly testified that "it's going to take a kind of change in our philosophy of approach" to address surface temperatures.[4]

Private standards-setters are most likely to protect against misuse when it involves children or the elderly. Private testing labs subject many consumer products to an articulate probe test intended to simulate an overly curious finger probing inside protective grates or openings in the appliance casing. The AGA/ANSI standard for space heaters simulates this hazard and the possibility of clothing ignition caused by contact with the heater. AGA Labs disagrees with Consumers Union about test methods—the proper fabric to use when testing flammability and the correct shape of the articulate probe—but both agree that these mishaps merit some protection.

Nevertheless, significant differences remain in how the two sectors view the responsibility of consumers. UL and AGA usually certify safety under conditions that assume full compliance with both the manufacturer's instructions and any applicable installation codes. AGA assumes, for example, that gas space heaters (1) will not be operated in bedrooms (because that is prohibited by the National Fuel Gas Code) and (2) will always be operated with proper ventilation (in accordance with the manufacturer's instructions). Injuries that might be caused by the failure of an adult to read the instructions or install an appliance with professional guidance are of little concern to AGA. Its regulatory philosophy does not encompass such paternalism. The CPSC, in contrast, takes the responsibility of manufacturers much more seriously than it takes the responsibility of consumers. When the CPSC staff drafted a proposal for the criteria to use "in considering requests for endorsement or recognition" of private standards, one of the only substantive conditions was that "information in the [standard] does not place the burden of safe use of the product onto the consumer in such a manner as to exculpate manufacturers or distributors from any liability associated with their product's use by the consumer."[5]

These different worldviews were highlighted clearly in the case of gas space heaters. According to a member of the Z21.11.2 committee, carbon monoxide poisoning occurs because "people do not use and maintain the product correctly." The CPSC had a different view. "Consumer misbehavior was not a problem with the unvented heater," a former CPSC commissioner asserts; "it was a dangerous product." The private sector's position is factually correct. No one has ever been poisoned by carbon monoxide while using a space heater correctly. But whether it is desirable to require the ODS depends on your philosophical view of government paternalism and individual responsibility. Thus, in the case of gas space heaters, woodstoves, and many other products, the CPSC sees problems where UL does not.

Defining the Range of Acceptable Solutions

The case studies suggest that even when public and private organizations address the same or similar "problems," the range of acceptable solutions varies considerably. These differences involve what might be called solution definition, a process analogous to problem definition. Defining the range of acceptable solutions is also a matter of philosophy, beyond the scope of the deliberative process. NFPA does not spurn housekeeping rules for economic or functional reasons. In fact, several firms require in-house what they so strongly oppose in external standards imposed by OSHA or NFPA. The objection is to any industrywide standard infringing on what is perceived as management prerogative. The same phenomenon exists with matters of less consequence than housekeeping. UL avoids certain types of warning labels, not because they would be too costly, but because they conflict with its philosophy of regulation. Similarly, most private standards-setters refuse to apply standards retroactively. The logic is predominantly economic. But NFPA's position, stated in the grain elevator proceedings, against making retroactive any provision requiring "even a dime of investment" suggests that more than economics is at issue.

Perhaps the most familiar example of "defining the solution" to a safety problem is deciding whether standards should specify design requirements (such as metal thickness) or performance levels (such as an "action level" for housekeeping).[6] Another design choice concerns the extent to which standards should (a) modify products or processes or (b) communicate information about risk to the consumer or user. These alternatives are not mutually exclusive, though they are often treated that way. The difference in how public and private standards-setters tend to view these questions is not well understood. Government is often accused of favoring design requirements over performance standards, adopting rigid rules that stifle technological innovation. Business interests, on the other hand, are presumed to favor performance standards. The case studies belie these characterizations. In none of the four cases was the government standard as detailed or lengthy as the private standard. UL and AGA standards are filled with detailed *design* requirements, and these requirements meet with the general approval of industry. In contrast, OSHA's "action level" for grain elevator housekeeping—a pure performance standard—was strongly opposed by industry.

The case studies suggest many more subtle differences in public and private conceptions of safety regulation. Five examples are detailed below. Some apply exclusively to consumer products, others to industrial processes and practices; a few apply to both. The discussion that follows this description unifies these seemingly disparate examples by considering the common links to professional ethics.

Banning a Product or Process

Perhaps the most fundamental difference in public and private conceptions of safety regulation is that only the government gives serious consideration to prohibition as a regulatory strategy. The private sector tends to assume that the object of regulation is socially desirable and is (or can become) sufficiently safe to be "acceptable." UL begins with the assumption that a product is *not* inherently or unreasonably safe. If it is too unsafe, UL will not list it. But the issue rarely comes up. The electronic bucking bronco is the only example that several UL officials could name of a product that UL would not accept for testing. In contrast, public agencies generally assume practically the opposite: that the object of regulation is suspect and may not be sufficiently safe to be socially acceptable. The CPSC space heater rule began as a proposed ban on all space heaters. More recently, the agency proposed a ban on certain all-terrain vehicles.

Participants in private standards-setting, cognizant of the antitrust law, argue that private standards are never intentionally prohibitory. They rarely are—at least explicitly. But all standards of any substance prohibit something. This clouds the distinction between public and private conceptions of safety regulation. Both sectors utilize prohibition in some form. The difference in perspectives is more a matter of degree than a difference in kind. Nevertheless, the distinction is important because the public sector is more likely to favor this strategy.

Private standards-setters prohibit all sorts of specifics through requirements that alter products or processes incrementally. They often prohibit specific product features such as power lawn mowers without an automatic shutoff and foot guard. But they are reluctant to prohibit at a more general level. On rare occasions, however, they prohibit an entire line or type of product. The ANSI/AGA standard for gas space heaters falls somewhere in between: regulating enough specific product features to prohibit a whole type of heater, the small porcelain bathroom model. The prohibition is not direct, however; the porcelain model simply could not meet all of the provisions added to the standard. Although that model has fallen by the wayside, other types of space heaters have taken its place. A representative of the gas appliance manufacturers describes it as a "drop-out ban." Prohibition at a more general level is out of the question.

Forcing Technology

Public and private standards-setters also have fundamentally different conceptions of technology. They disagree about how the state of technology limits the range of possible provisions in safety standards. To the private sector, technology is usually seen as a constraint. It is a given.

Government agencies are far more willing to "force" technology through requirements that are unattainable with technology currently in use.[7] The private sector, by contrast, seems unwilling to give technology even a gentle nudge. To private standards-setters, the current state of technology refers to what is generally in use, not to what is close at hand or on the so-called cutting edge. Hence, the ANSI/AGA committee was unwilling to require the oxygen depletion sensor on space heaters even after it was marketed by one company. The technology was still considered "speculative" and "unproven," so the committee deemed it an optional portion of the standard. In both of those cases, the government illustrated a willingness to do what the private sector would not. The FAA and the CPSC considered, and later required, solutions that moved beyond the technologies that were widely available. There was a feeling at the FAA, according to one staff member, that "the market would respond to the need for smoke alarms designed especially for aircraft." Similarly, when questions were raised about the feasibility of the largely unproven oxygen depletion sensor, CPSC staffers were equally convinced that the market would adapt.

Work Rules and Other Operational Controls

Safety standards are often thought of as technical in nature, taking the form of either performance or design requirements. But technical provisions are only part of safety regulation. Work rules, maintenance schedules, and other *operational controls* play an important role, especially in the kind of standards written by NFPA. To be effective, technical standards must work in tandem with operational controls. Sometimes, operational controls can even substitute for engineering solutions.

To more fully understand the distinction between engineering standards and operational controls, consider the example of safety standards for a hydraulic system.[8] Safety standards could incorporate any of the following four types of controls. First, a *technical performance standard* might specify that the bursting strength of hydraulic lines be equal to or greater than four times the working pressure. Second, a *technical design standard* might require that hydraulic lines be equipped with safety valves to prevent loss of system pressure in the event of a ruptured line. Third, behavioral rules could be adopted instead of these technical solutions. For example, the safety standard might include the following *operational control:* the hydraulic system must be inspected for leaks after each one hundred hours of operation. Finally, a *work rule* could be adopted requiring that hydraulic controls be checked every time the machine is started. These technical and behavioral approaches all provide possible solutions to identified hazards. The prevailing conception of safety regulation in the private sector generally excludes the latter two approaches. In response to pressure from business, ANSI formed a Safe Work Practices Task Group aimed at ensuring that "safe work practices are not included in the body of standards."[9] This philosophy accounts for why the appendix contains important provisions in both NFPA standards studied. It also helps account for the storm of protest over housekeeping. Maintenance procedures (particularly housekeeping practices) clearly have a significant effect on safety, but the prevailing view at NFPA is that housekeeping should be left entirely to managerial discretion. Standards for almost any operational controls, even those intended to complement specific technical requirements, make private standards-setters uncomfortable. We try to avoid "'how to' standards," notes a committee member. The provisions of NFPA 61B that address operating procedures are vague and relegated to the appendix, where all provisions are couched in the disclaimer that "this Appendix is not part of the requirements of this NFPA document but is included for information purposes only." The same is true of NFPA 408 for aviation fire safety. Several committee members agree that training requirements are vitally important to the successful use of Halon extinguishers. The standard even includes a (vague) chapter on flight crew training, something quite unusual for the NFPA. More typical is what was relegated to the appendix: "Although not required by this standard, it is highly recommended that live fire training on representative aircraft fires be conducted for all flight crew members during both initial and recurrent training sessions."[10] In contrast, public standards-setters embrace operational controls. The FAA tells commercial airlines "how to" do all sorts of operations and routine maintenance. The essence of the OSHA standard for grain elevators, the "action level" for housekeeping, is an operational control. So, too, are provisions on safety training, evacuation drills, and hot work permits.

Information Disclosure and Labels

Public and private standards-setters also appear to have different positions concerning information disclosure and warning labels. Government sometimes relies on warning labels as its major regulatory strategy. The woodstove labeling rule relies exclusively on information disclosure as a regulatory strategy. The agency defended this standard over the private alternatives on the grounds that its provisions had stronger language and were more likely to be effective. Labeling provisions were also a significant part of the gas space heater rule. In both cases the label was intended to change people's behavior. The private sector is less enamored of information disclosure and does not share in the public sector's penchant for trying to change people's behavior. There is a sense among many private standards-writers that warning labels should not even be included in standards. Historically, many of these organizations shied away from warning labels entirely. The labeling and marking requirements for the gas space heater filled less than a page in the 1963 version of Z21.11.2. There are almost five pages in the 1983 version. Warning labels and other instructions have become more prominent in private standards, but they tend to be written by lawyers who do not otherwise participate in the standards-writing process. A representative on AGA's unvented space heater committee takes labeling questions to in-house counsel at his firm before attending meetings. The Standards Department at UL oversees the warning and labeling provisions in all UL standards, but the engineers do everything else. These provisions are added more to provide a defense against lawsuits than to prevent injuries. It is inconceivable that UL would respond to a problem it considered serious by changing the labeling requirements. Only the government seems intent on what a former CPSC commissioner refers to as a fool's errand: trying to change the behavior of millions of consumers.

When Regulations Take Effect

Finally, public and private standards-setters have disparate views about when standards should take effect. This issue was controversial in all four cases. Government tends to favor the earliest possible effective date, being intolerant of industry claims concerning the feasibility of compliance. Like the stereotypical boss, they want it done yesterday. In contrast, it is outside the realm of possibility for private standards-writers to make standards effective immediately. They tend to allow much more lead time than government. "As long as one company has a device," complains a UL official, "the CPSC is inclined to make it an immediate requirement." The problem, in his view, is twofold. First, the device has not always been evaluated by an independent organization, so its usefulness is in doubt. Second, "other companies may not even have a prototype," meaning that an immediate requirement would grant a temporary monopoly to one firm. UL takes its cues from the market. Until something is widely available, particularly from more than one supplier, UL is reluctant to require it.

Government sometimes even favors the past over the present—making standards retroactively effective. Most private groups have an explicit policy against adopting retroactive standards. This was the most critical difference between the public and private standards for grain elevators: NFPA 61B applies only to facilities built after the standard was adopted, while the OSHA rule applies retroactively. This means that 61B affects, at most, only a few percent of all grain elevators. Changing that provision would probably have greater safety implications than any other single change in the NFPA standard. But the idea of such a change is outside the realm of conceivable solutions and has never been seriously discussed. Even when NFPA made a rare exception, applying its vague housekeeping requirements retroactively, there was opposition on principle. One committee member recalls that he "didn't want to be on record as requiring this even though [he] agreed with it." His rationale: "Let OSHA do it."

Regulatory Philosophy and Professional Ethics

These observed differences in regulatory philosophy appear to be more institutional than transient. That is, they were not produced by situational bargaining or compromise. Rather, they are working assumptions that are rarely the topic of discussion. The case studies suggest that two institutional features help shape the prevailing regulatory philosophy: professional ethics and organizational self-interest. (Organizational self-interest varies by regulatory environment—the topic of chapter 9.) The remainder of this chapter focuses on the important role of professional ethics in distinguishing public and private conceptions of safety.

In his collection of studies on public regulation, James Q. Wilson maintains that specific *types* of employees are important in shaping regulatory behavior. One category discussed by Wilson is professionals. Professionals "have distinctive ways of thinking about problems," and they care deeply about "the maintenance of professional esteem."[11] Of course, no single profession dominates government. Rather, as Frederick Mosher contends, a "very wide variety of professions and professionals in diverse fields" influence the leadership of government. However, in well-established agencies, Mosher continues, there is often "a single occupational group whose knowledge, skills, and orientation are closely identified with the missions and activities of the agency."[12]

A recent survey of "risk professionals" involved in environmental issues suggests that diversity reigns in this field, which accounts for a wide array of professionals from lawyers and economists to engineers and toxicologists.[13] The trends observed by Thomas Dietz and Robert Rycroft provide a solid basis for describing the prevailing ideology in the government agencies examined in the case studies. These risk professionals share an ideology described below as the "enforcement ethic." This ideology emphasizes formal legal rules. It is often associated with lawyers, although many nonlawyers share its premises. But this study did not consider private standards-setting. Rather, it examined professionals housed largely inside the Washington Beltway—in government agencies, law firms, consulting firms, environmental organizations, and trade associations

Beyond the Beltway, where most private standards-setting actually occurs, the patterns of professionalism are distinctly different. Engineers are much more dominant. UL has several hundred engineers and only a handful of lawyers (or nonlawyers fitting the profile of "risk professionals"). Engineers outnumbered all other professions on the technical committees for NFPA 408, 61B, and ANSI Z21.11.2. None of these committees includes a lawyer or an economist. A study for the Administrative Conference makes special note of the "surprising lack of lawyers" in many private standards-setting committees.[14]

The Engineering Ethic

Engineers have a distinct ethic, and it appears to explain several aspects of the regulatory philosophy observed in the private sector. The contours of the engineering ethic are sketched below, following two caveats about this analysis. First, the forces of professionalism vie with other political and economic influences operating on private standards-setters. Many participants simply register "directed votes" at committee meetings—votes that reflect the economic interest of their employers. Others operate with more independence, however, acting without specific instructions or in arenas where they have no direct stake. The fire protection engineer for a major airline participates not only in NFPA committees for aviation safety but also in those for railroad fire safety.

Obviously, proprietary considerations play no role in the latter. Similarly, there is no commercial link between Factory Mutual and the subject matter of NFPA 408, even though a Factory Mutual employee played a pivotal role in developing the standard. The FAA employee on the committee, although listed with his government affiliation, is actually an individual member who "joined for [his] professional development." A pilot for another major airline remained active on several NFPA committees long after his retirement. Although it is rare that engineers operate with such free rein, the professional influences apparent in such situations probably affect other standards as well.

Second, generalizations about groups as large as the engineering profession are necessarily stereotypes—they are suggestive of general themes but should not be taken too literally. Obviously, engineers do not all share the values discussed below. There are competing ethics in the private sector; but it would take dramatic changes in the structure of standards-setting or the profession of engineering for them to dominate. One competing ethic comes from science. Though the distinction between science and engineering has lessened as engineering schools have become more "scientific," there remains a distinct difference in how engineers and scientists approach standards-setting.[15] Researchers at the National Bureau of Standards, for example, sometimes take "scientific" positions that the engineers at AGA or UL consider unrealistic. This kind of conflict, which often pits principle against practicality, has been documented in other policy arenas where scientists and engineers interact.[16]

There are also factional divisions within the engineering profession—a profession more fragmented than is often realized.[17] The values described in this chapter characterized most of the engineers involved in the four case studies, but a small fraction of the profession espouse a different value system. The prevailing ethic would certainly change if these "human factors engineers" played a more prominent role in the process.[18] This seems unlikely, however, as the field is looked upon with suspicion by many engineers and rarely works its way into engineering education.

Instead, the prevailing view, seldom discussed but consistently applied, is that safety standards should not be paternalistic, "engineering for" things such as consumer misuse and poor maintenance. There are several reasons why engineers as professionals might take this view. In some cases, they may have a trained incapacity to recognize the problem. It was not until the American Gas Association Labs conducted some tests with consumers that its engineers realized that the lighting instructions for gas appliances were unclear to almost everyone but the gas appliance engineers who wrote them. The rigors of product testing can cause a similar failure of imagination. UL tests woodstoves under such carefully controlled conditions that its engineers have been unable to *create* creosote. It is hard for UL's engineers to conceive of a problem they have not been able to recreate. It follows that UL is less concerned about metal chimney tolerances than the National Bureau of Standards, which has not only created creosote but has measured the intensity of subsequent chimney fires.

Although this may explain differences in *recognizing* problems, it says little about those situations in which a problem has been recognized (or placed on the public agenda) but remains unaddressed by the private sector. UL may not appreciate *why* people have chimney fires, but it certainly knows that it happens frequently. Here, too, professional norms may explain why some of these issues go unaddressed. UL's engineers have a very different sense of professional duty and responsibility than the lawyers and other standards-writers in government agencies. Engineering to prevent misuse, at least at some point, is abhorrent to the professional engineer. Samuel Florman, an engineer and author, deplores those "who seek salvation for society through the moral conversion of the engineer."[19] "Why design a toaster that cannot burn you," asks a UL engineer, "when you can achieve the same result by not touching it when it is hot?" Expecting a "certain amount of prudence" by people, as another UL engineer puts it, is part of the engineering ethic.

Engineers generally consider issues such as warning labels or standards to battle product misuse as "political." As such, they fall outside the "technical" arena in which engineers operate most comfortably.[20] Engineers involved with grain elevator safety have a similar view: regulating safety devices is their job, but housekeeping is a "management" issue. The prevailing professional norm is to leave politics to the politicians (who are, quite frequently, lawyers) and management to the managers. Lawyers may mandate housekeeping or add warnings to products, but engineers are not in the business of trying to change people's behavior.

The engineering ethic also affects how private standards-setters define the range of acceptable solutions. Engineers appreciate the benefits of technology but, contrary to popular opinion, are often humble about its prospects. New technologies must be proven to be accepted by engineers. Smoke detectors for airplanes might be a good idea, but engineers want proof. They are all too aware of the factors that could cause malfunctions in the aviation environment. Accordingly, private standards-setters are slower to adopt certain safety measures. It takes more than a prototype or a good analogy to change a private standard. Caution does not necessarily mean restraint. Although engineers may be slower than others to endorse new technology, they are often less restrained when safety issues are cast in economic terms. To many engineers, "feasible" has only a technical meaning, not an economic one.[21] "There are those of us who go overboard," admits a professional safety engineer who sits on several NFPA committees. "It is easy to do in the name of safety." This is apparently why NFPA 408 is more demanding than the FAA standard for hand-held fire extinguishers. When deciding the appropriate number and type of extinguishers, the engineers who drafted NFPA 408 turned only to professional norms. The additional cost of Halon extinguishers was not an issue; neither was the marginal benefit of adding more extinguishers, Halon or otherwise.

The Enforcement Ethic

The engineering ethic does not pervade the public sector. With the exception of OSHA, where a fire protection engineer was in charge of the grain elevator rule, none of the key rulemaking personnel or official decisionmakers were engineers. Lawyers played an important role at the CPSC and OSHA. Their influence was less great at the FAA, where the Office of General Counsel reviewed the rule but did not influence the content. The prevalence of lawyers does not of itself denote a commonality of values like that which prevails in the engineering profession. Encompassing both the plaintiffs' and the defendants' bar—ardent adversaries in litigation concerning public safety—the profession is too fragmented to have common values on questions such as how to divide responsibility between consumers and manufacturers. There appear to be common values among most public standards-setters, however, and that regulatory ethos is described below as the "enforcement ethic." This ethic appears to infuse the hearts and minds of many government lawyers and other rulemaking personnel in the public sector. The enforcement ethic seeks to eliminate harm wherever possible; it tolerates few excuses, and demands near-total compliance.

The enforcement ethic is legalistic. It favors rules as a response to problems. Just as personal injury lawyers seek a remedy for every injury, some agencies propose a standard for every identified hazard. The process is routinized at the FAA, where accidents beget regulations. National injury estimates drive the CPSC. The magnitude of the hazard matters more than the cause. Fault and responsibility on the part of the consumer do not play an important role in this value system. Public agencies seek to prevent injuries, whether caused by misuse, poor management, or product design.

The enforcement ethic also tolerates few excuses, and business concerns are generally not among them. Some CPSC commissioners seek to determine whether issues are "technical" or "economic." Technical arguments can forestall action; economic arguments rarely do. The CPSC staff had little patience for industry arguments concerning the effective date of the woodstove and space heater rules. In both cases, industry was concerned about disposing of existing inventories before the rule took effect. Privately, CPSC staff members admit that they did not consider the concern a valid one. The FAA summarily dismissed the argument that false alarms from smoke detectors might panic passengers. "That is not a safety issue," according to an FAA staff member.

Finally, the enforcement ethic stresses compliance at all costs. Total compliance is often an end rather than a means. The CPSC staff was inclined to go ahead with a woodstove labeling rule so long as there was anything short of total compliance on the private side. "I don't buy the argument about 85 percent compliance [with the UL standard]," commented one staff member, "because it says nothing about the other 15 percent." Undue emphasis on total compliance led the CPSC to adopt a woodstove labeling rule that had doubtful marginal benefits and a minuscule chance of actually improving compliance. Similarly, for the rulemaking staff at OSHA it mattered not that the cost of proposed safety measures would be highest at those facilities where the benefits would be lowest—country elevators. To exempt smaller facilities from housekeeping requirements would have gone against the enforcement ethic, and the idea of doing so was never seriously entertained by the OSHA staff.

EIGHT

Regulatory Decisionmaking: Public and Private Standards in Action

Given these differences in regulatory philosophy, public and private standards-setting systems, even when they address the same general subject, seem somewhat like regulatory apples and oranges. Though similar in form and purpose, they are difficult to compare in substance. Economists and policy analysts, unfazed by this predicament, look to the bottom line. They compare the seemingly incomparable by thinking in terms of aggregate costs and benefits. This approach facilitates the normative comparison of outcomes, an important element in evaluating public and private standards, but it obscures the nature and workings of the decisionmaking process. The private sector almost never engages in cost-benefit analysis. In contrast, the public sector produces plenty of cost-benefit analysis—it is required to by law—but mandated analysis tends to provide rationalizations rather than bases for decisions. The task is further complicated, of course, by the uncertainties attendant to complex regulatory decisions.

This chapter examines the outcomes of public and private standards-setting and the nature of the underlying decisionmaking process, with the goal of evaluating the relative performance of the two systems. The cases partially confirm the conventional view that public standards are stricter than private ones and are sometimes prone to overzealousness. But there are contrary indications as well, suggesting that the private sector is more diverse than is commonly presumed. The private sector even exhibits surprising tendencies toward strictness on occasion. Understanding these patterns of behavior is critical to predicting how the private sector might act in the future. This chapter analyzes the cases in two ways: first, in terms of the *tendencies* of each sector in handling the uncertainties about regulatory costs and benefits; second, on the basis of overall *reasonableness,* making some important assumptions explained below. Both approaches suggest that private standards-setting is more diverse than is often imagined. Various explanations for this regulatory behavior are ventured in chapter 9.

Decision Rules and Routines

Within the constraint of regulatory philosophy there is considerable room for discretionary judgment. Given the inherent uncertainties in setting safety standards, however, it is unclear how standards-setters structure and exercise this discretion. In other words, what are the rules of evidence, formal and informal? Some version of cost-benefit analysis is the formal answer in the public sector, although agencies are often accused of circumventing the requirement. The mystery widens in the private sector, where cost-benefit analysis is almost never done. Private safety standards often precede any information on accidents or injuries. UL listed woodstoves for decades without the benefit of any injury estimates. So what does the private sector do instead? How does it actually make decisions? The cases suggest that heuristics and other standard operating procedures have evolved to simplify the resolution of these complex safety questions in the private sector.

One technique is to defer to "professional judgment" within certain constraints. In other words, so long as particular provisions do not cost too much, engineers are given free rein in making the decisions. This strategy requires only rough estimates of costs and not necessarily any formal assessment of benefits. It also results in a substantial amount of guesswork. UL prefers to call this "engineering judgment." Others use the phrase "educated guess," with the stress on *educated.* In either case, the implication is that guesses are guided by a combination of education, experience, and values. This explains both the importance of engineering ethics and the potential for unreasonably strict (but economically inexpensive) provisions in private standards. More costly and salient issues are not resolved so informally; they are subject to the political process described in the next chapter.

A related approach that also does not require extensive information about costs and benefits is to concentrate on ominous hazards such as electrocution and amputation. As a staff engineer at NFPA put it: "I can tell you how to protect against a hazard. I can't tell you how likely it is to happen." With ominous hazards, the probabilities are unimportant. Participants in both public and private standards-setting express the sentiment that certain hazards are obviously worth regulating. "One case can give you the answer," explains a UL employee. "Somebody loses a finger, let's fix it. I don't need information on a thousand cases." A former CPSC employee agrees: "If the problem is really significant, like the amputation of fingers or hands in the snowblower, you don't have to do a cost-benefit analysis to say that a twenty dollar control is going to pay for itself."

"Through almost intuition you can come up with cost-benefit analysis," explains an NFPA employee, who boasts that this intuition resulted in the requirement for ground-fault circuit interrupters. These devices, added to the National Electric Code in 1975, automatically trip the circuitbreaker when there might otherwise be serious or fatal shock. The irony is that a subsequent cost-benefit analysis conducted by the National Bureau of Standards casts doubt on the wisdom of the standard, concluding that the cost per life saved could exceed $7 million.[1]

Considering these tendencies in two dimensions—that is, separating estimates of cost from evaluations of benefits—suggests that there are different *patterns of preference* in the public and private sectors concerning whether and when to err on the side of safety. Four combinations of estimation errors are possible. Two of these patterns are suggestive of regulatory outcomes; the other two are ambiguous. A standards-setting system might tend to *under*estimate costs and *over*estimate benefits. Because both estimation errors favor regulation, the resulting standards, relative to other combinations of estimation errors, would tend to be the strictest, bordering on overly protective (see table 6). Public standards-writing is generally thought to have these characteristics. Conversely, a standards-setting system in which costs are *over*estimated and benefits *under*estimated would tend to be most lenient, with a danger of being too lax. That is the conventional wisdom about private standards-setting. The other combinations of estimation errors are ambiguous because the errors are in different directions.

Two caveats are necessary before carrying this analysis further. First, these descriptions are not meant to be pejorative. Overestimation, in this context, is not deliberate puffery, nor is underestimation intentionally deceptive. Rather, these terms describe tendencies that are akin to

TABLE 6   POSSIBLE COMBINATIONS OF
CUMULATIVE ESTIMATION ERRORS
BY STANDARDS-SETTERS

BENEFITS

		Underestimate	Overestimate
		I Ambiguous	II Strict, leaning to overprotective
COSTS	Underestimate		
	Overestimate	III Lenient, leaning to underprotective	IV Ambiguous

legal rules of evidence—they encompass various presumptions and informal rules concerning the burden of proof and the resolution of scientific disputes under uncertainty. Second, the typology illuminates differences in the direction, not the magnitude, of these tendencies. Standards classified in any of the four quadrants might be socially desirable, depending on the magnitude of the errors. Even with this ambiguity, the observed tendencies in the two sectors are quite revealing.

Moving first to how costs are estimated in both sectors, it is widely assumed that private standards-setters err on the high side, while government generally errs on the low. Private organizations have first-hand knowledge of costs and are likely to be sensitive to them, erring in the direction of the industry's concerns about profitability. In contrast, government lacks this first-hand knowledge and is likely to discount industry estimates of costs for fear they have been exaggerated for strategic purposes. Government also has no direct interest in, and often little actual concern about, how regulations affect profitability.

This much of the conventional wisdom is largely supported by the case studies. Government probably underestimated costs in all four cases. OSHA's estimates of the costs of the grain elevator rule were widely criticized as being too low. The cost estimates in the other cases, although much closer to the industry consensus, involved various minor errors in the "low" direction. The CPSC used a low figure for testing costs in the woodstove proceeding. The FAA assumed that airlines would buy the most inexpensive smoke detectors and, more significant, did not even calculate the additional training costs of Halon.

As expected, a tendency to underestimate costs does not characterize the four private cases. What occurred instead, however, is not readily apparent from the record. Documentation is scant, and many participants obscure the issues because arguments "against safety" are considered either unsavory or impolitic.[2] The one apparent exception is NFPA 408, where costs were never explicitly discussed. The standard was set practically without regard to cost. Nevertheless, it appears that the NFPA Agricultural Dusts committee tended to overestimate, not underestimate, the cost of safety measures. Members of the National Grain and Food Association surely did so in lobbying OSHA.[3] Manufacturers generally agree that UL and AGA "understand" the cost of various proposals and do not tend to underestimate them.

The surprise is on the benefit side, where it is generally assumed that private standards-setters underestimate benefits while government overestimates them. This characterization appears to fit government. Estimates of benefits in the woodstove labeling case, for example, were wildly exaggerated. W. Kip Viscusi argues that the estimated benefits of the gas space heater standard were also exaggerated, although the mistake was probably not very large.[4] There is good reason to believe that the FAA and OSHA overestimated benefits as well. The private sector, by contrast, did not behave as expected. In only one of the four cases did the private sector play down the benefits of taking additional safety precautions. Members of the NFPA committee for grain elevator safety seem resigned to the notion that few, if any, safety measures can affect the number of explosions. But in the three remaining cases, there was a marked tendency for the private sector to err on the "safe" side. This tendency varied by hazard but was unmistakable in overall terms. There is no substantive basis for believing that most aspects of UL 1482 have any real effect on woodstove safety. Similarly, the AGA/ANSI standard for gas space heaters is filled with requirements that have no obvious effect on safety. The same is true of the NFPA standard for aviation fire extinguishers. All available evidence suggests that the benefits of adding more Halon extinguishers and increasing the training procedures for personnel are likely to be very small. That was not the view of most NFPA committee members, however, who tacitly assumed that the benefits were worth the cost.

In short, government standards-setting was true to form, tending in all cases to the combination of errors that promotes overprotective regulation. By contrast, the private standards-setters were all over the map (see table 7). Only one of the four cases, grain elevators, falls into

TABLE 7   THE PATTERN OF ESTIMATION ERRORS
IN THE CASE STUDIES

BENEFITS

		Underestimate	Overestimate
		I	II NFPA 408 FAA: Fire safety CPSC: Woodstoves CPSC: Space heaters OSHA: Grain elevators
COSTS	Underestimate		
	Overestimate	III NFPA 61B	IV UL 1482 ANSI Z21.11.2

the category where underprotective regulation is most likely. In two cases, the results were ambiguous. Although it appears that UL and AGA tend to err in the favor of industry when estimating the *cost* of safety measures, they also erred on the side of safety in estimating the *benefits* of various provisions for woodstoves and gas space heaters. Finally, one of the private standards, NFPA 408, falls into the quadrant dominated by government. Based on the available evidence, this standard probably errs farthest in the direction of overprotectiveness, mandating even more than the FAA in an area where the likely marginal benefits are, by any reasonable measure, minuscule. The unexpected diversity of private standards carries over to the normative evaluation of outcomes.

Measures of Overall Performance

Distinct regulatory philosophies confine and direct the task of setting standards. Overlapping but different decisionmaking rules characterize the private and public sectors. But outcomes are not as easily differentiated as the philosophies and operating procedures that produce them. There are four reasons why it is difficult to draw policy conclusions from regulatory philosophy alone. First, regulatory philosophy constrains but does not determine outcomes. It leaves plenty of room for discretionary decisions. While regulatory philosophy keeps UL from addressing the creosote problem, it leaves considerable latitude in setting other requirements in the standard. These discretionary decisions result in a variety of outcomes. UL 1482 is probably too strict on glass doors, but too lax on metal grates. Similarly, the stability requirements in ANSI Z21.11.2 are undoubtedly stringent, while the clothing ignition test is not.

Second, however distinct these philosophies, the universe of potential outcomes overlap. The public and private sectors are capable of producing very similar outcomes. The FAA and NFPA, acting practically in isolation of each other, developed several similar provisions for aviation fire safety. There were pockets of agreement in the other cases as well—areas where both sectors agreed on the content of particular provisions. The CPSC approved the basic technical and performance provisions in UL 1482 and most of those in Z21.11.2. OSHA did not quarrel with the NFPA provisions for fire safety in grain elevators.

Third, even when regulatory philosophies dictate distinct regulatory outcomes, the normative implications are unclear. The same regulatory philosophy can perform well in one circumstance and poorly in another. Paternalism led the CPSC to adopt a seemingly desirable standard for gas space heaters, but an ill-advised one for woodstoves. Similarly, refusing to make standards retroactive practically gutted NFPA 61B, but had little adverse effect on NFPA 408 or UL 1482. The only way to evaluate regulatory philosophies, then, is by examining outcomes and seeking to understand the conditions under which they perform best.

Finally, it is difficult to draw substantive conclusions about regulatory philosophy because it is multifaceted and signals sometimes conflict. Safety standards are usually polycentric in nature, raising an assortment of complex issues. Under these circumstances, the manifestations of regulatory philosophy are varied and sometimes contradictory. The engineering ethic, for example, helps explain UL's reluctance to address the creosote problem in woodstoves, but it also explains its more stringent structural requirements. In sum, regulatory philosophy shapes the standards-setting process in several important ways, but the normative implications of these differences cannot be stated in simple terms that clearly favor one form over the other.

What is needed, then, is a measure of overall performance to facilitate the comparison of public and private outcomes. Whether that is possible strikes at the heart of a long-standing debate about process versus substance. Dispensing with pesky substantive issues, those disposed to the legal perspective turn exclusively to process (that perspective is examined in chapter 11). Those venturing substantive conclusions usually couch the analysis in terms of either strictness or reasonableness. Both concepts encompass important social considerations. Strictness generally refers to absolute benefits; reasonableness, to the relationship between benefits and costs. These frames of reference differ significantly, creating conflicting impressions of many standards. Public standards are usually considered stricter, but less reasonable, than private ones. That is, they probably generate more absolute benefits than private standards, but at a cost higher than many considered acceptable. By contrast, almost no one argues that private standards impose unreasonable costs. But reasonableness is thought to come at the expense of strictness. Obviously, these substantive measures should be merged in some manner. Standards should be compared through an aggregation of strictness and reasonableness.

In theory, cost-benefit analysis facilitates the task. But there are practical and philosophical objections to even the roughest forms of cost-benefit analysis. The dearth of reliable data, particularly on benefits, dims the potential for such analysis. Part of the problem is forecasting. Much depends on implementation. For example, OSHA's "action level" for grain elevator housekeeping will produce benefits if it is implemented through a reasonable inspection scheme. It will foster unreasonableness if implemented poorly. On a more philosophical level, cost-benefit analysis requires that monetary values be placed on life and limb, something both methodologically difficult and politically explosive. Cost-benefit analysis is out of the question for current evaluative purposes. The data necessary to support it are not available. Nothing remotely resembling cost-benefit analysis was undertaken by any of the private standards-setters. And the economic analyses conducted by OSHA, the CPSC, and the FAA are easily faulted for reasons elaborated in the case studies.

One way to evaluate outcomes directly despite the significant uncertainties about costs and benefits is to indulge in liberal evidentiary presumptions and seek only to separate the obviously bad outcomes from the possibly good ones. In those terms, a standard is within the "zone of reasonableness" if there is credible evidence that benefits are (1) nontrivial and (2) not significantly in excess of costs. This overly inclusive notion of "reasonableness" avoids the almost intractable disputes about the precise magnitude of uncertain benefits and costs. This approach also permits a surprising number of normative conclusions about the cases. The results, based on the summary evaluation in the case studies, are summarized and explained below:

Overly Strict	Within the Zone of Reasonableness	Too Lax
CPSC: woodstoves	OSHA: grain elevators	NFPA 61B
FAA fire safety	CPSC: space heaters	
NFPA 408	ANSI/AGA Z21.11.2	
	UL 1482	

On the public side, two of the standards were clearly too strict. There was no evidence that the CPSC's woodstove labeling rule would result in *any* measurable benefits; and fire protection engineers agree that the FAA's standard for aviation fire safety is very unlikely to generate benefits in excess of cost. The other two public standards were well within the zone of reasonableness. The need for grain elevator regulation is supported by the evidence, and the OSHA standard, although it could be improved, is reasonable in several respects. The CPSC's standard for gas space heaters is probably the best of the bunch. It seems to be responsible for the widespread use of ODS technology, an inexpensive and effective method for dealing with a problem of uncertain dimensions. The private sector was also divided. Two of its standards were clearly undesirable, although one was too strict and the other too lax. The NFPA went even further overboard than the FAA on aviation safety. NFPA officials privately admit that these standards are not supportable in economic terms. The NFPA also missed the mark on grain elevators, adopting a standard that is so weak that it barely addresses the most serious problem: grain dust.

Two tentative conclusions can be drawn from this normative evaluation. First, neither sector is clearly better than the other. Both sectors appear as capable of failing as they are of succeeding, although the public sector seems more likely to be overly strict, while the private sector is more likely to be too lax. Nevertheless, *private standards should not be rejected solely on the theory that they tend to be underprotective.* Sometimes they are not. This analysis also suggests that there is no simple answer to the question whether the public or private approach is generally better. Private sector behavior is too varied. NFPA 408 and 61B are cases in point. Second, the cases suggest that particular issues can foster distinct patterns of regulatory behavior. It is no coincidence that both the public and private standards for aviation fire safety seems "overly strict."

Both of these observations underscore the importance of understanding the reasons behind the observed results—the subject of the next chapter. Given the unusual nature of the "paired" case studies, however, it is appropriate to consider first whether these observations are intrinsic to overlapping standards. In other words, to what extent is the behavior of either sector affected by the activities of the other?

Accounting for Regulatory Overlap

As with most instances of overlapping standards, the private standard came first in all four cases. The most pertinent question, then, is whether the public sector tailored its behavior to the private standard. How the private sector responded to government intervention is also important, given widespread concern that public standards will "drive out" private ones.

In two of the cases, grain elevators and aviation fire safety, the public sector acted almost independently of the private sector. In neither instance was the public sector trying to influence the private. OSHA did not seriously pursue a strategy of trying to improve NFPA 61B, and the FAA did not even know about NFPA 408 until well into its own rulemaking proceedings. Therefore, the observations from those cases can safely be said to represent inherent traits, not ones unique to overlapping standards.

The most curious aspect of these cases concerns the private sector, which apparently did not alter its behavior in response to the threat of public intervention. The NFPA did not respond to the FAA, other than to send a brief letter to the public docket. Several committee members interviewed while the FAA regulation was in the proposal stage knew almost nothing about the regulation. In contrast, committee members considering revisions to NFPA 61B in July 1985 were acutely aware of the proposed OSHA rule. But they, too, took little action aimed at forestalling OSHA regulation. The committee seemed resigned to government regulation and was not willing to enact serious grain-dust controls in order to prevent it. This relatively independent behavior bolsters the conclusions already set forth about public and private standards-setting, but it does not necessarily bode well for public policy. The government's failure to exploit existing standards or to try to influence them seems wasteful. The FAA's actions certainly violated the OMB directive to consider existing private standards before adopting government ones.

Both cases involving the CPSC were interactive from the start. The agency acted with full knowledge of the relevant private standards, attempting in both cases to supplement them with beneficial government regulation. The private sector responded in both cases as well. To what extent does this interaction alter the conclusions about public and private behavior? It is impossible to know without somehow comparing this "interactive" behavior to cases in which there is no private standard. Some effects are obvious, however. The CPSC tailored its regulations to supplement private standards. Whether it would have proposed more comprehensive standards in the absence of private ones is uncertain, but the agency would have been hard pressed to justify the technical judgments contained in, say, UL 1482. A close examination of these cases suggests that the most significant effects of this interactive behavior went largely unnoticed. In the case of woodstoves, not only did UL alter its warning labels to placate the CPSC, but the percentage of certified woodstoves rose dramatically after the CPSC proposed its regulation. With gas space heaters, significant changes were made in ANSI Z21.11.2. The small porcelain bathroom heater was eliminated as a result of numerous improvements in structural requirements and performance standards. These changes in private standards should rightly be credited to government action, and conclusions about the private sector must be adjusted accordingly.

In sum, the CPSC cases suggest that the power of government to influence private standards is significant. Unfortunately, government's capacity for recognizing these improvements is apparently not as large. In neither case did the government clearly recognize the improvements in the private standards. Instead, driven by an enforcement ethic that was apparently unaffected by the private standards, government went ahead with regulations that produced minimal marginal benefits. The next chapter looks beyond these interactive effects to broader explanations of the differences in decisionmaking and performance.

NINE

Explaining Regulatory Behavior

Whether public or private, safety standards generally impose concentrated costs and confer dispersed benefits. "It may be astonishing that [regulation] of this sort is ever passed," observes James Q. Wilson, who advances a theory of entrepreneurial politics to explain its emergence in the public sector.[1] The theory, which relies on latent public opinion and anti-business sentiment, helps explain the government's behavior in at least three of the four case studies. Aviation safety seems to be a case unto itself. Wilson's theory does not explain private regulation, however. Private standards are not foisted on the private sector the way public standards are. Instead, private regulation is usually explained by some form of "capture" theory. The notion of capture is almost redundant, since private standards-setting is a form of self-regulation.[2] Private standards are often thought to reflect "the lowest common denominator" or "the path of least resistance." But the varied and sometimes stringent behavior observed in the private sector challenges these notions. The expected politics of private regulation prevailed in only one case, resulting in the lax standard for grain elevators. Moreover, there are puzzles about the behavior of the private sector in all four cases. Why was the Z21.11.2 committee willing to upgrade its requirements, substantially adding to retail costs, but unwilling to add the inexpensive oxygen depletion sensor? Why are certain provisions in UL 1482 and NFPA 408 overly stringent in the view of independent experts with no commercial axe to grind? Moreover, why weren't economic concerns ever voiced when NFPA 408 was upgraded?

This chapter explores two traditional explanations for regulatory behavior, along with three more powerful ones suggested by the case studies. The most conventional explanation of private regulation builds on the metaphor of the path of least resistance. Forestalling government regulation is the other motive most commonly attributed to the private sector. Other explanations suggested by the cases include: the political economy of product testing, the peculiar politics of aviation safety, and the legal constraints of the regulatory environment.

The Political Economy of Safety Regulation

The Path of Least Resistance

Private standards-setting is widely thought to be controlled by those who want the least done. Most private standards are "consensus" standards, a process noted for the rule that there be no "unresolved negatives" among those participating. This process seems practically designed to ensure that standards-setters follow the path of least resistance. The need for consensus, Eads and Reuter argue, leads to a "watering down" of many standards.[3] The process is abetted, others add, by the lack of consumer representatives agitating for increased safety.

The case studies provide selective support for the conventional wisdom. Business interests often express concerns about the cost of upgrading standards. Manufacturers of woodstoves and gas space heaters complained that the costs of certain UL and AGA requirements were unjustifiably high. Grain elevator operators sing the same refrain. There may be a realm in which engineers reign, but it is most likely to encompass provisions that would not add costs perceived to be significant by producers.[4] "People who don't have instructed votes still know who they work for," observes an NBS official familiar with many private standards-setters.

Concerns about "imbalance" among participating interests also find support in the cases. Organized consumer groups had a meek voice compared to manufacturers in all of the private cases. "Numbers count," according to an engineer at Consumers Union, "and I have been at a lot of meetings where I am the only negative vote—and that is the end of it." UL and some ANSI-sponsored committees pay lip service to "consumer participation," but consumer groups actually play only a minimal role in the process.[5] It is not that private standards-setters specifically exclude consumers—although attorneys have occasionally been excluded—so much as that consumers are unorganized and rarely have the resources to participate.[6]

But the "path of least resistance" is not a predictive explanation, since it says nothing about when resistance will or will not occur. Moreover, it leaves unanswered the question why pro-safety results sometimes obtain over the objections of some business interests. The cases suggest two reasons why the lowest common denominator might not prevail: (1) there are unlikely pro-safety interests in the private sector, and (2) there are institutional impediments to the "watering down" process hypothesized by Eads and Reuter.

Unlikely Safety Interests. Although the range of interests on most committees is limited by the paucity of consumer participants, the cases highlight several largely unrecognized advocates of safety in the private sector. For example, representatives of the insurance industry have an interest in controlling losses. Insurance representatives pushed UL to upgrade its requirements for metal chimneys.[7] Vendors of safety equipment also carry the pro-safety flag. Manufacturers of dust-control equipment speak out for improved housekeeping measures on the NFPA Agricultural Dusts committee. Labor representatives on some committees also favor various safety measures. The Air Line Pilots Association is active on NFPA's aviation committees; a representative from a Grain Workers Local sits on its Agricultural Dust Committee.

Installers and servicers also care about safety, often more than they care about cost or selection. An outspoken member of the National Chimney Sweep Guild was almost successful in getting NFPA to ban large stoves that require clearances of more than the traditional thirty-six inches.[8] Representatives of gas utilities, whose employees must confront the victims of product injuries, frequently argue in favor of additional safety features for gas appliances. The J. C. Penney testing lab, designed to incorporate considerations about the consumer into purchasing decisions, also suggests occasional improvements in UL standards. Finally, "the fire service" itself, as it is known around NFPA, is well represented on NFPA committees. Firefighters spread what the NFPA president recently called "the gospel of fire protection."[9] A Washington lawyer familiar with private safety standards agrees that "most NFPA committees have a bias toward the fire services." Needless to say, cost-benefit analysis is not one of the commandments.

The most intriguing examples of unlikely safety interests are committee members who appear to act against the interest they represent.
Staff members at AGA Labs, for example, favored a ban on space
heaters, while the AGA at large—overseer of the labs—opposed it.[10]
The representative of a major airline takes positions on NFPA aviation
committees that are sometimes opposed by his superiors. The simple
explanation is that an "interest" is rarely homogeneous. Just as consumers are not interested only in safety, manufacturers are not interested only in costs. Take a commercial airline, for example. Part of the
organization is interested in keeping operating costs down, while other
parts are interested in reducing insurance and liability costs. The latter
are likely to favor increased expenditures for safety. The Maintenance
Department probably wants a larger budget, and the Marketing Department might be interested in adding those safety items that matter
most to passengers (for example, smoke detectors but not fire-blocking
seat covers). In the case of NFPA 408, the airline representative cited
above works in the Engineering and Safety Department. His professional interest is in safety, with little regard for cost. And since it is more
likely that a safety engineer than an account executive will sit on the
relevant standards-setting committee, organizational interests are likely
to be subtly slanted in favor of safety in many cases.

Institutional Considerations.   The second problem with "capture"
theory is more fundamental: there are institutional reasons why standards-setting does not always reflect the conventional wisdom. Primarily, standards used by product testing labs are not written by "consensus." They are written by in-house engineers and only later sent
through a "canvass" process leading to ANSI approval and the designation "national consensus standard." Fatal to the "watering down"
theory, delays in the ANSI canvass process have no effect on the testing
labs. UL uses (and revises) its standards long before they are distributed
by ANSI for comment and review. UL officials privately confirm that
failure to achieve ANSI approval would not affect this situation. In
other words, UL is happy to go ahead without ANSI's imprimatur.
Accordingly, no participants have an influence akin to veto power.
While UL seeks comments from industry, it also adopts standards that
do not enjoy the "consensus" of all manufacturers. The "least common
denominator" argument also lacks an explanation for the role of the
staff. A study of the Association of Home Appliance Manufacturers
concluded that the staff has its own sense of mission and its own in-

terests, pursuing some goals that are not necessarily in the interest of the general membership.[11]

Forestalling Government Regulation

Private regulatory behavior that does not follow the path of least resistance is often explained as an effort to forestall government regulation. This theory allows for stricter results without attributing altruistic motives to the private sector. The theory both overexplains and underexplains private regulatory behavior. It overexplains to the extent that virtually any outcome, lenient or strict, can be attributed to the threat of government regulation. As David Garvin states:

> Only if firms were able to identify both the standards that would be established under government regulation and the precise amount that voluntary standards could fall below this level without inducing government action would [the lowest possible level] automatically follow. This information is seldom available. As a result, risk-averse firms, anxious to deter government regulation, might unknowingly set standards as rigorous—or, conceivably, even more stringent than—those that the government would demand.[12]

Accordingly, the theory is not predictive either. Almost any outcome might result from the desire to forestall government regulation. The "forestalling theory" also underexplains private regulatory behavior, since private standards generally predate and significantly outnumber government regulations. The threat of CPSC regulation, for example, cannot possibly be relevant to more than a small number of UL standards.

Even if the forestalling theory does not have wide application, it is most likely to apply to paired cases. Although private standards usually predate public ones—as they did in all four of the case studies—it seems likely that the private sector might upgrade its standards in response to the threat of government regulation. At first glance, the private participants seemed to be motivated by the possibility of government influence. UL changed its labeling requirements in response to the CPSC. The same motive helped move AGA Labs to upgrade Z21.11.2. Even the NFPA Agricultural Dusts committee upgraded 61B in a few respects with the hope of forestalling OSHA. But these motivations were not particularly strong. Although UL changed its labeling provisions, the bulk of the standard has nothing to do with labeling or the threat of CPSC regulation. Committee members considering revisions to NFPA

61B seemed resigned to government regulation and certainly were not willing to enact serious grain-dust controls in order to prevent it.

Forestalling government regulation was a dominant influence in only one case: gas space heaters. The AGA/ANSI standard was upgraded in several significant ways while government contemplated regulatory action. But, as with NFPA and grain elevators, the private sector was unwilling to mandate what the government obviously wanted: an ODS requirement. It added that only after the CPSC did. This is not to say that forestalling government regulation is always a weak motive. The case studies suggest that this motive is largely subordinate to other factors, such as the demand for private standards. That demand and the broader political economy of private regulation suggest that product testing labs have different motivations than other private standards-setters. Product testing labs have a financial interest in eliminating competing government regulation, before or after the fact. That is why AGA/ANSI adopted the CPSC's ODS requirement and why UL was willing to alter its labeling requirements. Other standards-setters seldom have this strong an interest. The political economy of product testing is discussed below, followed by consideration of the peculiar politics of NFPA and the special problem of aviation safety.

The Business of Product Testing

Hypotheses based on the assumption that private standards-setting involves some form of collective deliberation and democratic decision-making are inappropriate for the hundreds of standards developed by testing labs. Unlike government agencies, these organizations do not operate on an issue-by-issue basis. Standards are an ongoing business. And being in the business of certification affects the approach one takes in promoting the goal of product safety. Motivated by the financial interest in certification and bolstered by the market power attendant to such a position, testing labs have different regulatory incentives than are often attributed to the private sector. Testing labs have unusual incentives for making standards demanding, although they experience countervailing forces as well. The tendency toward stringency is particularly strong when it comes to compliance.

Testing labs generally do not develop standards unless there is a proven and profitable market.[13] These labs are in a responsive position, responding to a demand for a given standard. UL does not seek out clients, clients seek out UL. They come for various reasons. Sometimes product certification is required by law (as in jurisdictions mandating listed woodstoves), sometimes the demand originates with product liability insurers or retail stores, and on occasion an industry voluntarily seeks certification to bolster consumer confidence.[14] These forces combined to compel compliance with the Z21 standard. They were weaker in the case of woodstoves, probably owing to poor building code enforcement, although the pressures for compliance increased over time.

The economic realities of product testing help explain one of the major differences in public and private conceptions of safety regulation. To private testing organizations, it is almost always a "given" that the product will be marketed. UL and AGA Labs never seriously consider whether a product is best banned altogether (or "unlisted," in lab parlance). Even though some staff members at AGA Labs felt that unvented gas space heaters should be banned, it was a foregone conclusion that AGA Labs would continue to list them. The certification business can be very profitable. It is not in the interests of AGA Labs or UL to eliminate a testing market.

Testing labs are also particularly sensitive to the cost of developing and implementing standards for certification. This business equivalent of cost-benefit analysis further limits the kinds of standards that get written. The process is akin to the problem of "orphan drugs."[15] Insufficient demand for certification causes testing labs to overlook certain problems. Aviation safety is a case in point. There are sound scientific arguments for testing aviation fire extinguishers to special standards. UL advanced these arguments when opposing the FAA rule. UL has even received requests to develop such standards. But from UL's point of view, the limited market for aviation fire extinguishers does not justify the cost of developing special standards and test procedures.

Considerations attendant to the business of product testing help explain other aspects of UL's problem. In order to maintain support and credibility for their business, testing labs must take care that their test methods are defensible, reproducible, and relatively inexpensive. Developing test methods is inherently difficult, since the goal is a simple procedure that provides information useful in a complex world where products are used (and misused) in countless ways. UL and other testing labs generally handle the problem by deferring to accepted definitions of proper use. This means following the applicable use and installation codes as well as the manufacturers' instructions. This helps explain why UL is so reluctant to factor consumer misuse into its standards. There is often no defensible way to do it, especially when the misuse concerns the most basic conditions of installation and use. UL tests kerosene heaters, for example, using certified K-1 kerosene fuel as specified in the manufacturer's instructions. Testing for the "flare up" problem would require the addition of some amount of gasoline to the fuel. Should this be trace amounts, as would occur if a consumer put kerosene into an old gas can, or some larger amount that would simulate even grosser misuse? There is neither an obvious nor an easily defensible answer. Similar problems are posed by the fact that misuse can occur in a variety of different ways. Should UL also add tests for other improper fuel mixtures? Including "representative" examples of misuse could expand the cost of testing significantly, raising objections from manufacturers. It could also force some products from the market entirely, eliminating the market for certification. If enough gasoline is added to the fuel, all kerosene heaters will fail the test.

Simulating misuse can also be technically difficult, particularly if the hazard is related to poor maintenance. For example, it would be difficult to design practical and reproducible tests to simulate the kind of lint buildup that can, after six to eight months, impede the performance of a gas space heater. Creosote buildup poses a similar problem. It would be extremely time-consuming to build up actual creosote for testing. Yet without such an approach, there would surely be criticism of the test method intended to simulate the problem.[16] In sum, organizations such as UL sometimes resist recognizing misuse problems because of the implementation problems that would occur in testing. Product certifiers must think ahead to the implementation problems involved in developing test methods. Accordingly, they are sensitive to problems that the CPSC often overlooks in its desire to "do something."

Beginning with a demand for their service also endows the testing labs with certain regulatory power. It may be certain that the product will be listed, but the listing agency has considerable discretion in determining the requirements. There is almost never competition between labs using different testing requirements. Hence, a manufacturer who disagrees with, say, the UL standard for woodstoves has little choice but to comply. A lawyer who criticizes many private standards for being too lenient agrees that "the UL staff, from a professional point of view, can often set a level just because they think it is right." Market power does not create unbounded discretion, however. Opinions vary about the power of the staff at organizations such as UL. Most observers agree that proposed standards must enjoy the support of a critical mass of manufacturers. Even though UL has market power, it cannot afford to lose industry support. The credibility of the UL label would be called into question if firms were moved to challenge its standards openly. Accordingly, UL engineers speak of "what they can get away with" in their safety standards.

Several additional factors constrain the commercial testing labs. Product certification also involves a considerable degree of deference to manufacturers. The only way UL can provide certification quickly, particularly for new products, is to incorporate many prevailing business practices into its standards. The impression of most observers is that AGA and UL can "push" a recalcitrant firm marketing a product below widely accepted levels of safety, but must "follow" the determination of what is generally acceptable. "We are always following the crowd," comments an engineer at AGA Labs. The ability of testing labs to "push" is also affected by the availability of information. UL and AGA do not write product standards so much as review existing products. The certification business is prospective; products are often certified before they are marketed. Armed with specific information about product problems, UL is most effective in gaining overall improvements in standards. Absent such information, however, anyone urging a change in UL standards is likely to be rebuffed for failing to present evidence "from the field."[17]

Product certifiers take a similar view of research: it is expensive and will not be undertaken unless the payoff is clear. Research projects are occasionally undertaken that might improve numerous standards at once, such as research on shock hazards and sharp surfaces. But research to improve some aspect of a single standard is much less likely. UL is not inclined to investigate the qualities of catalytic combustors for woodstoves unless industry sponsors the work. UL 1482 will continue to generate revenue without this research.

A final aspect of product certification that distinguishes it from other private standards is compliance. Compliance is the business of product testing. The income received from these "follow-up" services, combined with the threat of liability if products do not actually meet the stated requirements, prompts the testing labs to implement comprehensive inspection schemes. Testing labs go to extraordinary lengths to ensure that products bearing their label comply with their standards. UL inspects producers at least four times a year, regardless of their track record—an approach that far exceeds any public enforcement scheme. But product testing labs are also more willing to phase in requirements over time. Since they demand total compliance from their clients and charge dearly for certification, the best way for testing labs to placate angry customers is to allow ample time for compliance. Unlike the CPSC, UL is usually receptive to adjusting the effective date to production cycles, assuring minimal problems with retrofitting or disposing of existing inventories.

NFPA Standards: Economics, Politics, and Process

While independent labs are both bolstered and constrained by the market for certification, the forces affecting membership organizations are clearly different. But the underlying reality, as observed by Anthony Downs, is essentially the same: "No bureau can survive unless it is continually able to demonstrate that its services are worthwhile to some group with influence over sufficient resources to keep it alive."[18] This support need not come directly from the most obvious source, the membership. Membership dues account for 41 percent of ANSI's revenues; the sale of publications accounts for 54 percent.[19] Other membership organizations are even more dependent on those purchasing their standards than on those writing them. Membership dues account for less than 8 percent of NFPA's revenues; publication sales account for almost 60 percent.[20] Sufficient support from those who rely on standards can empower private standards-setters vis-à-vis their membership.

Beyond these market-based forces, other sources of support "such as the state subsidizing the organization or legally enforcing its policies" can supplement and transform constraints imposed by the membership.[21] As a result, the demand for NFPA standards, and hence the nature of NFPA politics, is extremely variable. The National Electric Code, given the force of law in virtually every state in the country, generates intense interest from a wide range of groups. So does the Life Safety Code. In those instances, NFPA standards-setting is apparently characterized by lively interest-group politics. The health care industry battles with the building trades; the makers of plastic pipe oppose those who sell metal. Both standards were the source of scandals earlier this decade when specific commercial interests attempted to "pack" the annual convention to change the standard through an unusual floor vote.[22] NFPA has since vested greater authority in its Standards Council, making it impossible to write code text on the convention floor.

This is not to say that NFPA standards are merely a reflection of the most powerful interests on the relevant technical committees. First, these committees have a "balanced" membership designed to prevent any single group from dominating. Some of these interests, as discussed earlier in this chapter, are advocates of safety regulation. Second, installation and use standards permit a modicum of leeway unavailable to testing labs. Use standards are broader in scope than product standards, so that a demand for the standard will still exist even if it prohibits certain products or practices. Although NFPA desires to sell as many standards as possible, and this certainly affects which standards get written and how often they are updated, it is not beholden to particular interests in the same way as product certifiers. Accordingly, the National Fuel Gas Code prohibits propane cabinet heaters (and could do likewise with gas space heaters) without affecting the demand for the standard.

Unfortunately, the demand for other NFPA standards, including 61B and 408, is considerably weaker than that for the National Electric Code. The NFPA liaison to the grain elevator committee could not name a single organization or firm that actually uses NFPA 61B. The only apparent interest in NFPA 408 is from foreign countries. The stakes are much lower for standards with such little demand. These standards are more likely to fall behind the times as weak demand is reflected among the committee members. NFPA is also unlikely to pour organizational resources into standards that generate little income. The resulting politics are quite varied. But without a strong demand for the standard—created through, say, use by some government agency—NFPA committees lose an important source of leverage in determining how strict to make standards.

The politics of NFPA regulation also differ from what Wilson has described on the public side in one glaring respect: antibusiness sentiment does not drive private regulation. As a consequence, private regulation is largely unaffected by the injury statistics and major catastrophes that entrepreneurial politicians use to mobilize public support for regulation.[23] NFPA investigated the Air Canada incident, but there were no apparent repercussions for any of the aviation safety committees. The series of grain elevator explosions in 1977 probably prompted the NFPA Agricultural Dusts committee to meet—revision of the standard was already overdue—but the explosions did not cause significant changes in the standard. The limited role of public sentiment in private regulation seems to account for the less hurried and often more thoughtful approach to standards-writing in the private sector. The kind of pressure that motivated the FAA staff to want, above all else, to complete the rulemaking proceeding for aviation fire safety does not exist on the private side. The reduction in hastiness might come at the expense of timeliness, however. Lacking external pressure to "do some-thing," the private sector sometimes does nothing at all. NFPA 408 was so neglected that by the late 1970s it was considered practically useless.

Lacking what Wilson calls the most potent method for overcoming opposition to regulation—the public sentiment that follows any catas-trophe—the NFPA committees apparently do whatever can be accom-plished through political compromise. This suggests a grim reality, with standards taking whatever shape business interests desire. Hence the conventional wisdom that private standards-setting organizations are "captured." The grain elevator case supports this hypothesis. The Na-tional Grain and Feed Association opposes any regulation of grain elevator housekeeping, and NFPA 61B is obliging. But this hypothesis has limited explanatory power. The political "compromise" reached in aviation safety, and possibly in many other NFPA standards, is surpris-ingly strict. More NFPA standards should be examined before general conclusions are drawn about the politics of NFPA standards-setting in specific, and of membership organizations in general.

Risk and Culture: The Peculiar Fear of Flying

The politics of aviation safety are unusual, possibly unique. The polit-ical forces favoring increased public regulation are formidable, partic-ularly during a proclaimed era of deregulation. Many congressmen favor increased safety regulation, practically without regard to cost. (They travel frequently by air, and so do their most influential constit-uents.) The NTSB, a zealous advocate of increased regulation, provides Congress with recommendations that carry the weight of "expert advice." The powerful Air Line Pilots Association also joins several unions representing flight attendants in urging Congress to adopt reg-ulations proposed by the NTSB. Virtually nobody but the Airline Trans-portation Association argues against increased expenditures for avia-tion safety, and its voice is muted by the fact that many airlines generally favor government regulation. That is, they often prefer to have the government specify necessary safety precautions than to decide themselves. There is also widespread popular support for airline safety. It is one of those rare issues that motivates hundreds of citizens to write cards and letters directly to an administrative agency in support of new regulations. More common are the CPSC proceedings, which attract little public interest.

Aviation safety is, quite simply, a political sacred cow. This explains much of what happened with the respective NFPA and FAA standards. The unusual alliance of political interests favoring aviation safety regulation accounts for the FAA proposal and its quick adoption. Mobilized by the Air Canada fire, these forces motivated Congress to establish strict oversight procedures in 1984 to ensure the quick enactment of various regulations, including the fire extinguisher and smoke detector rule. The special status of aviation safety apparently dulled the OMB's normally critical senses about new regulations. There were no challenges to the cost-benefit analysis, no delays to seek additional justifications or modifications from the agency. Similarly, without serious objection, NFPA enacted regulatory provisions that committee members agree will cost more than what can be justified rationally. But apparently the fear of flying is pervasive. The politics of aviation safety produces regulatory outcomes unlike those commonly associated with social regulation.

Legal Constraints on Standards-Setting

Political and economic factors only partly explain regulatory behavior. The law is a powerful external influence, placing very different constraints on the two sectors. Only private standards-setters are subject to the antitrust laws—unless they can cloak their activity under the guise of a "public purpose." And lacking the sovereign immunity defense, private organizations are far more vulnerable to liability suits than their public counterparts. But public agencies are subject to more frequent and intrusive judicial review of their regulatory decisions. These legal influences, explored below, help explain the observed differences in regulatory philosophy.

Antitrust Law

Critics of private standards charge that the activity is prone to anticompetitiveness and that, owing to lax antitrust enforcement, the law does not sufficiently discourage such activity.[24] Proponents counter that the combination of liability law and antitrust law keeps private standards within an acceptable range of results. The argument goes as follows: private standards must be reasonable because liability attaches if a product is not reasonably safe, while the antitrust law assures that standards will not be arbitrary or anticompetitive. The case studies suggest that antitrust concerns are voiced by committee members more openly than those about liability, but their perceptions of antitrust law are often uninformed.

The accusation that anticompetitive purposes lurk behind private standards is understandable given the unsavory history of product standards. Standardization schemes involving everything from ice cream to carpets were struck down by the courts in the 1940s as thinly veiled efforts at price fixing.[25] AGA Labs was implicated in one of the most famous legal decisions in the field, *Radiant Burners v. Peoples Gas,* for allegedly withholding product certification for anticompetitive reasons.[26] Economic considerations certainly influenced the AGA/ANSI committee's decision about requiring the ODS device when there was only one supplier. Ironically, while pleading antitrust concerns, most committee members were actually worried about putting U.S. companies at a competitive disadvantage. But popular perceptions to the contrary, there are several reasons why safety standards are unlikely to be infused with anticompetitive purposes. First, price fixing schemes tend to involve the shape or size of a product, not its safety features. The former are necessary to standardize prices, the latter are not.[27]

More important, anticompetitive motives are most likely to be a problem in interpreting or applying safety standards, not in writing them. Anticompetitive implications are the clearest in applied situations, where outside scrutiny is minimal compared to standards-writing. The most celebrated case in the field, *American Society of Mechanical Engineers v. Hydrolevel Corp.,* involved a conspiracy between two volunteers on a small subcommittee that helps issue thousands of annual interpretations to the Boiler and Pressure Vessel Code.[28] In 1988, the Supreme Court declined to apply the "governmental action" immunity and upheld a verdict against a producer of steel conduit that had "packed" an NFPA meeting in order to keep polyvinyl chloride from becoming an accepted substitute under the National Electric Code.

There is somewhat less here than meets the eye. There has never been a successful antitrust suit alleging that a *safety* standard itself, as opposed to an interpretation, violated antitrust laws. The recent Supreme Court cases involved unusual circumstances and are unlikely to have widespread effect on private standards-setting, although they suggest a trend that might be counterproductive. *American Society of Mechanical Engineers v. Hydrolevel Corp.* involved an *interpretation* of the Boiler and Pressure Vessel Code, something that focuses directly on a single product, not on the formation of general standards. *Allied Tube and Conduit Corp. v. Indian Head* involved a decision on the floor of an NFPA meeting, not in a committee or subcommittee, where almost all policy decisions are actually made. Morever, as a result of changes prompted in part by these cases, standards-setters are providing fewer "interpretations" and the decisive "floor vote" is a thing of the past at NFPA.[29]

This leaves vast regions of standards-setting largely unaffected by antitrust considerations. In fact, the law tolerates a great deal of private activity, some of it questionable by almost any measure. By applying the so-called rule of reason to cases involving standards-setting proper, courts have sanctioned several private standards acknowledged to stifle technological innovation. Absent a showing of bad faith, there is almost always an "objective" reason for a standard that can pass judicial muster.

Private responses to antitrust law often seem out of proportion to the actual requirements of the law. Antitrust law is a popular excuse for almost every negative decision in the private sector. Since standards exclude things by definition, there is always an intuitively appealing argument that proposed requirements might illegally exclude something from the market. The law is not actually this restrictive. Even standards of obviously questionable scientific merit have been treated with great deference by courts and agencies.[30] "We give the benefit of the doubt to the standards setter," according to a Federal Trade Commission official.[31] The makers of low-tolerance metal chimneys or high-clearance woodstoves would have a valid antitrust claim only if they could prove the standards to be "manifestly anti-competitive and unreasonable."[32]

Antitrust law is nevertheless influential in standards-setting, according to participants. Fear of the antitrust law, well founded or not, apparently helps explain the reluctance of private organizations to ban specific product types or push technology. A representative of the Gas Appliance Manufacturers Association argues that the Z21.11.2 committee could not require the ODS device, which was manufactured solely by a European manufacturer, without raising "serious antitrust problems." UL, beset by a controversy about the temperature tolerance of metal chimneys, argues that the antitrust law is one of the reasons it cannot upgrade the standard.[33] Similarly, after the NFPA general membership agreed in an unusual floor vote to ban woodstoves requiring more than thirty-six-inch clearances, the Standards Council overturned the action, citing antitrust concerns.[34] These concerns are both wide-spread and overstated.

Liability Law

Unlike antitrust law, liability law is seldom cited as an official reason for doing anything in the private sector. Yet the case studies suggest that liability is a more significant factor than antitrust law in explaining regulatory behavior. Liability concerns help explain why so many pro-visions in NFPA 61B are vague and why, in both 61B and 408, NFPA pushes the distinction between "requirements" and "appendices." More generally, liability law seems to explain the reluctance of the private sector to (1) recognize or address issues of consumer misuse, (2) embrace certain new technologies, and (3) include work rules or oper-ational controls in safety standards.

Turning first to misuse: incorporating misuse considerations into standards can nullify the one effective defense to product liability suits that product certifiers and manufacturers still retain in some states—the misuse defense.[35] This defense works only if the plaintiff's use of the product was unforeseeable to the manufacturer. Accordingly, the more misuse is acknowledged in standards, the more manufacturers and product certifiers might be held responsible for it (no matter how im-possible the task). In other words, because of liability law it is not in UL's interest to think too much about potential consumer misuse.

There is a similar reluctance to adopt certain new technologies. The failure of a new safety device might leave a manufacturer or certifier in a worse legal position than if it had not addressed the problem to begin with. The argument, advanced to explain the slow diffusion of antilock braking technology, appears to explain the reluctance to require the ODS for gas space heaters. Committee members admit privately that data on failure rates of the device in Europe were considered legal dynamite.[36] Even if it significantly reduced the number of carbon mon-oxide deaths, as expected, manufacturers worried that the occasional injury it failed to prevent—as a result of equipment failure or poor maintenance—would be seen as the fault of the manufacturer, not the consumer.

Standards-setters also worry that "upgrading" a standard leaves ex-isting products more vulnerable to product liability suits. Improvements can be cited in some jurisdictions as evidence that the old standard was inadequate. When, as in the case of UL's metal chimney standard, hundreds of thousands of products manufactured under the existing standard are still in use (and will be for many years to come), there is considerable reluctance to "upgrade" the standard. This reason, admitted privately by UL officials, makes much more sense than the stated concern about excluding low-tolerance chimneys from the market.

Finally, liability concerns help explain why the operational controls were placed in the appendices of NFPA 408 and 61B. Technical and engineering standards are much easier to control. Third-party certification assures compliance with many product standards. Compliance with other provisions in NFPA 408 and 61B involves fairly discrete acts—carrying a certain type and number of fire extinguishers, attaching devices to conveyor belts in grain elevators, using specified building materials. Operational controls, on the other hand, require unfailing implementation. They are dependent on the goodwill and reliability of employees. They are also where corners are likely to be cut in the face of various economic pressures. Either way, liability fears apparently keep the private sector from mandating operational controls.

The Burden of Justification

The most important legal influence on public regulation appears to be the specter of judicial review. There is no analogy in the private sector. Except for violations of antitrust law, there is no possible basis for challenging the substance of private standards in court (and the antitrust law, as already explained, gives substantial deference to private safety standards in the absence of proven bad motives). With the CPSC, standards are not just reviewable by court, the statute allowing such review is intended to encourage closer judicial scrutiny than under the traditional, more deferential approach.[37] The agency has not fared well in the courts. A standard for swimming pool slides was rejected because the CPSC "provided little evidence that warning signs would benefit consumers."[38] The court rejected arguments based on "common sense" and faulted the agency for not having tested the effectiveness of the required signs. That same year, another court, rejecting portions of a safety standard for matchbook covers, practically demanded that the agency justify all of its decisions with cost-benefit analyses.[39]

This sort of judicial review creates a burden of justification on public agencies that does not hinder their private counterparts. "We cannot go to court on engineering judgment," notes a CPSC staff member with dismay. This suggests a major difference between public and private standards-writing. Public agencies cannot "get away with" what forms the basis for most private standards: engineering judgment, common sense, and educated guesses. The burden of justification probably helps explain why the government agencies shied away from technical issues in the case studies, seizing issues for which technical proof is least significant, such as warning labels and effective dates.

The final three chapters assess the policy implications of these observations and explanations. Chapter 10 aggregates the institutional considerations, setting forth the comparative institutional advantages of each system. Chapter 11 examines the most common policy prescription for improving standards-setting: changing administrative procedures. Chapter 12 considers interactive strategies and alternative policy instruments that are also worthy of consideration but are often overlooked in discussions of standards policy.

TEN

Comparative Institutional Advantages

Conclusions about specific safety standards are like snapshots—in order to be understood, they must be placed in context. The analysis thus far has been particularized and static, concentrating on the dynamics and outcomes of specific cases. This approach is suggestive but fragmentary. It points out specific differences between public and private approaches but says little about them as *systems*. This mirrors one of the main shortcomings with most discussions of "standards policy"— they amount to little more than empty calls for case-by-case decision-making. The problem is that policymakers have little understanding of the *institutional* differences between the public and private sectors. The goal of this chapter is to transform the observations of this study into some general conclusions about the comparative institutional advantages of public and private standards-setting. This discussion will be followed (in the final two chapters) by an analysis of specific proposals for exploiting and improving these institutional features.

There are no widely accepted criteria for comparing regulatory regimes. In order to provide a rounded view of the comparative advantages of public and private standards-setting, three approaches are taken below. The first examines the costs associated with decision-making, an approach favored by those who believe that more substantive measures are either impossible or simply not worthwhile. The second examines information inputs, an approach favored by those partial to rational decisionmaking models. The third is an amalgam of the remaining factors stressed by Lester Lave and others.[1] It adopts an evolutionary perspective, comparing how the systems change and adapt over time.

Decisional Costs

One way to compare standards-setting systems is by the cost of the enterprise, what economists call the "transaction costs." Standards-setting takes time and money, and some systems are likely to run more smoothly and inexpensively than others. Of course, transaction costs say nothing about substance. Perhaps more expensive standards are better in other respects. Given the troubling uncertainties about the costs and benefits of safety regulation, however, it is often impossible to evaluate standards substantively. If having a standard, any standard, is preferable to not having one, then the system that produces standards most quickly and inexpensively should generally be favored. But the difference between public and private decisional costs, as explained below, is more complicated than is often imagined.

Government rulemaking is often criticized for being time-consuming and expensive. Government agencies can be notoriously slow. It took the CPSC two years to decide whether to grant the Banner petition and another three years to develop a relatively simple woodstove labeling rule. The gas space heater proceeding was no quicker. OSHA's grain elevator standard was almost ten years in the making. Only the FAA stands in notable exception, having adopted the aviation fire safety standard in less than a year—a dubious distinction, considering its content.

But the case studies also demonstrate that government has no monopoly on slowness. NFPA proceedings can drag on for years. "Decisionmaking by town meeting" is how one committee member describes the process. It took NFPA much longer than the FAA to revise its standard for aircraft fire extinguishers. The same problem apparently plagues ASTM, ASME, and similar organizations. And there is reason to think that they will become slower in the future. As measured by the number of appeals to the NFPA Standards Council and the ANSI Board of Standards Review, contentiousness is on the rise. Moreover, standards-setting is expensive, and groups such as NFPA do not always see a sufficient return on the cost (in staff time alone) of meeting frequently to revise them. Again, there is an important distinction between standards developed in conjunction with product certification and most other private standards. Testing labs have a business interest in assuring that product standards are readily available when new products are submitted for approval. Standards developed for certification purposes are written in very short order, often in a matter of weeks or months. The resulting "desk standards" at UL have been criticized as violative of due process, but they are to be credited with remarkable timeliness. When private standards-setters lack this economic incentive, or when the cost of developing standards gets too high relative to the income generated by product testing, their efforts are likely to be as slow as those of government.[2]

It is impossible to compare the total administrative cost of the two systems, because so many of the costs on the private side are decentralized. Practically everyone on the NFPA and AGA/ANSI committees is sponsored by his or her employer or trade association. Undoubtedly, the total of these costs is still lower on the private side because the total number of person-days involved in any single standard is so much less.[3] UL keeps close track of the costs and revenues associated with its standards, but the organization is unwilling to reveal these figures. However, private standards written for certification purposes are apparently cheaper than government standards, at least from the point of view of the standards-setting organization.[4] In short, the private sector appears to have the advantage in terms of money and, to a lesser degree, time—particularly in connection with product testing.

The verdict on adversariness is less clear. Although private standards-setting is often considered less adversarial than government regulation, the case studies suggest that adversariness may be more issue-dependent than sector-dependent. In the woodstove and aviation safety cases, there was no more adversariness on the government side than there was on the private. In the grain elevator and space heater cases, the antagonism that marked the government proceedings was also present in the private sector—it was just less open and publicized. There were strong disagreements within AGA about the space heater. Even stronger disagreements lurk behind NFPA 61B; the National Grain and Feed Association opposes practically everything about it. The observed tranquility in the grain elevator proceedings came at the expense of not addressing the most important safety issue: housekeeping. The private sector has one important advantage, however. The scope of private standards is so broad that there is no stigma attached to particular standards-setting activities. When the CPSC recently took an interest in metal chimneys, the industry felt it had been unfairly singled out. Nobody has ever felt that way about a UL standard. This is not to say that the private sector does not "miss" some issues. It does. Certain types of issues seem to fall through the cracks in private standards-setting, some warranting government attention. This is one of the ways (discussed in chapter 12) in which government standards-setting could profitably complement its private counterpart.

Institutional Knowledge

Harold Wilensky coined the term "organizational intelligence" to describe the institutional ability to process and utilize information.[5] The concept seems particularly relevant to standards-setting, since the activity is so information-intensive. Three kinds of information contribute to "organizational intelligence" in setting safety standards: technical know-how, information on real-world experience, and applied research and development. The comparative strengths and weaknesses of the two standards-setting systems are striking. Private institutions are most intelligent in the first respect, public institutions in the second and third.

Technical Know-How

The most basic information utilized in standards-setting is know-how; that is, elementary knowledge about how a product or process works. The private sector is not only, as attorney David Swankin points out, "where the bodies are" (tens of thousands of people participate in private standards-setting); it is also where practical and technical knowledge often originates. Private standards-setters have a marked advantage in this regard over their public counterparts. They usually have a working knowledge of technical terms and basic engineering considerations, and they understand the practical implications of commercial use. One of the most active participants in revising NFPA 408 supervised Factory Mutual's study of hand-held fire extinguishers (conducted under contract for the FAA). Similarly, engineers for producers of space heaters and component parts participated on the Z21.11.2 subcommittee.

The personnel of public agencies, on the other hand, seldom have technical backgrounds or previous experience with the products or processes they regulate. Few are engineers. Many are lawyers or former compliance officers. In 1985, three of the CPSC commissioners were lawyers; none were engineers. A similar imbalance exists on the staff.

Neither regulators nor rulemaking staff members accumulate much technical experience over time, because public agencies do not specialize to the same extent as private standards-setters. Even at the FAA, which has a narrow mandate compared to most regulatory agencies, a rule-making staff member might work on fire extinguishers one day, fire-blocking seat cushions the next, and tactile aisle markers thereafter. A staff member at the CPSC might work on woodstoves, gas furnaces, or a host of other "fire and thermal burn" hazards.

The result in all four public cases was ignorance and confusion over basic facts. Limited know-how led to longer and often more adversarial public proceedings. Woodstoves, described by a former CPSC commissioner as a "simple" issue, and airplane smoke detectors, described by Congressman Mineta as "straightforward," both involved issues that exceeded the technical capabilities of the respective regulatory agencies. The CPSC spent two years trying to decide whether to grant the Banner petition.

In the process of acquiring knowledge, government agencies often lose credibility and are put on the defensive. It took the CPSC years to differentiate in its injury statistics between the various types of space heaters; some say that many CPSC investigators still don't understand the difference between vented and unvented equipment.[6] The CPSC staff also did not understand the special problems posed by fireplace inserts until very late in the proceedings on wood and coal-burning stoves. The commissioners had an even worse understanding of the technical issues. Analysts at the FAA lacked a basic understanding of the different types of Halon extinguishers and the special training needed for their use. OSHA's proposal for smaller grates on grain-loading pits was apparently born of ignorance about the operating effect of grate size on grain throughput and about the availability of other options for removing hazardous debris. Lacking basic knowledge, public standards-setters also tend to gloss over difficult technical questions, concentrating instead on more accessible, but less important, issues. The FAA plowed ahead in ignorance on smoke detectors. "They may be a good idea," noted an engineer at Factory Mutual, "but the feds are jumping in without the technical background to do the right thing. They were too slow to recognize the issue, and now they are moving too fast." They knew there were serious technical questions about smoke detectors and fire extinguishers, but they chose to ignore them. In the woodstove and gas space heater proceedings, the CPSC left the significant decisions to industry, concentrating instead on issues that could not be resolved through technical knowledge—such as the wording of warning labels and the effective date of regulations—even though technical questions, particularly about creosote, seemed to have greater safety implications.

In short, how standards-setters approach the task appears to be partly a function of their technical knowledge and capabilities. Lacking specific expertise, government agencies try to avoid technical issues, concentrating on issues where the agency is at less of a disadvantage. When technical issues are unavoidable, however, limited technical knowledge tends to reduce the agency's credibility and to result in longer, more contentious proceedings.

Information about Real-World Experience

Obtaining feedback on real-world incidents is the second form of institutional knowledge essential to setting safety standards. Without information about the type and frequency of accidents, it is almost impossible to spot trends or even identify some hazard scenarios. As a UL vice president puts it, "The proof of the pudding is in the field evidence." The case studies suggest, however, that such evidence is rarely generated by the private sector. Government agencies, although far from ideal, have much better information systems than their private counterparts.

Private information sources are largely anecdotal and play only a negligible role in shaping safety standards. UL, for example, has institutionalized contacts with building inspectors in order to learn about problems "in the field." But a UL engineer acknowledges that the information is of limited use. UL also has a clipping service that collects newspaper stories on product-related injuries. The information is always sketchy and often inaccurate. How the injury actually came about is unlikely to be described in any detail; brand names are rarely mentioned, let alone model numbers; and a vented heater with clogged vents might be described as unvented. The AGA also has a national reporting system—dubbed the Gas Appliance Information Network (GAIN)—which relies on voluntary reporting from gas utilities. The system is much less impressive than its name. An earlier version was nicknamed N-FLOP by staff members at AGA.[7] GAIN is also a flop. Reporting is scattered and, according to an AGA staff member, only one report was forwarded to a standards-writing committee in 1985.

NFPA makes a greater effort to collect injury information, but with only slightly more success. It, too, has a clipping service as a supplement to reports received from local fire departments. This was the only available data base on grain elevator fires when the NAS began its study. Unfortunately, the information was of questionable reliability. NFPA also sponsors comprehensive investigations of major fire incidents, such as the MGM Grand Hotel fire and the Air Canada incident. These investigations can improve standards-setting by providing better information on specific hazard scenarios, particularly if they are not duplicative of government efforts (as they were with the Air Canada fire). Unfortunately, the investigative function of NFPA is generally limited and plays little role in standards-setting. The 408 committee drafted its requirements before the Air Canada fire, and the NFPA investigation did not result in any changes. Committee minutes do not indicate whether the 61B committee ever evaluated NFPA's survey of grain elevator explosions. Only anecdotal information was discussed during committee deliberations at the July 1985 meetings.

There are two reasons why the private sector collects so little useful injury information: information has the quality of a public good, and it often carries worrisome liability implications. Public goods have value to those beyond the immediate purchaser. National defense is the classic example of a good that benefits all, whether or not they pay for it. A similar phenomenon affects the collection of injury information. Many private organizations would benefit from reliable national information on consumer product injuries, but the cost of any given organization collecting such information is prohibitively high. Since private standards-setting organizations are decentralized, there is also no easy mechanism for spreading the cost to all those who would benefit from a national information system.

Injury information also carries threatening legal implications. Lawsuits are rarely discussed openly in standards-setting committees, although Eads and Reuter report that such discussion might occur off the record.[8] Most firms keep records of consumer complaints involving allegations of injury, but it is unlikely they would share such information, given the adverse effect it could have in court. Even trade associations— according to staff members at the CPSC, the Outdoor Power Equipment Institute, and the Gas Appliance Manufacturers Association—generally do not receive this kind of information from their own members. NFPA's fire investigators are also inhibited by liability concerns, sometimes stopping short of certain conclusions or recommendations because the organization does not want to become embroiled in the litigation that inevitably follows the kinds of disasters they investigate.

Public information systems, though obviously flawed, are vastly better than private ones. The public sector does much more than clip newspapers. The CPSC has several information systems to provide feedback on consumer product safety. The agency collects injury data daily from hospital emergency rooms around the country and, through its field offices, conducts hundreds of in-depth investigations each year on selected hazards.[9] The hospital data provide the basis for national injury estimates; the accident investigation reports provide details of specific hazard scenarios. Similarly, the FAA maintains an extensive computerized file of Service Difficulty Reports, and the NTSB investigates all serious airplane accidents. In both the grain elevator and aviation fire safety cases, the government paid particular attention to accident investigations. OSHA deferred drafting its grain elevator standard so that the NAS could collect explosion data and conduct in-depth studies. Many of the recommendations from the NAS study were incorporated into the OSHA proposal.

Applied Research and Development

Applied research is the third type of knowledge essential to a standards-setting system. It is the only method short of actual experience for determining whether new technologies are actually feasible and reasonably effective. Such questions were prominent in all four case studies. The oxygen depletion sensor had a track record in Europe, and the question was whether the device would be as reliable with American fuels.[10] Similarly, questions were raised about the effectiveness of using household smoke detectors in airplanes. In the grain elevator case, there was significant controversy over whether pneumatic dust control could achieve airbone dust levels below the lower explosive limit. And with woodstoves there were a surprising number of technical questions, including the extent to which catalytic combustors could minimize creosote production.

Some standards-setters in both sectors have the in-house capability to conduct such research. The FAA Technical Center is well respected by industry. So is the National Bureau of Standards, which conducts applied research under statutory agreements with several agencies, including the CPSC. On the private side, UL and AGA conduct applied research both for in-house purposes and under contract. NFPA also supports a limited fire safety research effort.

The case studies suggest, however, that government does a better job of generating the kind of applied research that can inform standards-setting. The NBS conducted numerous helpful studies on wood-burning appliances. Its study on wall pass-through systems, a major source of fires related to woodstoves, filled a gaping hole in the private standard. Experiments conducted at the NBS also convinced the CPSC of the reliability of the oxygen depletion sensor—something that AGA Labs was reluctant to admit. The FAA funds extensive research into aviation safety, including the investigation of hand-held fire extinguishers, prompting the president of a major airline to declare at a recent Flight Safety Foundation conference that "airlines and manufacturers rely on the government to do development and testing."[11] There were only scattered instances of private research efforts connected with the case studies. Two airlines and a major airframe manufacturer conducted tests on Halon fire extinguishers. The other major research effort, considered a public relations ploy by some, was undertaken by the National Grain and Feed Association. In the woodstove case, however, the lack of private research was notable. Catalytic combustors, a possible method of reducing creosote formation, were not (and have not) been considered by UL because, as a UL engineer said, "Nobody [in the industry] wanted to spend the money."

Research is expensive and private organizations generally do not do it unless someone else pays. Some private groups simply have no resources. "ASTM is just a building with rooms and secretaries," quips a former CPSC commissioner. It relies on its members to bring to the standards-setting process any information about relevant research. NFPA does much the same. Committees do not have budgets; nor does NFPA at large conduct applied research to support its standards-setting activities.

Product certifiers are also reluctant to undertake research aimed at improving standards. This research can have the quality of a public good. If UL improves a standard through applied research, other testing labs might be able to capitalize on the expenditure. Since UL must ultimately pay for such research efforts through its certification fees, the organization is not likely to conduct research in those areas, like woodstoves, where it shares the certification market with other labs. According to a UL spokesman, however, woodstoves are unusual in this respect. "We are often a monopoly for all practical purposes."

The funding of public research depends on the politics of the budgetary process, but there is certainly the potential (realized in several of the cases) to fund projects not likely to be done privately. Many research budgets have been cut on the public side, particularly at the CPSC, but there are also indications that funding might actually increase for the FAA. The need for more public research and information collection is discussed in the final chapter.

The Evolutionary Perspective

More important than any single institutional feature is how an organization changes over time. Aaron Wildavsky has stressed the importance of "resilient" approaches to safety regulation.[12] Others have emphasized the advantages of "flexibility" and "responsiveness."[13] These concepts place standards-setting in an evolutionary context. What matters is not so much how individual cases are resolved as how results change over time. A regime that generates standards that are considered "too lenient" (at the time of adoption) might actually be more desirable than one that generates standards closer to the social optimum (at the time of adoption) *depending on when the respective standards are adopted and how they are adjusted over time.*

The case studies suggest that there are significant evolutionary differences between public and private standards-setters, differences that indicate several previously unrecognized advantages of the private sector. In short, private standards-setting is prospective and ongoing, while public efforts are usually corrective and singular. Private standards-setters tend to intervene relatively early in the life cycle of an issue, adjusting the standard subsequently over time. Public standards-setters, by contrast, are likely to get involved later, often after a major disaster, adopting a "one-shot" standard without the benefit of subsequent adjustments. The evolution of standards-setting systems can vary in two important ways: (1) in the timing of interventions and (2) in the nature of any subsequent adjustments.

The Timing of Regulatory Interventions

Turning first to intervention, the case studies suggest a major difference between the public and private sectors. The private sector appears to intervene relatively early in the life cycle of an issue, often in anticipation of problems rather than in direct response to them. Private standards often flow directly from engineering decisions. They are usually written in anticipation rather than in response to accidents. NFPA 408 and 61B were in place long before the first serious in-flight fire or the well-publicized series of grain elevator explosions in 1977–78. UL and AGA initiate the development of standards as products are submitted for certification, which is almost always before they are marketed. The implications of this difference depend critically on how (and whether) these standards are adjusted over time.

In contrast, government interventions appear to occur relatively late in the life cycle of an issue and are usually reactive. Grain elevator safety was considered a problem by fire prevention engineers and insurance companies in the 1920s. OSHA did not get actively involved in the issue until after the disastrous Christmas of 1977. NFPA formally considered questions about aviation fire extinguishers more than ten years before the FAA first issued its advisory circular, and almost thirty years before it adopted a formal standard on the matter. Government standards also tend to respond to specific problems identified through real-world experience. For every serious airplane accident, there is a new FAA rule. This means that decisions are often made under pressure and with emotion, as in the months following the Air Canada fire. The pressure to "do something" becomes so overwhelming that valid concerns, such as whether household smoke detectors will work reliably on airplanes, too easily get brushed aside. Conversely, once "something" is done, there is little or no pressure to follow up on the action and reassess its wisdom in light of subsequent field experience.

Private standards-setters are also generally more comprehensive in defining "the problem," although the grain elevator case demonstrates that there are certain problems that only the government is likely to address. Private standards are more likely to be conceived as a total package, covering most aspects of the product or process from design and performance to labeling and production. In contrast, both of the CPSC standards addressed a single issue or single solution. So, too, with the FAA. Whether comprehensiveness is an advantage depends on the relationship between private and public standards. If the two were mutually exclusive, the private approach would probably be preferable. "It is generally better to regulate a range of problems satisfactorily than to do one in great detail," admitted a former CPSC commissioner who often favored government regulation.

Adapting Standards over Time

Over time, private standards-setting appears to be more flexible and adaptable than government regulation. Private standards are continually being revised. Many government standards are one-time interventions. Public standards rarely evolve the way private ones do. The "regulatory ratchet" characterizes some government standards, while the mechanisms for revising standards remain unused in others.[14]

In none of the public sector case studies was standards-setting seen as an evolutionary process. There was little expectation that a standard, once adopted, would be altered in the foreseeable future. To the contrary, attaining closure was an important goal in its own right—one that took OSHA almost nine years in grain elevator safety. The FAA brushed aside technical questions about smoke detectors in order to avoid going through the requirements of "notice and comment" rulemaking all over again. In the gas space heater proceeding, the prospect of "gearing up" for a new rulemaking proceeding seemed so onerous to one CPSC commissioner that when the commission decided to revoke the space heater rule—in light of good evidence that it was no longer needed—she objected strenuously on the grounds that "restoration of the protection previously provided by the mandatory standard would require initiation *anew* of the *entire* time-consuming, resource-intensive process" (original emphasis).[15]

Whether or not their perception of the rulemaking process is accurate, government agencies seem to operate on the principle that "it's now or never." As a result, public standards are often confined in scope, and they tend to stay fixed in their original form. The CPSC, for example, had reason to believe that gas space heaters might pose a chronic nitrogen dioxide hazard. But lacking an ongoing process for standards-writing, it saw the choice as either delaying the ODS rule (possibly for years) or not addressing this hazard at all. Revisions are always possible on the public side, but the process is ad hoc and seldom used. Several problems with the woodstove labeling rule have come to light since its adoption, but the idea of amending the rule has not been seriously considered. According to CPSC staff members, the effort required to enact the rule in the first place is the reason amendments are not seriously being contemplated. Instead, the agency has tried to amend the rule informally by working directly with the testing labs.[16] Some of the advantages of a formal adjustment process might be captured through such informal efforts, but on the whole it seems likely that the public sector suffers significantly from the lack of revisions.

The revision process is institutionalized on the private side. NFPA standards are supposed to be reviewed and, if necessary, revised every five years. For product testing labs, the process is continual. There is some merit in this attribute alone. The ongoing nature of private standards-setting may facilitate the resolution of conflicts by tilting the strategy of participating parties in the cooperative direction. Periodically revising standards is also the only way to keep up with changes in information, technology, and preferences. But whether and how standards-setters take advantage of this opportunity is of paramount importance. The evidence from the case studies is mixed. On the positive side, the "ratchet effect," described by Eugene Bardach and Robert Kagan in their study of government regulation, does not seem to characterize the private sector.[17] Through the adjustment process, private standards are made stricter in some respects and more lenient in others. On the negative side, such flexibility can foster nonchalance. Private standards-writers are often willing, sometimes even anxious, to postpone addressing certain complex or controversial problems until the next time the standard is supposed to be revised. In 1980 the NFPA Agricultural Dusts committee decided that action on several controversial proposals should be postponed "for further study." These proposals were summarily dismissed at a meeting five years later.[18] UL convinced members of the canvass on woodstoves to withdraw their opposition on the assurance, still unfulfilled, that the creosote problem would be handled soon. At AGA Labs, the surface temperature of space heaters has been a "continuing agenda item," without apparent effect, for over twenty years.

Comparative Summary

The difference between public and private standards-setting is not just a matter of degree, it is a matter of kind. Public efforts are not simply stricter or more lenient than their private counterparts. The systems are too different to be compared one-dimensionally (see table 8). There are important differences in how public and private standards-setters (1) resolve philosophical questions about the appropriate scope of safety regulation, (2) estimate costs and benefits, and (3) act over time and in the context of a larger regulatory program. These observations are troubling because they cast doubt on the reasons most commonly given in favor of one form of regulation over the other. Public regulation is not always stricter; private regulation is not always more reasonable. The performance of the two sectors is mixed, and there are different reasons to favor each.

The conventional wisdom about strictness and leniency is only par-

TABLE 8   GENERAL DIFFERENCES BETWEEN PUBLIC
AND PRIVATE STANDARDS-SETTING SYSTEMS

	Public Sector	Private Sector
Economic perspective	Often too strict Overestimates benefits, underestimates costs	Mixed results Rarely underestimates costs, sometimes overestimates benefits (and costs)
Regulatory philosophy	Paternalistic Technology-forcing Enforcement-oriented	"Buyer beware" Technology-based Protective of managerial discretion
Evolutionary perspective	Intervenes after a crisis One-shot interventions with few changes Selective	Intervenes early Adjusts often, usually in the "right" direction Technologically comprehensive

tially correct. Although public agencies appear to err systematically on the side of safety, their private counterparts do not always err in the other direction. Three of the four private cases studied are characterized by decisions that also err on the "safe side." At least one of these cases, the NFPA standard for aviation fire extinguishers, is unreasonably strict, providing reason to conclude that the private sector occasionally makes the same mistakes as the public sector. A rough estimate of overall economic efficiency suggests that, for the standards studies here, neither sector has a clear advantage. On the public side, two of the standards were unreasonably strict (the CPSC on woodstoves and the FAA on aviation fire safety), and two were within the "zone of reasonableness" (the CPSC on space heaters and OSHA on grain elevators). On the private side, two of the standards were also in the zone of reasonableness (UL and AGA), while the others were split: one too lenient (NFPA on grain elevators) and the other too strict (NFPA on aviation fire extinguishers).

But these conclusions capture only a portion of the interesting differences between the two sectors. Public and private standards-setters do not just select different outcomes. They have entirely different ways of looking at problems. Public agencies are more paternalistic in defining "the problem" for regulation. They are also more willing than private standards-setters to select early deadlines, require unproven technologies, and regulate in a manner that interferes with traditional notions of managerial discretion.

Finally, aside from the specific standards, the two sectors vary over time and in the relationship between single standards and the standards-setting system. Sometimes private standards-writers do not have adequate information; they do not even know that a "problem" exists. At other times, they do not agree that "the problem" should be addressed. When changes are made, they are most likely the result of either government information or anecdotal evidence. Private standards are rarely unreasonable, however, in the sense of requiring something that is not generally feasible both technically and economically.

Public standards-writing, on the other hand, is reactive and rarely adaptive. Standards-writing is usually prompted by accidents or injuries. Standards are viewed as one-time corrections and not, with the exception of the FAA, as something likely to be amended in the future. Government standards are generally narrower than private ones. Although prompted by specific problems, it is questionable whether the resulting standard will address them effectively. Information about potential costs and benefits is assiduously compiled, but seems to play only an indirect role in decisionmaking. Technical issues are generally avoided in favor of "softer" issues, such as how strong a warning should be or when a regulation should take effect. But government is willing to do things the private sector will not—protect people against their own mistakes, "push" technology—and in some cases it is successful.

The remaining two chapters examine proposals for improving public and private standards-setting systems. Chapter 11 examines popular proposals for altering procedural requirements, particularly in the private sector. Chapter 12 examines more promising alternatives, including interactive strategies, niches for public standards, and methods of improving private standards-setting.

PART FOUR

Policy Implications

ELEVEN

Reforming Standards-Setting:
The Procedural Perspective

Most policy prescriptions concerning standards-setting reflect a procedural view inspired by legal formalism. The evolution of more detailed and formal administrative procedures in the public sector reflects deep distrust of discretionary decisionmaking.[1] Administrative procedures are seen as a method of constraining this discretion. There are two related approaches: one emphasizes rules of participation, the other rules of analysis. *Rules of participation* circumscribe who can participate in a proceeding and in what manner they can do so. In the public sector, the Administrative Procedures Act (APA) sets forth the requirements for federal "notice and comment" rulemaking.[2] The private sector is widely thought to be less desirable than the public sector primarily because the balance of participating interests is perceived as more "skewed." A popular policy prescription is to establish a private sector version of the APA and do something to "improve" the balance of participating interests. The Administrative Conference of the United States recommends, for example, that private standards be utilized by government only when written by "a broadly based and balanced array of relevant interests."[3]

Rules of analysis, on the other hand, attempt to prescribe the criteria used by the ultimate decisionmaker. A series of controversial executive orders mandate that administrative agencies conduct some form of cost-benefit analysis.[4] Those concerned with the rules of analysis also tend to consider the private sector worse than the public sector because analytical procedures in the private sector are obscure and occasionally unorthodox. While few argue that analytic rules can assure desirable results, many agree that such rules represent an improvement over the informal approach of the private sector. The fashionable policy pre-scription: more cost-benefit analysis.[5]

The case studies suggest that the procedural perspective provides only limited insight into the differences between public and private standards-setting. There is little reason to think that these prescriptions will be effective or desirable. Of course it matters who participates and what analytical procedures they use, but the differences between the two sectors are not as big as often imagined. Moreover, efforts to alter the balance of "interests" or to force more rational analysis probably will not make much difference. The procedural perspective is worth considering in more detail, however, because it remains so dominant in policy discussions about improving standards-setting.

Rules of Participation

The most popular view of standards-setting is based on what Richard Stewart calls "the interest group model of administrative law."[6] The underlying notion is that standards-setting, and almost any other policy decision by an administrative agency, is a political process shaped largely by the "balance" of participating "interests." The process is often described in terms of "capture." The Administrative Procedures Act is supposed to provide some protection against capture by opening the process to all interested parties.

Although some have argued that activist judicial interpretations of the APA have resulted in "capture" by consumer and environmental groups,[7] most legal commentators believe that the act has helped insu-late agencies from "capture" by business. Stewart concludes that im-proving interest group representation is not a universal solution but is nevertheless an important "technique for dealing with specific problems of administrative justice."[8] Under this view, there is widespread suspi-cion that private standards-setting is less desirable than the public al-ternatives because it is dominated by "business interests." After all, the activity is, by its own terms, private, not public.

Others favor the procedural approach simply because of the im-mense difficulties in judging actual outcomes. Herbert Simon has argued that agencies should pursue "procedural rationality" when "problems are immensely complex, and where crucial information is absent."[9] These conditions characterize much of the terrain of safety regulation.

Under either view, the private sector is widely assumed to be worse than the public sector. Surprisingly, the conventional wisdom is incorrect. Most private standards-setters boast a set of procedural requirements that require a "balance" of participating interests. Many also emulate the requirements of the APA by providing notice of their proceedings and allowing the opportunity to comment. The case studies suggest that these "balance" provisions do not necessarily produce the intended results, but many private participants are nevertheless more safety-conscious than expected. The case studies also suggest, contrary to most legal commentary, that the private sector is not much different from the public sector in its "notice and comment" requirements. In a few surprising ways, the private sector is probably better.

Notice Requirements and "Openness"

It has been alleged that private standards-setting is biased in favor of industry because consumers and other related interests are not even aware that some private standards are being written. A lobbyist for the Association of Flight Attendants objects that he cannot follow developments in NFPA 408 as easily as he can monitor the FAA. The case studies suggest that NFPA is not to blame. In fact, rules concerning "notice" barely distinguish the public and private sectors, much less explain any differences in their approaches to standards-setting. Pursuant to the APA, government agencies publish notice of proposed actions in the *Federal Register*. Private groups do much the same. In an unusual agreement with the National Bureau of Standards, NFPA actually publishes notice of its rulemaking activities in the *Federal Register*. UL and AGA notify the public through trade journals and in-house bulletins as well as ANSI's *Standards Action*.

The case studies suggest that any differences in "notice" rules are unimportant. In the case of woodstoves, for example, UL received comments from more people on its canvass list than the CPSC heard from at its public hearing. In fact, a CPSC commissioner commented at the public hearing that the agency did not do a very good job of publicizing its actions.[10] By holding regional hearings in Texas and Florida, the CPSC heard from more members of the public in the space heater proceedings, but the number was still much less than those reached by the comprehensive comment system employed by AGA Labs.[11] In the two cases where more people participated in the public proceedings than in the private ones—grain elevators and aircraft fire safety—the difference in participation cannot be attributed to procedure. Both the public *and* the private proceedings were announced in the *Federal Register*. And in neither case, incidentally, did the additional participation seem to affect the public agency.[12]

The Importance of Being "Balanced"

Even if private standards-setting is as "open" as its public counterparts, what really matters under the interest group theory of administrative law is who *actually* participates, not who theoretically could. In this respect, most private organizations lend credence to the theory by placing a premium on the appearance of "balanced" decisionmaking. NFPA is the extreme case, conducting what one NFPA member calls "standards-setting by town meeting." The membership at large virtually makes the final decision on whether to adopt a standard. (The Standards Council actually has the final say, a power it has exercised in response to efforts to "pack" votes on the convention floor.) At the committee level, NFPA goes to great lengths to classify its members according to their "interest." The Standards Council reviews assignments to ensure that committees are "balanced" and that no single interest dominates the proceedings. As a practical matter, this usually means that no more than two representatives on a committee are ever from a single category of interests. But the Standards Council looks at specific issues as well as overall numbers. On the Fire Sprinkler Committee, for example, "balance" also means equal representation from metal and plastic interests, and the Standards Council has recently decided that "balance" on another committee requires both union and nonunion representation. The importance played by NFPA members on the makeup of committees is evident in the increasing number of formal appeals over committee membership decisions.

Whether any of this really affects the quality of standards-setting is unclear. Three questionable assumptions underlie the application of "interest group theory" to private standards-setting. First, standards-setting is assumed to be a legislative-type process, in which voting is the ultimate method of decisionmaking. That is not the case with UL standards. It probably is not an accurate description of most "consensus" decisionmaking. Second, the balance of participating interests on the private side is thought to be weighted heavily in favor of business rather than consumer interests. That is not true in many private standards-setting efforts. Various "business" interests advance the cause of safety.[13] Finally, the underlying assumption is that adding more "consumers" or consumer advocates would have a beneficial effect on the process. The case studies provide several reasons to discount this hypothesis.

Appearances Can Be Deceiving

"Balance" requirements notwithstanding, there might be, as is often alleged, a lack of meaningful diversity in the interests actually represented in the private sector. In fact, the case studies suggest that the "balance" of interests in private standards-setting looks much better on paper than it does in reality. First, the requirement that interests be "balanced" seldom applies at the primary level of decisionmaking, where the standard is actually written. "Balance" tends to be required at the reviewing stage, not the writing stage. The general Z21 committee is "balanced," for example, but technical subcommittees, such as Z21.11.2, which are not, do all of the work. Similarly, UL's canvass lists are "balanced," but the standards themselves are written in-house. The significance of balanced participation depends, then, on the scope and significance of review. The more deference given to technical committee decisions, the less significant any "balance" requirements. Since review in the private sector tends to be highly deferential, the practical significance of current "balance" requirements appears minimal at best. (They may still have symbolic value, of course.) The real decisions are made by technical committees or individual engineers who operate outside these requirements.[14]

Even when "balance" is required, the process is riddled with practical problems. The categories are too crude. For example, under the most elaborate classification system—NFPA's—insurance company representatives complain that brokers, who really represent the interests of their clients, not of the insurance industry, are classified as "insurance" representatives. It would take a classification scheme as complex as the Standard Industrial Classification system to begin to capture the important differences in business interests. Even then, unless participants were also classified by intraorganizational affiliation (for example, Engineering and Safety Department, General Counsel's Office, Marketing), it would be impossible to capture many of the significant differences in interests.

The problem is worse with consumer interests. The category "consumer" is so broad as to be practically meaningless. Everyone is a consumer. For a standard written by the Hydraulic Institute, both the Chemical Manufacturers Association and the American Water Works Association were considered "consumer" representatives.[15] This kind of flexibility led an NFPA member active on several aviation committees to conclude that "classification of members in NFPA is a joke." Moreover, consumers care about more than just safety. "Good coffee," points out the manager of the J.C. Penney Testing Lab, "is as important as the quality of the handle on the pot." Cost can also be as important as safety. Not everyone wants or can afford the "Rolls Royce of coffee pots," or any other appliance for that matter. Styling is also important to consumers, as suggested by the marketing adage about 1956—the year Ford sold safety and Chevrolet sold cars.[16]

Still, concerns about the "balance" of participating interests appear to be validated by the modest voice that organized consumer groups have relative to manufacturers in private standards-setting. UL and some ANSI-sponsored committees pay lip service to "consumer participation," but consumer groups play only a minimal role in the process.

The Opportunity to Comment

Whatever the significance of *who* participates in standards-setting, what may be most important is *how* that participation occurs. This raises the second part of "notice and comment" rulemaking. On the public side, participation is often in written form. Pursuant to the APA, agencies request written comments on rules proposed in the *Federal Register*. Some agencies choose to hold public hearings as well, but this is not required under the "informal rulemaking" procedures of the APA.[17] Responses to written comments are routinely published in the *Federal Register* before a rule becomes final. On the private side, contrary to popular conceptions, participants, whatever interests they represent, generally have better access than in the public sector. Most organizations also offer an opportunity to respond to proposals with written comments. NFPA utilizes a procedure almost identical to that of the APA. ANSI mandates similar procedures as part of the larger requirement that private standards reflect a "consensus" of affected interests. Many of the APA-like rules in the private sector were adopted in the wake of the FTC's investigation of standards and certification. There are examples in both sectors of seemingly legitimate concerns being ignored. This suggests that rules governing "comment" might not be very effective in either sector.

Surprisingly, the forms of participation are often more limited in the public sector than in the private, leading an attorney for the FTC to conclude that "government standards-writing is less open." "The only idea of process in the public sector," he complains, "is holding hearings." Such hearings were held in all of the public sector cases but aviation fire safety. (Written comments were solicited in all four cases.) Yet many participants in the CPSC proceedings complain that participation is stifled because observers cannot communicate with the commission during the many important briefing sessions conducted by the staff.

Direct dialogue between commenters and decisionmakers is more common on the private side. This has led some to conclude that private standards-setting holds the advantages sought in proposals for public "regulatory negotiation."[18] There were opportunities for informal dialogue in all of the private sector cases. UL engineers met with the Industry Advisory Council several times while converting UL 1482 to published form.[19] The minutes of the AGA/ANSI Z21.11.2 committee indicate that outsiders often attend meetings as guests. ANSI rules provide that "affected interests," a term subject to some dispute, can always attend committee meetings.[20] In short, those who want to participate appear to have better access to the standards-setting process. UL's canvass method is a bone of contention because it allows only industry participation during the formative stages of standards-setting, relegating other parties to commenting in writing on a proposal developed in their absence.[21]

Under the comment process specified by the APA, public agencies are expected to provide "reasoned responses" to all comments on the proposed rule. In theory, this should force the agency to face its critics. In reality the process is supervised by agency lawyers whose main concern is to ward off judicial review. Responses to comments are tailored to protect the agency, not to answer the commenter. The same appears to hold true on the private side, where the demands of the commenting process are greater. Most private standards-setters aspire to develop "consensus" standards, meaning that "unresolved negative comments" must be addressed in a convincing manner. But the response to comments in both sectors is prone to superficiality.

In the private sector, the process that unfolded in all four case studies was far from responsive. Like government agencies, UL delegates the task of responding to commenters to a special department that does not write the standards and whose main interest is in gaining approval, not changing the standard. In the case of woodstoves, the "response" to several comments was unresponsive; in a few cases, it was actually misleading.[22] NFPA has a similar problem. According to an NFPA official, commenters often complain that "committees claim to 'accept a comment in principle' but then go off in another direction." Another tactic, used in the grain elevator proceedings, is to hold over controversial comments for study and then dismiss them summarily several years later.[23]

Given their more technical orientation, however, private standards-setters might actually do a better job than their public counterparts in responding to comments. A detailed study of public and private standards for liquefied natural gas facilities concluded that "responses by the [NFPA] technical committee were far more specific than responses given by the [Department of Transportation]."[24] In neither case does the requirement to respond to comments appear to have a significant effect on the quality of decisionmaking.

Rules of Analysis

The procedural perspective has evolved into a broader effort to force "comprehensive rationality" in administrative decisionmaking.[25] This "analytic imperative," as Colin Diver describes it, is embodied in a combination of executive orders and statutes mandating that public agencies analyze the economic impact of proposed standards. There are no similar rules in the private sector. Cost-benefit analysis is almost universally avoided. Leland Johnson of the RAND Corporation has identified this as a major shortcoming of private standards-setting.[26] In short, there appear to be significant differences in the rules of analysis governing standards-setting in the public and private sectors.

Beginning with outward appearances, systematic economic analysis seems to pervade public standards-setting and elude private efforts. The CPSC prepared preliminary and final economic impact statements in both cases, quantifying costs and describing possible benefits. The FAA's full-blown economic analysis, comprising the bulk of the *Federal Register* notice announcing the proposed rule, quantified costs and benefits in a detailed fashion. OSHA contracted for two risk-benefit analyses of the grain elevator rule, with the second addressing criticisms of the first.

By contrast, private standards-setting appears much less structured and systematic. A member of the NFPA committee on chimneys and venting—a man with a doctorate in physics, widely acknowledged to be an expert on woodstoves—recalls his initial shock at the "casual and off-handed way in which many decisions are made." Decisions made at the NFPA committee meetings on grain elevators in 1985 were similarly informal, often based on anecdotes, if on any information at all. The very notion of estimating overall benefits or costs, let alone explicitly trading them off against one another, is opposed by many in the private sector. "I don't know of any time that we have consciously gotten into cost-benefit analysis," comments a UL vice president.[27] An NFPA executive committee has spent seven years considering the appropriateness of cost-benefit analysis.[28] Many members share the feeling expressed at the organization's 1985 annual meeting that "cost-benefit analysis is not relevant to the actions of NFPA."

Of course, decisions packaged as cost-beneficial do not necessarily embody the concept of comprehensive rationality. Agency subterfuge is one reason. Procedural requirements can spur defensive tactics instead of substantive changes. For example, many agencies faced with the analytical requirements of environmental impact statements successfully repackaged their decisions without changing the outcome.[29] The same phenomenon is likely when cost-benefit analysis is mandated by statute, regulation, or executive order. What Stephen Breyer is quick to observe about public standards-setting is equally true of private efforts: the process "as it might exist in the world of the rational policy planner" almost never happens in reality.[30]

In none of the public sector case studies did the economic analysis, so prominent in the official record, appear to shape the content of the standard. The people "downstairs" write the rules at the FAA; the people "upstairs" do the cost-benefit analysis. The tasks are done more or less at the same time, and no one interviewed on either floor thinks that the cost-benefit analysis affects the substance of the rule. (Of course, it might help justify what ends up being proposed, and it certainly delays the process to some extent.) Many OSHA officials are similarly skeptical of systematic attempts to quantify costs or benefits. They view such efforts largely as methods for justification, not decisionmaking. The risk-benefit analyses funded by OSHA were done after the grain elevator standard was written. In short, analyzing public and private standards-setting in terms of their rules of analysis is an invitation to frustration. On the public side, it is clear that the rules do not tell the whole story, while on the private side it is not even clear what the rules are. The ideal of comprehensive rationality provides little basis for evaluating or comparing standards-setting systems in a manner that illuminates the observations in chapters 7 and 8.

Summary

Standards-setting is often analyzed through the lens of administrative law. Decisionmaking processes are evaluated by reference to the rules of participation and the rules of analysis—rules intended to promote such lofty goals as "balance" and "comprehensive rationality." Most public policy initiatives concerning private standards-setting reflect this perspective. The underlying assumption seems to be that the more private standards-setting looks like public standards-setting, the better. Recommendations from both the FTC staff and the Administrative Conference of the United States come close to requiring a private version of the APA.

The case studies suggest that some common conceptions about the differences between public and private standards-setting are incorrect. Notice is not necessarily better in the public sector, nor is the form of participation. More significantly, the case studies suggest that the procedural perspective is inadequate for understanding the standards-setting process. The fundamental flaw with this perspective is summed up in the fact that the public and private systems, which vary in myriad respects detailed in chapters 7 and 8, look practically alike in the language of administrative procedure. Under the veneer of "due process" and "consensus," the many institutional arrangements for standards-setting—from the trade association that writes its own standards, to the product certifier that writes them for others to use, to NFPA's "town meeting" and the various approaches taken by government—all appear to be more or less equivalent.

In short, the procedural perspective seems to gloss over, rather than illuminate, the most important aspects of standards-setting. Many of the procedural devices attendant to standards-setting, particularly those adopted on the private side in response to the threat of FTC regulation, are apparently like "grafts on a scheme of government to which they are intrinsically foreign."[31] They may improve outward appearances, but they make little difference to the underlying dynamics of decision-making. The procedural perspective, although popular, is elusive because it does not speak to the important differences between public and private standards-setting. Some alternative avenues of analysis, with related policy prescriptions, are contained in chapter 12.

TWELVE

Interactive Strategies and Alternative Policy Instruments

Policy choices about public and private standards are often framed in mutually exclusive terms; the choice is either public standards or private ones. Given the predominant number of private standards, the most common public policy question is whether government should supersede (or defer to) private standards. Reflecting broader sentiments about government and business, the answer has varied from favoring preemption of private standards in the 1970s to deferring to the private sector in the 1980s. But policy choices are rarely as stark as political rhetoric. The two systems of standards-setting are not mutually exclusive. Public standards do not necessarily "drive out" private ones, as is often alleged. The two sometimes even work in concert. Public and private standards coexisted to different degrees in all four of the case studies. This was part of the research design, of course, and is not representative of the general relationship between the public and private sectors. But *interactive strategies* are a potentially valuable policy tool, given the comparative institutional advantages of public and private efforts. If the two sectors interact in a complementary fashion, rather than being redundant or self-defeating, they hold the potential for producing the best of both regulatory worlds.

The first part of this chapter chronicles the failure of existing "standards policy." The second part examines interactive strategies for government to take in a world heavily populated by private standards. Since determining the appropriate role for public and private standards depends on the full constellation of instruments and institutions that operate in a given policy space, the chapter concludes with a brief consideration of alternative policy instruments for influencing standards-setting.

The Failure of "Standards Policy"

A major facet of "standards policy" in many federal agencies involves how government participates in private standards-setting. Several agencies have been preoccupied with whether government employees should cast formal votes on private sector committees.[1] This issue is symbolic rather than consequential, diverting attention from policies that could have a much greater effect on private standards. It makes little difference whether government representatives who otherwise participate in private standards-setting cast a formal vote. Issues are rarely decided by vote, and the stringent opposition of almost any participant, voting or not, usually gives pause to the entire group. The issue has attracted so much attention at the CPSC because it is seen by many as indicative of the agency's overall regulatory mission. To those actively involved in writing public standards—a group generally skeptical of the private sector—voting represents an endorsement they fear will weaken the agency's regulatory resolve. To the small number assigned to participate in private standards-setting, voting would legitimate their uneasy mission.

Rather than worry about voting, it would make more sense simply to increase government participation in private standards-setting. OSHA did not participate in NFPA 61B. Similarly, in the case of liquefied natural gas facilities, the Materials Transportation Bureau (of the Department of Transportation) chose not to participate on the relevant NFPA committee.[2] Better communication between the public and private sectors could improve standards-setting in several ways. This is probably a much more effective way of influencing private organizations than, say, trying to increase consumer participation. Government participation is more reliable over time, and its representatives tend to be more knowledgeable than most consumer representatives. Most participants in the private sector interviewed for this study agree that consumer participation is often not very influential, but they expressed a different view about government. Benefits from increased participation would also flow to government. Participation is a form of education that can help an agency better understand its own regulatory choices.[3]

Aside from the issues of participation and voting, most current statements of "standards policy" are vague, bordering on useless. The OMB circular, for example, directs administrative agencies to rely on private standards "whenever feasible and consistent with law."[4] The amended version of the CPSC's authorizing statute requires deference to voluntary standards if:

> (1) it is likely that there will be substantial compliance with the voluntary standard, and (2) compliance with the voluntary standard is likely to result in the elimination or adequate reduction of the risk of injury.[5]

Neither of these policies contains much real guidance for deciding when private standards are "adequate," and neither speaks to the institutional differences between public and private approaches. Instead, agencies are left to devise their own ad hoc policies. Most seem uninterested in developing any kind of general standards policy. A report on the implementation of the OMB circular notes the sentiment that many agencies "have not yet heard of the circular, or not done anything about it, or don't really care."[6] The Interagency Committee on Standards Policy, charged with implementing the circular, virtually disbanded in 1987 owing to a lack of interest among participating agencies.

In lieu of a general policy, the most popular way of evaluating the adequacy of private standards, when agencies have to decide, is to scrutinize compliance rates. Standards that do not engender "high enough" compliance are considered suspect. This perspective provides two omnipresent justifications for public regulation. First, public standards have the force of law. Unlike "voluntary" standards, they command the authority of the state. Second, at the federal level agencies can enforce standards nationwide. This is an important advantage if problems are national in scope or if states might otherwise engage in undesirable competition to lower regulatory requirements. Business interests sometimes support federal regulation as a method of eliminating conflicting state or local requirements, which are often taken directly from private standards.

The perceived advantages of the mandatory and national nature of certain government standards, more than anything specific about their content, underpin many public policies concerning private standards. In neither of the consumer product cases was the CPSC trying to improve the *content* of private standards so much as the enforcement. The real hope for the woodstove labeling rule was that it would increase certification to UL 1482. The CPSC standard depended heavily on UL for its content. The oxygen depletion sensor was already an "optional requirement" in Z21.11.2. The CPSC simply sought to make it mandatory, again leaving technical specifications and details to the private sector. These do not seem to be isolated examples of the government seeking to combine its enforcement power with the standards written by the private sector. HUD turned NFPA's standard for mobile homes into a federal regulation (much to the dismay of NFPA), and OSHA did likewise with hundreds of ANSI standards shortly after the agency was created. This enforcement-based strategy is popular because the public agency has a standard to work with, rather than starting from scratch. The government acts more as an editor than as an author, taking existing provisions and (sometimes) tinkering with them. Starting with a private standard is not only more convenient for government, it also provides the built-in credibility that distinguishes first guesses from second ones. The importance of such credibility cannot be understated in the case of "trans-scientific" issues.[7] What a government agency may not be able to justify alone can attain instant credibility with the right private sector credentials. UL decisions are practically accepted as gospel. How many provisions of the Uniform Building Code, for example, are ever challenged on safety grounds?

Although persuasive in some contexts, the enforcement rationale does not always provide a sound reason for government intervention. First, the cases demonstrate that the marginal benefits of making private standards mandatory are often overestimated. Public standards are only as good as the incremental benefit they add to existing private ones. The size of this increment is no problem if the private standard generates very few benefits (as in the case of NFPA 61B) and the government version is both stronger and better enforced. More commonly, however, compliance with so-called voluntary standards is practically mandated through a combination of local codes and other incentives. Before government took any action, at least 50 percent of the airlines complied with the FAA's advisory circular, upward of 85 percent of the woodstove market was in compliance with UL 1482, and close to 100 percent of the unvented gas space heater market was in compliance with the "requirements" in Z21.11.2. In the latter two cases, the marginal benefit of perfect compliance would be minuscule. Both the FAA and the CPSC made the mistake of calculating the benefits of their own proposals without subtracting the existing benefits of private standards. In the case of woodstoves, the marginal benefit of the CPSC standard was very close to zero. Ironically, the CPSC justified its standard under a statute intended to force deference to the private sector "whenever appropriate." Beneath the irony, these cases reveal a major shortcoming in basing standards policy on compliance rates.

A second problem with current efforts is that nationwide standards are not always better than regional ones. In the case of gas space heaters, some states and localities wanted to take a stricter approach than the CPSC by banning the product altogether. Their petitions for exemption from preemption were the undoing of the CPSC standard. The topic of regulatory federalism is just emerging, and there is no comprehensive theory about when the federal government should preempt state efforts.[8] But the CPSC's experience in both cases suggests federal intervention was the wrong approach.

Given these problems, it would probably be best if government minimized the use of the "enforcement rationale." What is needed instead is a standards policy that builds on the comparative advantages of public standards-setting. Two major components of such a policy are discussed below: (1) identifying uniquely public objectives and policy instruments and (2) defining niches for public standards that complement private ones.

Defining a Role for Public Standards

Promoting "Public" Values

All the attention paid to enforcement and compliance issues obscures a more basic reason for government to intervene in the world of private standards. There are some things the private sector simply does not want to do. These lines between public and private are not readily obvious, but their contours are suggested by the regulatory philosophies sketched in chapter 7. Certain approaches to safety regulation are favored almost exclusively by the public sector. The government may call them protective; the private sector considers them overzealous or paternalistic. In either case, government should not waste time waiting for private standards-setters to implement this part of the public agenda. Rather, public agencies should identify and pursue the strategies and goals that set them apart from the private sector. Paternalistic regulation and "technology-forcing" stand out from the case studies. Concerns about consumer misuse distinguish the CPSC from both UL and AGA Labs. A willingness to engage in technology-forcing distinguishes the public standards for space heaters and aircraft smoke detectors from the private ones. And both NFPA standards underscore the reluctance of the private sector to regulate operating procedures, maintenance schedules, training routines, and other "managerial" issues.

Government should proceed with caution, however, since the case studies also suggest that some strategies disfavored by the private sector do not always work well in practice. Paternalistic regulation can be self-defeating or ineffective. To have been worth the effort, the CPSC woodstove rule would have had to have been dramatically more effective than any previously studied information strategy. Similarly, the desirability of operational controls depends on the quality of enforcement. It remains to be seen whether OSHA inspectors will apply the "action level" for housekeeping in a flexible but firm fashion. The agency certainly has a reputation for unreasonable enforcement.

The verdict on technology-forcing is at least partially in the government's favor. The CPSC apparently advanced the introduction of safer technology for gas space heaters. A trade association representative familiar with gas appliances admits that there is no evidence of the technological problems industry predicted while refusing to adopt the "unproven" technology. The jury is still out on smoke detectors for the passenger compartments of commercial aircraft. Whether the FAA rule will spur the development of better detectors remains to be seen. The FAA rule was written in ignorance of several matters of importance, however, and the gas space heater was successful primarily because the CPSC had the support of the National Bureau of Standards. This suggests that technology-forcing should only be undertaken when an agency has strong technical support.

Whether government should engage in either of these strategies is ultimately a question of values. Whatever the answer, it would be an improvement if these matters were highlighted and debated rather than concentration being put on contrived issues such as those raised in the woodstove proceeding.[9] The CPSC has never given any real content to its mandate to protect against "unreasonable risk of injury." As with most administrative agencies with broad mandates, the agency has left its regulatory mission rather vague. The issue of public policy toward private standards provides an ideal opportunity for facing these value questions directly.

Niches for Public Standards

An interactive standards policy should also be based on identifying *niches* for public standards. This strategy targets issues or areas that private standards do not cover. Some oppose this effort at interactive regulation, fearing that public standards will "drive out" private ones. That has happened several times on a programmatic level. The emergence of federal automobile safety standards displaced the safety program of the Society of Automotive Engineers. (The SAE still writes test methods that are referred to in government standards, however.) Similarly, the creation of the Civil Aeronautics Board ended UL's involvement in airplane certification. But the argument does not provide a valid reason for avoiding overlap in individual standards. Public and private standards-setters can and do operate in the same policy space. They sometimes even cooperate. UL works with the Food and Drug Administration in regulating microwave ovens and with the Coast Guard in regulating marine safety equipment. But even when the two sectors compete—attempting, as they did in all four case studies, to regulate the same subject independently—the efforts of one sector do not necessarily detract from those of the other. In none of the cases did the public standard "drive out" its private counterpart, although both UL and AGA Labs argued that they would. Identifying areas where public standards would best complement private ones is difficult because there are so many private standards. Nevertheless, the case studies suggest three possible niches.

Orphan Standards.   One promising niche for public standards is similar to that of "orphan drugs"—efficacious drugs that private companies decline to produce.[10] The most common examples of orphan drugs are treatments for rare diseases, where the number afflicted (the potential market) is too small to justify the expense of producing the drug. A similar condition obtains with safety standards: market forces limit the development of possibly useful private standards. The case studies suggest two types of market failure in the market for safety standards. First, as with orphan drugs, some standards are not written because the development costs are too high, given the anticipated income. There is such a limited market for, say, aviation fire extinguishers that the cost of developing special requirements for the aircraft environment are not worthwhile. Yet a standard of this type would probably do more to improve aviation fire safety than the specific actions taken by either the FAA or the NFPA. UL officials are quick to point out that some of its standards are "charitable." The standard for septic tanks, for example, apparently generates far less income than it costs. Yet there are undoubtedly other areas where standards would help promote the public interest but do not currently exist for economic reasons. Second, there is a related type of market failure involving chronic hazards. The cost of developing standards to control truly long-term hazards is simply prohibitive. The private sector readily admits its failure to address such safety problems. Engineers at AGA Labs agree that the hazards of long-term exposure to combustants from space heaters should be studied, and possibly regulated, by the government. An enlightened government standards policy would seek to identify and address these gaps in private standards.

Comparative Standards and Information.   Another possible niche for public action involves comparative standards and information. Economists argue that optimal levels of safety can be achieved when consumers select their own levels of risk.[11] That only works, however, if comparative safety information is available. A wider range of choices will also be available to the public if graded standards are favored over "pass-fail" ones. An assistant attorney general in the Carter administration cautioned: "A single quality level standard if set too high may unjustifiably exclude substitute products from the marketplace. Pass-fail standards may also blunt the incentive for further product development and innovation."[12]

Standards that facilitate safety comparisons are also desirable when information on causal links is weak. For example, there is significant uncertainty about the connection between high-absorbency tampons and toxic shock syndrome. Given this uncertainty, a standard that allows consumers to compare absorbency rates and apply their own notion of risk aversion seems preferable to one that imposes a single, arguably unjustifiable, level of risk.

Private action of this type is highly unlikely given the competitive implications of comparative safety standards. Private standards are built on common interests. Comparative standards are antithetical to these common interests. UL assiduously avoids *rating* safety. Instead it maintains the myth that products fall neatly into two categories, safe and unsafe. After extensive negotiations, the major tampon manufacturers were unable to agree on a test method for rating absorbency. Each method was considered favorable to a particular brand, raising the ire of various competitors.[13] In sum, the private sector is generally unwilling to develop standards that distinguish levels of performance. To the extent that this strategy has a place in safety regulation, it is located in the public sector. Several comparative standards have been adopted by the federal government in the automotive field: octane ratings, fuel economy ratings, crash ratings, and tire treadwear ratings. Not all these standards have been successful, but this type of effort is worth considering and probably has a place in any enlightened standards policy.

Integration and Coordination.   Finally, there is a role for public standards to cut across private regulatory boundaries. The narrow focus of private standards-setting tends to eliminate safety judgments across products or programs. Neither AGA Labs nor UL, for example, considers the relative safety of gas appliances versus electric appliances. AGA concentrates on the former, UL on the latter. There is no equivalent to the OMB in private standards-setting, trying to ensure that the next regulatory efforts are undertaken where they will do the most good. The government could provide a valuable service in some areas by considering together the universe of products or processes regulated separately by the private sector. An overall policy of, say, banning certain propane appliances in favor of natural gas and electricity might create more benefits than individual standards aimed at making all three somewhat safer.

The case studies also include examples of assorted "holes" in private standards that could possibly be filled by public action. For years, NFPA 211, the installation code for chimneys, fireplaces, and woodstoves, required certified wall pass-through systems, even though none were actually available. A similar situation obtained with spark arresters and fire-resistant floor coverings. NFPA standards mandated a certified product that did not exist. Installation codes can also fall out of touch with reality. NFPA 211 calls for chimney specifications that few contractors ever follow. The portions of the National Electric Code incorporated into NFPA 61B are not really based on the conditions encountered in grain elevators. So, too, NFPA 408 is built on a rating system for fire extinguishers that has nothing to do with the aviation environment. The causes and possible remedies for these dysfunctional aspects of private standards are not clear. Private standards-setters admit that the relationship between product standards and installation codes is arcane and puzzling. Public scrutiny of the connections between private standards might provide insights and improvements.

Alternative Policy Instruments and Institutions

Developing public standards is not the only way for government to seek what safety standards have to offer. Government can also attempt to influence the development of private standards. Since private standards cover literally thousands of subjects unlikely to be regulated by government in the foreseeable future, this strategy may have a much greater effect on public safety than government could ever hope to achieve through the small number of standards that survive the political process and the courts. Unfortunately, standards policy has been almost silent on other methods of improving private standards-setting.

Safety standards interact with a host of other policy instruments and influences. Harter and Eads observe that liability law, workers compensation law, information, and wage differentials are among the array of instruments that affect workers' health and safety.[14] However these instruments and institutions are evaluated on their own account, they affect standards-setting and hold the potential for improving it indirectly. Harter and Eads emphasize the importance of taking these instruments and institutions into account when analyzing a specific policy space: "Policy instruments coexist and interact. Modifying one does not represent the adjustment of an isolated instrument, but a shift in the constellation of instruments and institutions affecting private behavior."[15]

It is beyond the scope of this study to examine the role of these "external" forces independent of their effect on safety standards, although they should certainly be considered in any analysis of specific standards. OMB raised such issues in the grain elevator proceedings, appropriately questioning whether the force of liability law and insurance provided sufficient incentives for safety. But, as Harter and Eads suggest, changing these policy instruments will probably alter the standards-setting system. These need not be mere side effects. They might form the basis for useful, purposeful changes in standards-setting. The case studies suggest many important linkages between these policy instruments and standards-setting. Several policy instruments and institutions whose relevance to standards-setting was suggested by the case studies are discussed below.

Reforming Liability Law

Liability law is probably the most widely recognized policy instrument that affects private standards-setting. It was an important influence in several of the case studies. The debate over "tort reform" encapsulates the familiar arguments about whether the direct effects of liability law hamper public safety objectives.[16] The case studies add to that debate by suggesting that liability law has undesirable effects on standards-setting. At least two reforms seem in order. Both would help ensure that improvements in standards are encouraged, rather than discouraged, by the law. These two changes would probably have a larger impact on private standards-setting than any aspect of the various "standards policies" offered in the past ten years.

First, improvements made in a standard should not be admissible in cases concerning mishaps *prior to the improvement*. Although there is some support for this position in the law, "the growing tendency," according to UL's general counsel, "is to admit into evidence post-accident revisions to standards."[17] This can only discourage improvements in standards. UL would be more willing to upgrade its standard for metal chimneys if doing so did not create the implication that thousands of existing chimneys are, by UL's apparent admission, inadequate. Similar concerns were apparent when the NFPA's Agricultural Dusts committee added provisions for motion-detection devices to the appendix of the standard in 1973. These provisions might have been made mandatory but for the implication that facilities without such devices were below the generally accepted industry practice. Protecting standards-setters and businesses against liability *for making improvements* would certainly advance public safety objectives.

Second, in assessing the reasonableness of the risk attendant to a product or process, the law should consider overall effects, not just specific incidents. In other words, the law should not impose liability when overall social benefits clearly outweigh specific adverse effects. This argument has been advanced in connection with innovation by individual firms such as drug companies.[18] There are implications for standards-setters as well. The most persuasive reason why AGA did not require the oxygen depletion sensor on space heaters without prodding by the CPSC—a reason never committed to paper in either the public or private proceedings—is that companies were afraid that an occasional failure of the device would create new liabilities. Similar fears have slowed the introduction of other technologies, from vaccines to anti-lock brakes, that would unequivocally increase overall levels of safety. The perverse result is that standards-setters rationally avoid some actions that would make the world safer because, unfortunately, these actions might also increase exposure to liability.

Loosening Antitrust Law

Though not thought of as an instrument of public safety, antitrust law is often considered a proper tool for controlling private standards-setting. Strengthening the influence of antitrust law is always a popular proposal. (Who wants to defend "trusts" or "combinations"?) Such proposals are particularly popular because more substantive suggestions for controlling private standards-setting are lacking. In the area of standards and certification, the FTC houses some of the strongest advocates of increased antitrust scrutiny. These staff attorneys place their hope in stricter antitrust enforcement largely because the proposal to regulate standards-setting by rule was abandoned by the commission under President Reagan.

There are two reasons for restraining this enthusiasm for controlling private standards-setting through antitrust law. First, reducing one type of error often increases another type. Stricter antitrust enforcement would probably eliminate some of the worst standards currently in use, but it would probably also eliminate some of the good ones. This study suggests that producers are increasingly crying "antitrust" to intimidate standards-setters from taking socially desirable actions. Stories about antitrust law inhibiting otherwise desirable actions are almost as common in the private sector as those about liability law. Certain metal chimney producers raised this argument with UL and were effective in keeping UL from upgrading the standard, even though research results from NBS support such a move. Antitrust considerations were also instrumental in keeping AGA Labs from adopting ODS technology that was produced by only one company. Increasing the strength of antitrust law may well decrease the propensity to upgrade private standards.

The second reason for restraint is that antitrust law threatens to heap undesirable administrative costs on the private sector. That is practically the intention of those pushing the due process argument. As two members of the Supreme Court realized in the *Indian Head* case, "insisting that organizations like NFPA conduct themselves like courts of law will have perverse effects."[19] One effect is that due process itself can be exploited for anticompetitive reasons. The number of appeals to NFPA's Standards Council has increased to the point where it threatens to overburden the system. Higher administrative costs are likely to result in fewer standards and less frequent updating. The antitrust influence also threatens to burden the private sector with perhaps the worst aspect of public regulation: the judicial second-guessing that follows on the heels on most standards. The current level of discussion about antitrust and standards-setting is uninspired, relying on contrived distinctions that classify NFPA as "commercial" and the CPSC as "political."[20] At the very least, antitrust doctrine should be reexamined in a manner that recognizes the relevant institutional similarities and differences between public and private standards-setting. It should also be recognized that proposals to strengthen antitrust enforcement might actually be counterproductive, eliminating more desirable standards than undesirable ones. As Maitland argues, there are good reasons to permit more collective action by business organizations.[21] Whether a loosening of sorts is possible without allowing an undue amount of undesirable activity is worth examining.

Public Information Systems

Perhaps the most promising possibility for government action suggested by this study is an information strategy. The government has a clear comparative advantage in generating two types of information particularly important to setting safety standards: applied research and feedback on real-world experience. The private sector is lacking in its capacity to generate such information. Government overcomes the "free rider" problem that plagues private efforts to produce so-called public goods. Government is also the only avenue for collecting vital information such as medical records that are otherwise protected by privacy laws.

The potential for influencing private standards-setting with information about real-world experience is significant. The private sector has demonstrated its willingness to alter standards in light of relevant information. A former CPSC voluntary standards coordinator cites numerous examples where the private sector responded to public information. Liability law also helps provide an incentive for the private sector to respond to injury information. Unfortunately, it also provides a countervailing incentive against collecting it. What you know *can* hurt you. In any case, the incentive to respond depends on the quality of information. Industry feels no need to respond to many of the existing CPSC data because they are so clearly inadequate.

Perhaps the most influential government organization involved in collecting information is the National Transportation Safety Board. The NTSB has no decisionmaking power, but its recommendations carry considerable weight. The NTSB was split off from the FAA "so that the same person . . . was not both promulgating civil air regulations and investigating the accidents they might cause."[22] Avoiding this "conflict of interest," whether real or imaginary, seems to have bolstered the NTSB's clout. The FAA adopts many NTSB recommendations in short order. Others are eventually adopted under pressure from members of Congress who use these authoritative recommendations to register support for the popular cause of aviation safety. "Without the NTSB," muses a lobbyist for the Association of Flight Attendants, "the FAA could turn all of these issues into technical mush." Devoting a specific organization to the collection and analysis of injury data would probably improve standards-setting in other areas as well.

Government could also exert a more positive influence on private standards-setting by doing more applied research. Most private standards-setting organizations would gladly replace various "engineering judgments" with decisions based more on science—so long as someone else shoulders the research costs. Voluntary associations such as NFPA do almost no applied research; they do not have the resources. Testing labs occasionally conduct such research, but seldom in connection with a single standard. Perhaps the best policy for government is to increase funding for the National Bureau of Standards. Not only does NBS have the necessary technical capability and reputation to conduct useful research and development, but it offers the right institutional setting for developing an intelligent research strategy. The cases demonstrate that prolonged NBS involvement can help improve private standards. The agency combined its technical knowledge and reputation to bring about beneficial changes in NFPA 211 and ANSI/AGA Z21.11.2. "Engineering needs a loyal opposition," argues Edwin Layton in a prominent book on the profession.[23] Engineers face issues that are technical and political, in an organizational context that profoundly shapes personal incentives. They can best be kept in check by other engineers with the technical knowledge and institutional independence to challenge them. The National Bureau of Standards (now the National Institute of Standards and Technology) fits the bill, although its budget is still minuscule compared to its potential agenda.[24]

Engineering Schools, Insurance Companies, and Other Influential Institutions

There are a host of institutions at the periphery of this study that obviously play an influential role in the achievement of public safety objectives. These institutions interact with private standards-setting in ways that are not well understood and deserve more attention. The rest of this chapter contains speculation about the policy implications of the influence of three "external" institutions on private standards-setting.

The discussion is organized in decreasing order of speculativeness. That is, the institutions most peripheral to the case studies, about which only the most tentative statements are possible, are discussed first.

Engineering Schools. One important institutional influence on standards-setting comes through engineering education. The influence is diffuse and difficult to measure but nevertheless important in shaping the ethics that predominate in the private sector. Engineering education has been criticized for being too narrow in focus.[25] This study does not examine the details of engineering education, but it supports the conclusion that revisions might improve private standards-setting. A greater educational emphasis on economic trade-offs and human factors might improve the reasonableness of standards in two ways, respectively making them less demanding when the benefits are low and more demanding when human factors account for significant injuries.

Building Code Organizations. By design, this study also concentrates on "paired" public and private cases. In reality, however, private standards typically come in *connected pairs* or interlocking webs. The tendency of the private sector to separate product standards from installation and use codes is exemplified by the division of labor between UL and NFPA. The symbiotic relationship between these organizations is somewhat mysterious, and at times problematic. Matters are complicated further by the process through which these standards most often become law: municipal building codes. Building codes draw on the efforts of NFPA and UL, as well as those of various regional building code conferences—organizations that draft model building codes. The importance of the linkages between all these standards is clear. How to improve building code enforcement and achieve better coordination between installation codes and product standards is not. Perhaps the recently abandoned federal housing code deserves reconsideration. Possibly the government should institute a mechanism for bringing together those who write installation codes and product standards. Without improvements in the enforcement of building codes or the integration of design and use standards, it appears likely that some improvements in private standards will ultimately prove ineffective.

Insurance Companies. Insurance companies are also key actors affecting public safety. Not only do they spread risk, but, through insurance underwriting, they determine which risks are insurable and at what rate. If premiums accurately reflect risk, then insurance can help internalize externalities and improve public safety. Several major standards-setting organizations, including UL and NFPA, trace their origins to the insurance industry. Safety standards help insurers in two ways: (1) they provide convenient underwriting criteria, and (2) they promote general loss control. But what about the reverse influence—that is, how insurance companies affect standards-setting? Two possible influences are indicated by the case studies. Both seem rather weak, however, suggesting the potential for improvement.

The first way insurers affect standards-setting is with information. Insurance companies identify problems and manage information. In theory, they should be able to provide standards-setters with helpful data on the size and nature of various hazards because insurers pool information on claims through institutions such as the Insurance Services Organization. In practice, however, insurers apparently contribute little useful information to standards-setting efforts. An insurance company representative testifying in favor of the CPSC woodstove rule was embarrassed by questions about the actual magnitude of the problem. In an analysis of residential fire insurance, David Hemenway concludes that "the insurance industry has not been especially helpful in providing useful [loss control] data." He suggests several policies that might improve the situation, but all require further study.[26]

Second, as one of the primary users of safety standards, insurers are potential watchdogs for the quality of these standards. Unlike many participants in standards-setting whose interests are vested in particular products, insurance companies have a purer motive: reducing losses. Insurers certainly make use of these standards. Product liability insurers require compliance with UL and AGA standards. Some grain elevator insurers require compliance with NFPA 61B. But the case studies suggest that insurers are not very demanding users of private standards-setters. They are seldom involved enough in the details of particular hazards to know a good standard when they see one. Insurers play almost no role in the NFPA committees on aviation fire safety, even though individual fires can be catastrophic. The grain elevator standard is sadly lacking in critical areas of grain elevator safety, but reinsurers are apparently unaware that more effective standards for safety are possible. Moreover, in neither the grain elevator case nor the woodstove case does it appear that the premiums charged by insurance companies reflect differences in risk. Airline officials also contend that their premiums have nothing to do with their loss control efforts.

This study suggests that insurance companies could improve the quality of private standards if they were more demanding. A small reinsurance company was apparently instrumental in getting UL to change its requirements for metal chimneys. But the low priority that many insurance companies seem to place on loss control has been noted by Hemenway.[27] How to maximize the potential of insurance as a regulator of risk has long been a puzzle in the area of workers compensation. Somehow, the critical role of insurers as assessors and regulators of risk should be more widely recognized so that these issues are addressed in various areas of public safety.

Conclusions

Both public and private standards-setting are more complicated than is often imagined. The popular characterization of the public sector as slow and rigid is sometimes true, but there are notable exceptions. The FAA moved quickly in adopting standards for fire extinguishers and smoke detectors; OSHA adopted flexible and reasonable standards for grain elevator safety. Similarly, private standards are not always weak and "watered down." Three of the four private standards in this study provided meaningful, if not stringent, safety regulation.

The relevant questions for public policy are also more complicated than is generally recognized. The choice is rarely between public and private standards. Rather, the challenge is recognizing ways in which the two sectors can interact beneficially. This study identifies the comparative institutional advantages of public and private standards-setting and suggests several ways to take advantage of them. One approach is to emphasize "public" values. In other words, the public sector should emphasize certain strategies shunned by the private sector. Second, government should identify niches where public standards are likely to complement private ones. A particularly promising strategy is filling "holes" in private standards. Finally, the importance of alternative policy instruments must not be overlooked. Standards-setting in both sectors is affected by a variety of "external" factors that are subject to influence by government action. Several of these factors hold the promise of improving standards-setting in ways that could never be mandated directly. Altering the product liability law and improving the education of engineers could both lead to significant improvements in standards-setting. Recognizing these subtle influences and pursuing strategies that build on the complex interaction of public and private safety standards is the key to an intelligent and productive standards policy.

Appendix: List of Interviews

Note: This list, organized in alphabetical order, includes only those interviews conducted in person and lasting more than thirty minutes. Telephone interviews and brief personal conversations are not included. Approximately half of the listed interviews were tape-recorded and transcribed.

Wade Anderson, Enforcement Directorate, CPSC, Bethesda, Md., December 7, 1984, and June 18, 1985.

Robert Barr, director of public protection, NFPA, Quincy, Mass., November 27, 1984.

Robert Benedetti, staff liaison for agricultural dust hazards, NFPA, Quincy, Mass., November 28, 1984.

Debbie Berkowitz, director of health and safety, Food & Allied Services Trades, AFL-CIO, Washington, D.C., June 6, 1985.

Henri Branting, Airworthiness Division, FAA, Washington, D.C., December 6, 1984, and June 11, 1985.

James Brenneman, fire protection engineer, United Airlines, San Francisco, April 24, 1985.

Kay Broughton, Standards Department, AGA Labs, Cleveland, May 20, 1985.

William Carey, research associate, Fire Protection Department, Underwriters Laboratories, Northbrook, Ill., July 17, 1985.

John Cedervall, associate managing engineer, Casualty & Chemical Hazards Department, Underwriters Laboratories, Northbrook, Ill., July 20, 1985.

Al Chabeck, vice president, AGA Labs, Cleveland, May 21, 1985.

Hank Collins, vice president, government affairs, Underwriters Laboratories, Washington, D.C., November 11, December 10, 1984; June 19, 1985.

Arthur Cote, vice president, standards, NFPA, Quincy, Mass., November 27, 1984.

Douglas Crane, owner, Crane Stove Works, Braintree, Mass., November 28, 1984.

Eugene Curry, staff attorney, Federal Trade Commission, Boston, November 29, 1984.

P. A. DeLeon, industrial standards manager, Honeywell Inc., Golden Valley, Minn., July 16, 1985.

Martin Eschelman, State Department (former USDA Special Task Force member), Washington, D.C., June 11, 1985.

Matthew Finucane, safety and technical director, Association of Flight Attendants, Washington, D.C., November 9, 1984.

Mark Goedde, director of engineering services, National Grain and Feed Association, Washington, D.C., June 18, 1985.

Forrest Hammacker, Standards Department, AGA Labs, Cleveland, May 21, 1985.

Bea Harwood, Epidemiology Directorate, CPSC, Bethesda, Md., June 19, 1985.

David Hemenway, professor, Harvard School of Public Health (author of *Industrywide Voluntary Product Standards*), Boston, November 29, 1984.

Bill Higgins, Interagency Standards Advisory Council, OSHA, Washington, D.C., November 7, 1984.

James Hoebel, manager, Office of Program Management, CPSC, Bethesda, Md., November 11, 1984, and June 19, 1985.

S. David Hoffman, vice president and general counsel, Underwriters Laboratories, Northbrook, Ill., May 17, 1985.

Jeffrey Horlick, National Lab Accreditation Program, NBS, Gaithersburg, Md., June 6, 1985.

Robert F. Hubbard, (retired) vice president, plant operations, Cargill, Minneapolis, July 15, 1985.

Larry Ingels, GAIN Program, American Gas Association, Arlington, Va., June 19, 1985.

Mike Jorgensen, staff engineer, Fire Protection Department, Underwriters Laboratories, Northbrook, Ill., May 17, 1985.

Carter Keithly, Wood Heating Alliance, Washington, D.C., December 12, 1984.

Lawrence Krasner, manager, Applied Research Department, Factory Mutual Corporation, Norwood, Mass., November 30, 1984.

Richard Kutina, director, building energy codes and standards, American Gas Association, Arlington, Va., June 6, 1985.

Escher Kweller, gas appliance engineer, NBS, Gaithersburg, Md., December 3, 1984.

Jack Langmead, Gas Appliance Manufacturers Association, Arlington, Va., November 6, 1984, and June 19, 1985.

Allen Lewis, Regulatory Analysis Division, FAA, Washington, D.C., December 6, 1984.

John Liskey, Outdoor Power Equipment Institute (former director of voluntary standards at CPSC), Washington, D.C., November 5, 1984.

John Locke, National Lab Accreditation Program, NBS, Gaithersburg, Md., December, 5, 1984.

Donald Mackay, Office of Standards Policy, NBS (former director of voluntary standards at CPSC), Gaithersburg, Md., October 31, December 6, 1984, and June 5, 1985.

John Mackey, assistant to Commissioner Terrence Scanlon, CPSC, Washington, D.C., June 6, 1985.

Warren Mathers, Human Factors Directorate, CPSC, Bethesda, Md., June 19, 1985.

Stan Morrow, Office of Program Management, CPSC, Bethesda, Md., November 5, 1984.

Doug Noble, voluntary standards coordinator, CPSC, Bethesda, Md., June 11, 1985.

Y. D. Oleksiw, manager, Merchandise Testing Center, J. C. Penney, New York, June 10, 1985.

George Papritz, standards engineer, Consumers Union, Mount Vernon, N.Y., November 14, 1984.

Richard Peacock, product flammability research engineer, NBS, Gaithersburg, Md., November 8, 1984, and June 5, 1985.

Donald Peyton, president, ANSI, New York, November 15, 1984.

Eleanor Perry, chemical engineer, CPSC, Bethesda, Md., December 4, 1984.

R. David Pittle, technical director, Consumers Union (former CPSC commissioner), Mount Vernon, N.Y., November 14, 1984.

Dale Ray, Economics Directorate, CSPC, Bethesday, Md., December 4, 1984.

Robert Schroeder, staff attorney, Federal Trade Commission, Boston, November 29, 1984.

Thomas Seymour, fire protection engineer, Office of Fire Protection Engineering, Directorate of Safety Standards, OSHA, Washington, D.C., June 7, 1985.

Jay Shelton, Shelton Research Labs, Sante Fe, N. Mex., November 22, 1985.

Max Spencer, vice president, operations and engineering, Continental Grain Company, New York, June 10, 1985.

Stephen Spivak, ANSI Board of Directors, National Bureau of Standards, Gaithersburg, Md., October 31, 1984.

Stuart Statler, commissioner, CPSC, Washington, D.C., December 14, 1984.

Diane Stern, program administrator, health and safety standards, ANSI, New York, October 2, November 15, and December 10, 1984.

David Swankin, ASTM Board of Directors, attorney and standards activist, Washington, D.C., December 14, 1984.

James Talentino, engineer, NHTSA (former CPSC engineer and former member of the Z21 committee), Washington, D.C., October 30, 1984.

Al Townsend, president, National Agra Underwriters, Camp Hill, Pa., June 13, 1985.

Dr. Stanley Warsaw, Office of Standards Policy, NBS, Gaithersburg, Md., June 5, 1985.

Notes

CHAPTER ONE

1. Charles Wolf, Jr., "A Theory of Non-Market Failures," *The Public Interest* 55 (Spring 1979):114–33.

2. James Q. Wilson, *The Politics of Regulation* (New York: Basic Books, 1980), 373.

3. For a description of the policy consensus on certain forms of economic deregulation, see Martha Derthick and Paul J. Quirk, *The Politics of Deregulation* (Washington, D.C.: Brookings Institution, 1985).

4. Robert B. Reich, "Looking Back at Regulation: Business Is Asking for Trouble Again," *New York Times*, November 22, 1981, sec. 3, p. F2. There recently has been considerable discussion of "reregulation," particularly in airlines and trucking. See, for example, Stuart Reginald, "To Regulate, to Deregulate, or, Now, to Reregulate," *New York Times*, October 29, 1984, 14; "Rumblings of Reregulation," *Fortune*, January 10, 1983, 17.

5. Wilson, *The Politics of Regulation*, x.

6. An important alternative to command-and-control regulation, frequently touted by economists but outside the scope of this study, is incentives such as taxation and subsidy. See, for example, John Mendeloff, *Regulating Safety: A Economic and Political Analysis of Occupational Safety and Health Policy* (Cambridge, Mass.: MIT Press, 1979).

7. Lester M. Salamon, "Partners in Public Service: The Scope and Theory of Government-Nonprofit Relations," in Walter W. Powell, *The Nonprofit Sector* (New Haven: Yale University Press, 1987), 100.

8. The name change was part of the massive Omnibus Trade and Competitiveness Act, signed into law on August 23, 1988. The new Institute (NIST) retains all of the old functions of NBS, along with several new ones concerning technology transfer.

9. Engineers refer to these standards as "M&Ms" because they specify

either materials or methods. Many simply set forth definitions, such as the meaning of two-by-four (a piece of lumber that, under the standard, is not actually $2'' \times 4''$). Others facilitate the interchangeability of items such as flashlight batteries and automobile parts. Scores of these private standards are used by government for procurement purposes.

10. See, generally, Steven M. Spivak, *Implementation of OMB Circular A-119: An Independent Appraisal of Federal Participation in the Development and Use of Voluntary Standards,* prepared for the National Bureau of Standards, NBS-GCR-85-495 (Springfield, Va.: National Technical Information Service, 1985).

11. See Timothy J. Muris, "Legalization of Standardization Under the Antitrust Laws"; John Boyer, "The Role of Due Process in Avoiding Antitrust Liability"; and Edward T. Buhl, "Antitrust Liability for Standards Developers," all in American National Standards Institute, *Standards and the Law* (New York: ANSI, 1984). A recent decision of the Supreme Court, in a case involving the National Fire Protection Association, concludes that the immunity granted for influencing legislation, known as *Noeer* immunity, does not apply equally to private standards-setting; rather, private organizations are bound to unspecified "safeguards" against "bias" and "stacking" (*Allied Tube and Conduit Corp. v. Indian Head,* 56 U.S.L.W. 4539 [June 13, 1988], 4543).

12. A 150-page report prepared for the Administrative Conference of the United States discusses several "horror stories" and presents "impressionistic" evidence from scattered meetings, but it contains no case studies. See Robert W. Hamilton, "The Role of Nongovernmental Standards in the Development of Mandatory Federal Standards Affecting Safety or Health," *Texas Law Review* 56 (November 1978): 1329, 1446. Similarly, a report on representation of interest groups that was commissioned by NFPA discusses many of the same "horror stories" but contains no detailed information for any single case. See Robert G. Dixon, Jr., *Standards Development in the Private Sector: Thoughts on Interest Representation and Procedural Fairness* (Quincy, Mass.: National Fire Protection Association, 1978). David Hemenway, author of the only book on industrywide voluntary product standards (*Industrywide Voluntary Product Standards* [Cambridge, Mass.: Ballinger Publishing, 1978]), confirmed in an interview in 1984 that he knew of no detailed case studies of voluntary standards-writing in this country. The only case study (subsequently located) compares two safety standards for regulating liquefied natural gas facilities: one developed by NFPA, the other promulgated by the Materials Transportation Board of the U.S. Department of Transportation. See John H. Young, "Direct Interest Participation in the Regulatory Decision Process: Lessons Learned from Two LNG Safety Standards" (Staff paper prepared for the Office of Technology Assessment, 1983).

13. UL has three kinds of standards: published, proposed, and unpublished. Unpublished standards (also known as "desk" standards) cover hundreds of products. These standards are somewhat controversial and are discussed in more detail in chapter 3. UL also distinguishes between "published" standards and "proposed" standards. "Proposed" standards are, in fact, published; they are a kind of intermediate step between unpublished and officially "published."

14. Hemenway, *Industrywide Voluntary Product Standards*, 78.

15. The proposal, *Federal Register* 49 (June 19, 1984): 25005, was withdrawn unanimously by the FTC in 1985. However, the CPSC chair vowed: "The recognition issue is not dead. I am not deterred in my efforts to find a viable plan . . . to promote voluntary standards" (CPSC, "Statement of Terrence M. Scanlon, Chairman," January 16, 1985).

16. Albert O. Hirschman, *Exit, Voice, and Loyalty* (Cambridge: Mass.: Harvard University Press, 1970).

17. John E. Chubb and Terry M. Moe, "Politics, Markets, and the Organization of Schools," *American Political Science Review* 82 (December 1988): 1067.

18. Grant McConnell, *Private Power and American Democracy* (New York: Vintage Books, 1966), 141.

19. George Eads and Peter Reuter, *Designing Safer Products* (Santa Monica, Calif.: RAND Corporation, 1983), 43.

20. George S. Stigler, "The Theory of Economic Regulation," *Bell Journal of Economics and Management Science* 2 (Spring 1971): 3.

21. McConnell, *Private Power and American Democracy*, 127.

22. Ibid., 120–26. See also Robert Michels, *Political Parties* (1915; reprint Glencoe, Ill.: Free Press, 1949).

23. Constance Smith and Anne Freedman, *Voluntary Associations* (Cambridge, Mass.: Harvard University Press, 1972), 54.

24. According to the acting director of the FTC's Bureau of Consumer Protection, the "staff recommends that the Commission terminate this proceedings, and continue to pursue a program of case-by-case enforcement against deceptive or anticompetitive practices" (Memorandum to the Federal Trade Commission from Amanda B. Pedersen, August 29, 1985).

25. Henry S. Kariel, *The Decline of American Pluralism* (Stanford: Stanford University Press, 1961), 73–74. These comments were specifically in reference to the National Recovery Act. For an interesting and alternative interpretation of these events, see Donald R. Brand, *Corporatism and the Rule of Law: A Study of the National Recovery Administration* (Ithaca: Cornell University Press, 1988).

26. Mancur Olson, Jr., *The Logic of Collective Action* (Cambridge, Mass.: Harvard University Press, 1965).

27. McConnell, *Private Power and American Democracy*, 6.

28. Theodore Lowi, *The End of Liberalism*, 2d ed. (New York: W. W. Norton, 1979), 116–19. As mentioned earlier, both the CPSC and OSHA turned to private standards-setters in their early years. OSHA adopted hundreds of ANSI standards wholesale; the CPSC utilized the "offeror process," which allowed outside organizations to propose safety standards for public adoption. Both policies were later rescinded.

29. See Samuel P. Huntington, "The Marasmus of the ICC: The Commission, the Railroads, and the Public Interest," *Yale Law Journal* 61 (April 1952): 467–509; Marver Bernstein, *Regulating Business by Independent Commission* (Princeton: Princeton University Press, 1955); Stigler, "The Theory of Economic Regulation."

30. Kariel, *The Decline of American Pluralism*, 94.

31. See, for example, Nina W. Cornell, Roger G. Noll, and Barry Weingast, "Safety Regulation," in *Setting National Priorities* (Washington, D.C.: Brookings Institution, 1976).

32. Wilson, *The Politics of Regulation*, 372.

33. *Underwriters Laboratories v. Internal Revenue Service*, 135 F.2d 371, 373 (10th Cir. 1943). UL subsequently regained its tax-exempt status from Congress.

34. *Eliason Corp. v. National Sanitation Foundation*, 614 F.2d 126 (6th Cir. 1980), cert. denied 449 U.S. 826 (1980).

35. See Petitioner's brief at pp. 43–47 and Respondent's brief at pp. 41–47 in *American Society of Mechanical Engineers v. Hydrolevel Corp.*, 456 U.S. 556 (1982).

36. Alfred E. Kahn, "Cartels and Trade Associations," in *International Encyclopedia of the Social Sciences* 2:320–25 (standardization is essential if collusively fixed prices are to be truly uniform).

37. Peter M. Blau and W. Richard Scott, *Formal Organizations* (San Francisco: Chandler Publishing, 1962), 42–58.

38. Robert Leone, *Who Profits* (New York: Basic Books, 1986).

39. Lowi, *The End of Liberalism*, 118.

40. McConnell, *Private Power and American Democracy*, 66.

41. Brand (*Corporatism and the Rule of Law*, 307) also concludes that the NRA actually favored small and medium-sized businesses, not large ones as argued by Lowi and others.

42. Less than six months after it began operations OSHA incorporated into law over 250 pages of private standards, mostly from ANSI and NFPA (*Federal Register* 36 [May 29, 1971]: 10466). For a discussion of the problems that ensued, see Phillip Harter, "A View from the OSHA Task Force: Voluntary Standards Used in Regulation," *ASTM Standardization News*, May 1977.

43. Henry Weinstein, "OSHA Will Place New Limits on 402 Toxics," *Los Angeles Times*, June 8, 1988, 1.

44. Bruce W. Owen and Ronald Braeutigam, *The Regulation Game: Strategic Use of the Administrative Process* (Cambridge, Mass.: Ballinger Publishing, 1978), 12.

45. Ibid., 3.

46. Lawrence S. Bacow, *Bargaining for Job Safety and Health* (Cambridge, Mass.: MIT Press, 1980), 45–46.

47. Bruce A. Ackerman and William T. Hansler, *Clean Coal/Dirty Air* (New Haven: Yale University Press, 1981), 113.

48. McConnell, *Private Power and American Democracy*, 120–21.

49. As Lipset et al. argue in their landmark study of the International Typographical Union, it is necessary to combine structural and historical analyses to understand the organization (Seymour Martin Lipset, Martin A. Trow, and James C. Coleman, *Union Democracy: The Internal Politics of the International Typographical Union* [New York: Free Press, 1956], chap. 18).

50. Michael S. Hunt, "Trade Associations and Self-Regulation: Major Home Appliances," in *Regulating the Product: Quality and Variety*, ed. Rich-

ard E. Caves and Marc J. Roberts (Cambridge, Mass.: Ballinger Publishing, 1975), 39–56.

51. Steven Kelman, *Regulating America, Regulating Sweden: A Case Study of Occupational Safety and Health Regulations* (Cambridge, Mass.: MIT Press, 1981).

52. David A. Garvin, "Can Industry Self-Regulation Work?" *California Management Review* 25, no. 3 (Summer 1983): 44.

53. Wilson, *The Politics of Regulation*, xi.

54. Mary Douglas and Aaron Wildavsky, *Risk and Culture* (Berkeley and Los Angeles: University of California Press, 1982).

55. Lester B. Lave, *The Strategy of Social Regulation: Decision Frameworks for Policy* (Washington, D.C.: Brookings Institution, 1981), 8–28.

CHAPTER TWO

1. National Bureau of Standards, *Standards Activities of Organizations in the United States*, NBS Special Publication 681, (Washington, D.C.: Government Printing Office, 1984), 1.

2. Paul B. W. Miller and Rodney Redding, *The FASB: The People, the Process, and the Politics* (Homewood, Ill.: Irwin, 1986), 20.

3. American National Standards Institute, *1984–85 Catalog of American National Standards for Safety and Health* (New York: ANSI, 1984).

4. For a description of these organizations, see National Bureau of Standards, *Standards Activities of Organizations in the United States*, 87–88 (ASAE), 92–93 (ASHRAE), and 93 (ASLE).

5. The FTC formally initiated an inquiry into private standards-setting organizations in 1974, two years after the staff recommended regulation to prevent trade restraints and consumer deception (FTC, "Preliminary Staff Study (Precis): Self-Regulation—Product Standardization, Certification, and Seals of Approval" [mimeographed, 1972]). The staff later proposed a rule that would mandate extensive procedural protections, including an appeals procedure, and require standards-setters to meet a substantive "fairness" criterion (FTC, Bureau of Consumer Protection, *Standards and Certification: Proposed Rule and Staff Report* [Washington, D.C.: Government Printing Office, 1978]). The subsequent proceedings on the proposed rule were controversial and divisive. Over twelve weeks of hearings, the staff heard from over two hundred witnesses. The FTC Improvements Act of 1980 removed Commission authority to issue a rule regarding standards and certification under section 18 of the FTC Act, concerning "unfair and deceptive acts or practices" (15 U.S.C. sec. 57a). The FTC proceeded with the Standards and Certification proceedings under section 6(g) of the FTC Act, the "unfair methods of competition" provision. The staff eventually recommended against a regulation, favoring case-by-case enforcement against unfair methods of competition (FTC, Bureau of Consumer Protection, *Standards and Certification: Final Staff Report*, [Washington, D.C.: Government Printing Office, 1983]).

6. For example, a recent dispute over which trade association had jurisdiction to certify log-splitting equipment had little to do with actual safety.

Rather, the dispute, according to several members of the Board of Standards of Review, stemmed from the income that would be generated through this service.

7. Barry I. Castleman and Grace E. Ziem, "Corporate Influence on Threshold Limit Values," *American Journal of Industrial Medicine* 13 (1988): 531.

8. ASME subcommittees provide approximately twenty thousand interpretations of the Boiler and Pressure Vessel Code every year. The case, *American Society of Mechanical Engineers v. Hydrolevel Corp.*, 456 U.S. 5556 (1982), involved an unauthorized and blatantly anticompetitive interpretation of the code by two subcommittee members who were direct competitors of Hydrolevel, a valve manufacturer. After an "unofficial" letter on ASME stationery warned that the Hydrolevel valve might be unsafe, the firm lost sales and eventually went bankrupt. For a detailed discussion of the facts in *Hydrolevel*, see Charles W. Beardsley, "The Hydrolevel Case: A Retrospective," *Fire Journal*, May 1985. The decision was strongly criticized. See, for example, William J. Curran III, "Volunteers . . . Not Profiteers: The Hydrolevel Myth," *Catholic University Law Review* 33 (1983): 147.

9. Chap. 21, Code of Federal Regulations, subchap. F. The estimate of the number of actual standards is from National Bureau of Standards, *Standards Activities of Organizations in the United States*, 451.

10. See, generally, Richard B. Stewart, "The Reformation of American Administrative Law," *Harvard Law Review* 88, no. 8 (June 1975): 1667–1813.

11. National Bureau of Standards, *Standards Activities of Organizations in the United States*, 1.

12. For example, the Refrigerator Safety Act, the Flammable Fabrics Act, and the Poison Prevention Packaging Act.

13. Eads and Reuter, *Designing Safer Products*, 2.

14. See Udo Staber and Howard Aldrich, "Trade Association Stability and Public Policy" (Paper prepared for the Albany Conference on Organization Theory and Public Policy, SUNY-Albany, April 1–2, 1982).

15. See John Bart Sevart and R. Lewis Hull, *Power Lawn Mowers: An Unreasonably Dangerous Product* (Durham, N.C.: Institute for Product Safety, 1982), and sources cited in the extensive bibliography at 195–207.

16. For example, two of the first safety standards developed by the agency were for—of all things—matchbook covers and swimming pool slides. Both standards were overturned in court. See, generally, Theresa M. Schwartz, "The Consumer Product Safety Commission: A Flawed Product of the Consumer Decade," *The George Washington Law Review* 51, no. 1 (November 1982): 32–95.

17. W. Kip Viscusi, *Regulating Consumer Product Safety* (Washington, D.C.: American Enterprise Institute, 1984), 106–8.

18. The article, which was about product testing in general, noted that "without question, UL's efforts have been a major force in preventing electric shocks and fires" but added, on the basis of a few "horror stories," that UL's record is "checkered" (Mark Dowie et al., "The Illusion of Safety," *Mother Jones*, July 1982, 35). The criticism is mild, particularly for this publication,

making UL's response—a staff member referred to it as "disastrous"—as revealing as the article.

CHAPTER THREE

1. See Bernstein, *Regulating Business by Independent Commission.* For a criticism of the life-cycle theory, see Owen and Braeutigam, *The Regulation Game,* 11–12.

2. See, generally, Paul J. Quirk, *Industry Influence in Federal Regulatory Agencies* (Princeton: Princeton University Press, 1981).

3. Country elevators, estimated to number 10,400, receive grain from farmers for later delivery to terminal elevators or grain processors. Storage capacity ranges from one hundred thousand bushels to over a million, and the average number of workers is approximately four. Inland terminals, numbering 710 by one count, receive grain directly both from farmers and from country elevators, holding it for delivery mostly to export facilities and grain processors. There are approximately eighty export facilities. Inland terminals and export facilities have large capacities, in the millions of bushels, and employ an average of forty to fifty workers each.

4. Bulk handling at storage facilities is more hazardous than grain handling at processing facilities (e.g., cereal plants) that have throughput. Feed milling involves a grinding and mixing process whereby grains are blended with protein concentrates, vitamins, drugs, and minerals. The receiving operations in feed mills are almost identical to those in grain elevators. Grain and feed handling is accomplished by bulk conveyors and bucket elevators, like in grain elevators, but the operations tend to be smaller and slower than in most grain elevators, resulting in less dust generation. On the other hand, the grinding and processing creates additional dust. A report prepared for OSHA by Arthur D. Little, Inc., estimates the following distribution of grain-handling facilities by type:

Country Grain Elevators	10,415
Inland Grain Elevators	710
Export Grain Terminals	75
Small Feed Mills	3,030
Large Feed Mills	1,040

5. Country elevators generally have lower throughput than other facilities, but those acting more as transfer points than as storage areas have unusually high throughput. Differences in elevator technology and design further complicate any assessment of grain elevator safety. Dust-control technology has improved considerably in the past twenty years, so higher throughputs are much safer in facilities with relatively new technology. Basic elevator design has improved as well. Newer facilities are built with a minimum of ledges, rafters, and other features that allow layered dust to accumulate. Some older facilities, retrofitted with faster handling equipment, still lack the benefit of safer building design. Compared to others of equivalent throughput, these facilities are safer in some respects and less safe in others.

6. For a discussion of the shortcomings of these data and a defense of the higher estimate, see U.S. Department of Agriculture, Office of the Special Coordinator for Grain Elevator Safety and Security, *Prevention of Dust Explosions in Grain Elevators—An Achievable Goal* (Washington, D.C.: Government Printing Office, 1980), 28. There are other hazards associated with grain handling as well. Workers have suffocated while inspecting bins, and the Environmental Protection Agency is concerned about outdoor dust emissions and fumigant use. Still, there is a consensus in government and industry that the explosion hazard poses the greatest danger.

7. The uneven correlation between production and sales further compounds the difficulty of evaluating injury data over time; for example, 1985 was a banner year for production but a bust for exports and, hence, for grain handling (see William Robbins, "A Barren Prospect for Wheat: As Exports Dry Up, Another Big American Harvest Goes into Storage," *New York Times,* June 16, 1985, sec. F, p. 4).

8. Most primary explosions occur because an ignition source comes in contact with a dense dust cloud. These "explosions" actually entail a rapid combustion in which flames spread through the dust cloud and heat is produced more rapidly than it is dissipated to the surroundings.

9. USDA, *Prevention of Dust Explosions,* appendix C, table 44, p. 110.

10. National Academy of Sciences, National Materials Advisory Board, *Pneumatic Dust Control in Grain Elevators: Guidelines for Design Operation and Maintenance,* NMAB 367-3 (Washington, D.C.: National Academy Press, 1982), 103–8 (Appendix C: "Results of an Experiment to Determine Whether Dust Suspensions in Bucket Elevator Legs Can be Kept Below the Lower Explosive Limit by Pneumatic Means").

11. Much of the uncertainty surrounding pneumatic dust control is due to its checkered past. A lot of ineffective systems have been installed and others have not been properly maintained. The dust control systems in many facilities were designed by the local air conditioning and furnace outfits. Heating and cooling principles do not lend themselves well to this application, leading the NAS to conclude that "contractors who design and install systems often are poorly qualified for the work."

12. National Academy of Sciences, National Material Advisory Board, *Prevention of Grain Elevator and Mill Explosions,* NMAB 367-2 (Washington, D.C.: National Academy Press, 1982), 18.

13. See note 6 above.

14. Only three of the fourteen major explosions examined in a USDA study occurred in facilities less than fifteen years old. There are no reliable figures on the number of elevators built since 1980, but sources in the grain industry agree that at least 95 percent of all elevators are older.

15. National Fire Protection Association, *Standard for the Prevention of Fires and Explosions in Grain Elevators and Facilities Handling Bulk Raw Agricultural Commodities,* NFPA 61B-1980 (Quincy, Mass.: NFPA, 1980) sec. 6-6.3, p. 20 (the various versions of this document are hereafter referred to as NFPA 61B, followed by the year of publication).

16. Ibid., sec. 5-1.5, p. 14.

17. See, generally, National Fire Protection Association, *Guide for Explosion Venting*, NFPA 68 (Quincy, Mass.: NFPA, 1984); NFPA, *Standards on Explosion Prevention Systems*, NFPA 69 (Quincy, Mass.: NFPA, 1984).

18. The specifications for dust-control systems provided by UL in 1926 have long since been deleted from 61B, although it is difficult to ascertain why from the committee minutes. The first edition of what later came to be called NFPA 61B required that air aspiration systems be installed in conformance with the UL Research Bulletin no. 37 on controlling floating dust. See National Fire Protection Association, *Regulations of the National Board of Fire Underwriters for the Prevention of Dust Explosions in Terminal Grain Elevators: Recommended by the National Fire Protection Association* (Boston: NFPA, 1925), sec. 33, p. 6.

19. NFPA 61B-1980, sec. 8-1.1, p. 23.

20. See, for example, *Secretary of Labor v. Valley Center Farmers' Elevator, Inc.*, 8 O.S.H.C. 1061 (1979) (violations for hazardous dust accumulations vacated for failure to establish the amount of dust necessary for the creation of an explosion); and *Secretary of Labor v. Cargill*, 7 O.S.H.C. 2114 (1979) (violations vacated for failure to establish that accumulations of one-eighth to one-fourth inch constitute a "recognized hazard" in the industry).

21. Testimony of William Phillips, assistant vice president, loss prevention and security, Continental Grain Co., informal OSHA hearing, *In the Matter of Grain Handling* (Kansas City, Mo., June 21, 1984, vol. III, transcript), p. 49.

22. NFPA 61B-1980, sec. 6-6.6, p. 20. Information on Continental's policy was obtained through interviews.

23. Ibid., sec. 7-2.4, p. 22; sec. 2-4.1, p. 10; sec. A-11-6.5, p. 41.

24. A one-page "divisional guideline" issued by the Continental Grain Co. states that dust accumulations exceeding one-eighth of an inch over a broad area constitute an unsatisfactory condition requiring "immediate attention." This guideline was not intentionally made public by Continental. It was introduced into evidence at an OSHA hearing, however, and a Continental official acknowledged its authenticity in an often hostile exchange with OSHA officials and a representative of organized labor. See informal OSHA hearing, *In the Matter of Grain Handling* (Kansas City, Mo., June 21, 1984, vol. III, transcript), pp. 47–59 and Exhibit 38. The one-eighth-inch standard is also incorporated into Canadian standards and a proprietary standard developed by the Factory Mutual Research Corp. See "Deadlock over Explosive Dust," *Science*, November 4, 1983, 485, 486.

25. NFPA 61B-1973, foreword, p. 5.

26. The committee's official response was that "a vast majority of elevators' legs require slow down switches [and it] would be difficult to identify those that could be run without such a device." See National Fire Protection Association, *Technical Committee Reports: 1986 Fall Meeting* (Quincy, Mass.: NFPA, 1986), "Report of Committee on Dust Explosion Hazards," Part I, Comment 61B-27-(5-1.9) (Log #71), 9.

27. Cheryl Cook, "AGRI Damages Called Unfair," *Council Bluffs Nonpareil*, May 29, 1985, 1.

28. Major explosions occur only when there is fuel to spread the explosion.

A specific requirement of almost any level of stringency would, in all likelihood, form the basis for liability in those cases in which the fuel, for whatever reason, was ignited.

29. NFPA 61B-1980, sec. 5-5.2, p. 16. This language was adopted at the July 1985 committee meeting after a proposal to add the italicized language in the following provision: "All bearings shall be properly maintained *as prescribed by the bearing manufacturer and/or the lubricating instructions*" (see attachment to Memorandum from Max Spencer to NFPA 61B Committee Members, June 20, 1985). The Cargill representative objected to "the bearing manufacturer dictating to the operator." "Put the responsibility on the person who owns it," he argued, "and he will maintain it well if he is running a good shop." The committee did not adopt the proposed change.

30. For example, one commenter suggested a new paragraph "with stronger wording which clarifies that this is an advisory guide not an industry standard." NFPA, *Technical Committee Reports: 1986 Fall Meeting,* "Report of Committee on Dust Explosion Hazards," Part I, Comment 61B-1-(1-1) (Log #4), 6. For a sample of similar proposals, see ibid., Comment 61B-4-(1-1.4 New) (Log #5) and Comment 61B-9-(1-2.4 New) (Log #12).

31. For example, compare NFPA 61B-1973, sec. 3011, p. 10 (explosion venting will "minimize damage to the building or equipment and injury to personnel"), with NFPA 61B-1980, sec. 4-1, p. 13 (explosion venting "so that structural or mechanical damage is minimized.)

32. See NFPA 61B-1959, introduction, sec. 1, p. 1.; NFPA 61B-1973, sec. 701, p. 19.

33. NFPA 61B-1980, sec. 2-2, p. 9, and sec. A-2-2, p. 36.

34. See, for example, *Secretary of Labor v. Cargill Inc.* (Conrad, Montana), 8 O.S.H.C. 1745, 1747 (1980) (appendix sections concerning tramp metal detectors "wholly advisory" rather than mandatory, and private advisory standard cannot form the basis of a violation).

35. Interbin vents reduce the danger of explosive dust clouds forming and igniting during bin loading. They are much cheaper, but less efficient, than attacking the problem through dust collection. The concern, particularly among insurance representatives on the committee, is that interbin vents can help spread a fire or explosion. Basically, punching holes in walls, for whatever reason, violates fundamental principles of fire protection. There are very few bin fires, however. The primary hazard in grain elevators is explosions, and experience indicates that explosions will get through a concrete wall with or without a vent. But the likelihood of explosion may actually be decreased by use of such vents. See NFPA 61B-1980, sec. 3-2.2, p. 12.

36. Dust explosions are so powerful that it is difficult, some say impossible, to use venting successfully in most facilities. Ongoing studies of explosion venting funded by the NGFA were slowed down when an experimental silo was unexpectedly destroyed in an explosion. Comments about the practicality of venting a silo roof in accordance with 61B are raised periodically by those arguing that in many designs the roof is too small to provide an adequate vent. "The roof vent [in most cases] will be about as effective as a rifle with a cardboard barrel," notes an NAS panelist. The committee does not take issue

with these arguments. It retains the requirements as an "ideal" that admittedly will not be effective in all circumstances. For an example of criticisms of the venting requirements, along with the official committee response, see NFPA, *"Technical Committee Reports: 1986 Fall Meeting,"* Report of Committee on Dust Explosion Hazards," Part I, Comment 61B-22-(4-2) (Log #28), 8.

37. NFPA, National Electric Code (ANSI/NFPA-70), Article 500.

38. Division 2 is supposed to represent conditions where there are not explosive concentrations of dust in the air but where there could be dangerous accumulations of static dust in electrical equipment. This makes sense for machinery operating in the most active parts of the elevator. "It makes no sense," notes an insurance representative, "for equipment on the third floor of an elevator head house."

39. NFPA 61B-1980, sec. 5-1.9, p. 14; sec. 5-2.2, p. 15; sec. 5-6.4, p. 16.

40. For an analysis of this provision, see Donald L. Morgan and Mark N. Duvall, "OSHA's General Duty Clause: An Analysis of Its Use and Abuse," *Industrial Relations Law Journal* 5 (Spring 1983): 283–321.

41. See, generally, National Academy of Sciences, National Material Advisory Board, *The Investigation of Grain Elevator Explosions,* NMAB 367-1 (Washington, D.C.: National Academic Press, 1980).

42. *Federal Register* 45 (February 15, 1980): 10732 (request for comments and information and notice of informal public meetings).

43. NAS, *Prevention of Grain Elevator Explosions,* 40. The panel also noted that collecting information about actual explosions "is difficult because of legal constraints" (35).

44. Ibid., 9.

45. U.S. House, Agriculture Subcommittee on Wheat, Soybeans, and Feed Grains, *Review of Grain Elevator Safety,* July 21, 1982 (Washington, D.C.: Government Printing Office, 1982.)

46. It included provisions for (1) emergency action plans, (2) employee training, (3) permit systems for hot work, (4) procedures for bin entry, (5) briefing of contractors, (6) housekeeping, (7) grate openings, (8) filter collection specifications, (9) bulk grain driers, (10) grain stream processing equipment, (11) emergency escape requirements, (12) preventative maintenance, (13) inside bucket elevator design, and (14) partially inside bucket elevator design.

47. Proponents and critics alike agreed that the housekeeping provision accounted for 70–75 percent of the initial cost of the rule and upward of 95 percent of the recurring costs.

48. NAS, *Prevention of Grain Elevator Explosions,* Appendix D: "Report of the Subpanel on Recommended Standards and Regulations," p. 130.

49. "False Sense of Security for Workers Should Not Be Created by Rule, OSHA Told," O.S.H. Rep. (BNA) (March 29, 1984), p. 1170.

50. National Grain and Feed Association, Petition for a Partial Stay of the Grain Handling Facilities Standard, *In the Matter of Grain Handling Facilities Standard,* March 14, 1988, 2.

51. For example, most industrywide estimates were based on a nonrandom survey of seventeen facilities. And the analysis of pneumatic dust control, according to a grain elevator insurer, was "uninformed and inaccurate."

52. Estimating the cost of the "grate opening" requirement, for example, depended on assumptions about (1) the number of facilities that currently have either pit magnets or perpendicular grate bars with appropriate spacing, (2) the percentage of those not in compliance that would choose magnets instead of grates, (3) the average product, installation, and maintenance costs for magnet systems, and (4) similar estimates for constructing metal overgrates.

53. On the grate opening requirement, for example, the OSHA study assumed that most facilities would add low-cost overgrates. The NGFA figured that most operators would add more expensive magnets.

54. For example, Booz, Allen estimated the total area of country elevators that would have to be swept or vacuumed at 49.4 million square feet. Industry estimated 77.5 million. Since there are not even reliable figures on the exact number of country elevators, both estimates are within a reasonable margin of error given existing data.

55. OSHA estimated that 10 percent of existing facilities already complied with the housekeeping requirements. The figure may be higher. Most of those familar with the industry agree that Cargill, for example, maintains comparatively safe facilities. The estimates offered by industry seem unrealistically gloomy in predicting that no facilities are in compliance.

56. Booz, Allen & Hamilton, Inc., "Some Impacts of a Proposed OSHA Standard on Grain Handling Facilities" (Report prepared for Office of Regulatory Analysis, OSHA, April 1984), II-4–II-35.

57. OMB estimated, for example, that country elevators and small feed mills cause 18.3 percent of the fatalities but would account for 53.1 percent of the compliance costs. See Office of Management and Budget, "OSHA's Proposed Standard for Grain Handling Facilities: April 1984," table 2, p. 27. This thirty-nine-page critique was enclosed with a letter to Francis Lilly, solicitor, Department of Labor, from Christopher DeMuth, OMB administrator for information and regulatory affairs, April 11, 1985.

58. *Federal Register* 49 (January 6, 1984): 996. The alternatives added by OMB are puzzling. They certainly did not add flexibility to the standard. The housekeeping requirements were already stated in performance terms that allowed sweeping, pneumatic dust control, or any other effective method. The "once per shift" proposal, as industry representatives privately admitted, meant almost nothing. All facilities do some sort of housekeeping once per shift. "The language here is so vague that you could sweep with a rake for five minutes and be in compliance," argued an AFL-CIO lobbyist. The pneumatic dust-control alternative was equally puzzling, as nobody argued seriously that all facilities should be required to install such equipment.

59. These "worksheets," intended to demonstrate the high cost of the standard, provided simple formulas with which operators could calculate their own compliance costs and send the results to their congressman.

60. U.S. Senate, Subcommittee on Labor of the Committee on Labor and Human Resources, *Hearing* (S. Hrg. 98-946) (Yukon, Okla., July 13, 1984, testimony of Joe Hampton, executive vice president, Oklahoma Grain and Feed Association), 20.

61. Joann S. Lublin, "Grain-Elevator Rule Forges Unusual Link as AFL-CIO Backs Labor Agency's Plan," *Wall Street Journal,* August 24, 1983, 50.

62. *Federal Register* 52 (December 31, 1987): 49592. For a report on Senator Harkin's efforts, see O.S.H. Rep. (BNA) (December 2, 1987), p. 999.

63. These areas are (1) floor areas within thirty-five feet of inside bucket elevators, (2) floors of enclosed areas containing grinding equipment, and (3) floors of enclosed areas containing grinding equipment. The standard is not limited to these areas, however. "Priority housekeeping shall include *at least* [these three areas]" (29 CFR 1910.272 [i] [A]; emphasis in original).

64. 29 CFR 1910.272 (p) (7).

65. *Federal Register* 52 (December 31, 1987): 49598.

66. Ibid.

67. Editorial, *Feedstuffs,* April 4, 1988.

68. *National Grain and Feed Association v. OSHA,* 858 F.2d 1019 (5th Cir. 1988). The court expressed "no opinion as to whether the agency underestimated the compliance costs of its standard" but agreed with industry challenges that the record was inadequate. Approximately one year later, OSHA "redetermined" that the one-eighth-inch action level is feasible, promulgating the "final rule" again with a "supplemental statement of reasons" (*Federal Register* 54 [December 4, 1989]: 49971).

69. Informal OSHA hearing, *In the Matter of Grain Handling* (Washington, D.C., June 14, 1984, transcript), 696.

CHAPTER FOUR

1. The analysis in this chapter is restricted to commercial airliners. The FAA regulates small commuter airlines and private aircraft separately.

2. A few major airlines have safety departments. Several of these airlines conduct occasional safety tests and participate in the development of some nongovernment safety standards. But most airlines do not do any of these things. The explanation of these differences is an important question for future research.

3. Federal Aviation Administration, Federal Aviation Regulation (F.A.R.) 121.309(c). See, generally, 14 C.F.R., part 121.

4. FAA, "Hand Fire Extinguishers in Transport Category Airplanes and Rotorcraft," Advisory Circular 20-42, September 1, 1965.

5. National Transportation Safety Board, Recommendation A-73-067 (closed on May 3, 1979, following "acceptable action" by the FAA).

6. FAA response (May 2, 1974) to NTSB recommendation A-73-067.

7. FAA, Advisory Circular 20-42A, July 29, 1980.

8. FAA, General Notice 8000.212, November 29, 1980.

9. Letter from W. B. Durlin, vice president, engineering and quality control, Frontier Airlines, to Sheldon King, FAA air carrier maintenance inspector, Aurora, Colo., December 16, 1983. Obtained through Freedom of Information request for correspondence concerning compliance with FAA General Notice 8000.212.

10. Boeing apparently concluded that Halon 1211 worked better than wa-

ter extinguishers in all simulated fire tests but a large newspaper fire. The company did not officially release the results of its tests, but an unofficial account appears in L. M. Krasner, Factory Mutual Research Corporation, *Study of Hand-Held Fire Extinguishers Aboard Civil Aviation Aircraft,* DOT/ FAA/Ct-82/42 (Springfield, Va.: National Technical Information Service, 1982), 20.

11. Hal Quinn, "A Burning Nightmare at 31,000 Feet," *MacLean's,* June 13, 1983, p. 19.

12. The NSTB is an independent agency charged with investigating transportation accidents and recommending regulatory changes. Its reports are often highly influential. NFPA, in cooperation with the U.S. Fire Administration and the National Bureau of Standards, investigates major fires of all sorts for the purpose of improving private standards.

13. See, generally, Thomas J. Klem, National Fire Protection Association, "Investigation Report: Air Canada DC-9 Aircraft Fire, Greater Cincinnati Airport, June 2, 1983" (photocopy, n.d.).

14. National Transportation Safety Board, Recommendations A-83-71 (thermal discharge extinguishers for lavatories) and A-83-72 (Halon extinguishant), forwarded to J. Lynn Helms, administrator, Federal Aviation Administration, October 31, 1983.

15. The three committees were the House Subcommittee on Transportation, Aviation, and Materials; the House Subcommittee on Investigations and Oversight of the Public Works and Transportation Committee; and the Senate Labor and Human Resources Committee.

16. U.S. House, Committee on Public Works and Transportation, *Legislation to Improve Airline Safety,* Hearings, July 26, August 1–2, 1984 (98-59) (Washington, D.C.: Government Printing Office, 1984), 161.

17. See, for example, H.R. 3264, 98th Cong., 2d sess. (requiring smoke detectors); H.R. 3793, 98th Cong., 2d sess. (requiring a "comprehensive, manually operated fire extinguishing system"); H.R. 5518, 98th Cong., 2d sess. (requiring high-buoyancy life vests).

18. U.S. House, Committee on Public Works and Transportation, *Legislation to Improve Airline Safety,* 2 (Congressman Mineta).

19. James Ott, "Smoke Detectors Start Conflict," *Aviation Week and Space Technology,* September 24, 1984.

20. The first digit in the number represents the number of carbon atoms in the compound molecule; the second digit, the number of flourine atoms; the third digit, the number of chlorine atoms; and the fourth digit, the number of bromine atoms.

21. To qualify for a Class A rating from UL, it is necessary to meet minimum performance criteria on an excelsior fire, a wood crib fire, and a wood panel fire. The excelsior fire test, for example, involves six pounds of fuel distributed over a $2'10'' \times 5'8''$ test area. The wood crib test involves extinguishment of a crib composed of fifty wood members arranged in ten layers of five members each. Specific details for test construction, arrangement, ignition, and fire attack strategy are contained in UL 711.

22. Charles Perrow disagrees, arguing that "we simply do a lot of driving

and very little flying, giving us the impression that the risk of the latter is much smaller. In terms of exposure (fatalities per hour) they may be very similar" (*Normal Accidents: Living with High-Risk Technologies* [New York: Basic Books, 1984], 126). While Perrow is correct that comparing absolute numbers of fatalities may be misleading, he is wrong in attempting to remedy the problem by comparing the number of fatalities per hour. That measure would make sense only if airplanes and automobiles traveled equally fast. An hour of "exposure" to airplane travel is not commensurate in any meaningful sense with an hour of car travel. An hour of airplane travel should be compared with the "exposure" necessary to accomplish the same distance in a car, since that is the choice faced by an individual. Under this measure, commercial airplane travel would have to be considered at least five times safer than car travel.

23. Robert J. Johansen, "Using Statistics in Aviation Underwriting," *Best's Review (Prop/Casualty)*, February 1982, 42.

24. U.S. House, Committee on Public Works and Transportation, *Legislation to Improve Airline Safety*, 58.

25. See, for example, Executive Order 12291, February 17, 1981.

26. For an explanation of the $350,000 value placed on a statistical traveler's life, see FAA, Office of Aviation Policy, *Economic Values for Evaluation of Federal Aviation Administration Investment and Regulatory Programs* (Springfield, Va.: National Technical Information Service, 1981), 12–27.

27. *Federal Register* 49 (May 17, 1984): 21010 21015 (notice of proposed rulemaking).

28. A phenomenon is characterized by a Poisson distribution if the average number of events during a given time period can be estimated from past experience. Further, if the time period is subdivided into much smaller intervals, the probability that an event will occur in such a small interval is extremely low and remains constant for every small interval, and the probability that two or more events can occur within such a small interval is so low that it can be assigned a probability of zero. Finally, the occurrence of an event within any small interval is independent of the occurrence of events in other small intervals and is also independent of when that small interval occurs within the larger time period.

29. Thomas Hopkins, "Economics of Safety" (Paper presented to the Flight Safety Foundation Conference on Cabin Safety, Washington, D.C., December 13, 1984), 154.

30. The error has been corrected in subsequent FAA analyses.

31. The Federal Aviation Regulation on Training States that each crew member must "operate" an extinguisher in training exercises during initial training and every twenty-four months thereafter. According to a report commissioned by the FAA: "Actual practice among the carriers varies broadly from brief discharge of agent on a makeshift fire to passing empty extinguishers around with individuals operating the discharge assembly" (Krasner, "Study of Hand-held Fire Extinguishers Aboard Civil Aviation Aircraft," 44).

32. H. M. Hollingsworth, U.S. Coast Guard Research and Development Center, *Obstructed Fire Tests on Hand-held Fire Extinguishers for Recreational Boats*, CG-D-133-75 (Springfield, Va.: National Technical Information Service, 1975).

33. The FAA employees do not both officially "represent" the FAA. NFPA, concerned about the "balance" of its committees, resisted the idea of having two FAA representatives on one committee. Through a compromise, an employee of the Airports Division participates as an individual, not as a representative of the FAA. He attends not so much to influence NFPA standards as to gain technical information and contacts helpful in his job at the FAA.

34. One representative was from the FAA's Research Facility. His primary interest was in the arcane dispute (described later) about various Halon extinguishing agents. The other was, as noted, from the Airports Division. He considered NFPA 408 entirely outside his area. "I am only concerned with fire extinguishers if they are inside an airport facility," he explained.

35. There are seventeen other NFPA aviation safety standards covering such items as aircraft hangars, airport terminals, loading walkways, and aircraft engine-testing facilities.

36. National Fire Protection Association, *Aircraft Hand Fire Extinguishers,* NFPA 408-1956 (Boston: NFPA, 1956), sec. 110 (scope), p. 6 (the various versions of this document are hereafter referred to as NFPA 408, followed by the year of publication).

37. The same engineer describes an intensive battle in the mid 1970s to get Boeing to consider supplying aircraft with Halon fire extinguishers. "For years Boeing was married to dry chemical," so it was not until the airline presented its own test data on the effectiveness of Halon that they made headway with Boeing.

38. An amendment to the 1970 version provided an exception to the general rule that extinguishers shall be carbon monoxide or water: "Extinguishers utilizing halogonated extinguishing agents classified by the Underwriter's Laboratories, Inc., as falling in UL Toxicity Group 5 or 6 may be substituted for the carbon dioxide extinguishers if it can be shown that there is sufficient free-air volume within the aircraft cabin space to avoid producing serious irritating effects on the occupants" (NFPA 408-1973, sec. 312, p. 5).

39. Sale of publications (primarily standards) accounted for almost $14 million in 1984, close to two-thirds of NFPA's income (NFPA Balance Sheet, *Fire Journal,* May 1985, 82).

40. NFPA 408-1980, sec. 3-1.3, p. 7.

41. Ibid., sec. A-2-3-4.1, p. 10.

42. For example, as discussed in chapter 4, if NFPA allows only metal chimneys passing the 2100° F fire test, UL will have to change its standard accordingly.

43. See, generally, Underwriters Laboratories, *UL 711: Standard for Rating and Testing Fire Extinguishers,* 3d ed. (approved as ANSU/UL 711-1979) (Northbrook, Ill.: Underwriters Laboratories, 1983). This standard sets forth performance requirements for the four classes now used universally in labeling fire extinguishers: Class A (wood, cloth, paper), Class B (flammable liquids), Class C (electrical equipment), and Class D (combustible metals). Extinguishers are rated by class and capacity. For aviation purposes, for example, NFPA 408

calls for a 5:BC rating, meaning a five-gallon extinguisher capable of extinguishing a UL Class B and Class C fire.

44. NFPA 408-1980, sec. A-5-3.3.

45. National Fire Protection Association, *Technical Committee Documentation: 1984 Annual Meeting* (Quincy, Mass.: NFPA, 1984), Comments 408-8-(2-3.3.1 [New]), 408-9-(2-3.6), and 408-10-(table 3-1.1), p. 5.

46. See, generally, Yair Aharoni, *The No-Risk Society* (Chatham, N.J.: Chatham House, 1981).

47. "Statement by Congressman Norman Y. Mineta," in *Proceedings of Cabin Safety Conference and Workshop: December 11–14, 1984*, DOT/FAA/ASF100-85/01 (Springfield, Va.: National Technical Information Service, 1985), 9.

CHAPTER FIVE

1. Schwartz, "The Consumer Product Safety Commission," 32, 71–73.

2. *Sunset Homeowner's Guide to Wood Stoves* (Menlo Park, Calif.: Lane Publishing, 1979), 5.

3. The Epidemiology Directorate of the CPSC estimates the following losses due to residential solid-fuel heating equipment:

	Fires	Deaths	Property Loss ($ millions)
1978	66,800	290	132.7
1979	70,700	210	177.7
1980	112,000	350	245.4
1981	130,100	290	264.8
1982	139,800	250	257.7
1983	140,000	280	295.7

Consumer Product Safety Commission, "FY 1984 Wood and Coal Heating Equipment Report" (transmitted to the Commission by cover memorandum from the Office of Program Management on April 4, 1985), 15.

4. For an example of the criticisms lodged against the CPSC's hospital survey information, see Edward Heiden, Allan Pittaway, and Rosalind O'Connor, "Utility of the U.S. Consumer Product Safety Commission's Injury Data System as a Basis for Product Hazard Assessment," *Journal of Products Liability Law* 5 (1982): 295.

5. A trade association representative complains that "there is a big thick volume on how to fill out the NFIRS reports but most of that stuff is ignored and there is a pattern of common answers." He reports that firemen have told members of the trade association that "design deficiency" is "just a buzzword we use" to categorize fires of unknown origin.

6. Richard D. Peacock, Center for Fire Research, National Bureau of Standards, *A Review of Fire Incidents, Model Building Codes, and Standards Re-*

lating to Wood-Burning Appliances, NBSIR 79-1731 (Springfield, Va.: National Technical Information Service, 1979), 5–6.

7. A study for the Department of Energy concluded that 10 percent of woodstove fires are attributable to "improper equipment design" and another 4.3 percent to "equipment malfunction." A Massachusetts study, attributed no more than 2 percent of woodstove fires to "defective or unsafe" appliances. The difference is partly definitional. Scenarios that were considered the users' fault in one study were considered design errors in another.

8. *Underwriters Laboratories v. Commissioner of Internal Revenue,* 135 F.2d 371, 373 (10th Cir. 1943).

9. Underwriters Laboratories, *1984 Annual Report* (n.p., 1985), 1, 9, 18.

10. Underwriters Laboratories, *UL 1482: Safety Standard for Room Heaters, Solid-Fuel Type,* 2d ed. (Northbrook, Ill.: UL, 1983), sect. 5.2, table 5.1, p. 8 (hereafter referred to as UL 1482).

11. Ibid., sec. 17.20, p. 35.

12. Ibid., sec. 6.7, p. 10.

13. The secrecy UL is famous for serves several purposes: it assures manufacturers with trade secrets that they will not be revealed through the product certification process; it facilitates discussion of matters that might involve product liability suits; and it hinders outside review and potential embarrassment.

14. Similarly, the proposed standard stated that the test structure should be "reasonably free of drafts." The revised version specifies that it is "to be erected within a room having ventilation capable of maintaining the buildup of carbon monoxide to less than 100 parts per million throughout the period of any test." Other revisions added flexibility to the standard, again with no obvious implications for safety. The original proposal specified the use of Type J (iron-constantan) thermocouples—the thermoelectric device for measuring temperature differences. The revised version allows Type K (chromel-alumel) as well.

15. For example, the January 1978 proposal included primarily installation instructions, with few operating instructions. The installation instructions did not provide details about floor protection or chimney connectors. There was no reference to creosote buildup and no caution about storage or use of flammable liquids. Underwriters Laboratories, "Report of Meeting of Underwriters Laboratories Industry Advisory Conference for Fireplaces, Fireplace Stoves and Solid Fuel Type Room Heaters and PROPOSED EFFECTIVE DATES" (Memorandum to the Fire Council, manufacturers, and others interested, January 18, 1979; capitalization in original), appendix B, B2–B5.

16. UL of Canada is unrelated to the UL in this country. There are apparently myriad differences between ULC and UL standards. Whether they reflect differences in testing philosophy or, as a UL spokesman claims, ULC's desire to protect its own turf is a topic for future research.

17. Underwriters Laboratories, "Proposed Revisions to Proposed First Edition of the Standard for Solid Fuel Type Room Heaters, UL 1482 and PROPOSED EFFECTIVE DATE" (Memorandum to the Fire Council, manufacturers, and others interested, April 25, 1979; capitalization in original), 1–3.

18. The same is true of NFPA. In both instances, ANSI "approval" is routine, and neither UL nor NFPA would be likely to change its standards were it

necessary for ANSI approval. One major standards-writer, the American Society for Testing and Materials, stopped sending its standards through ANSI several years ago.

19. See, generally, American National Standards Institute, "Procedure for the Development and Coordination of American National Standards (Approved by the ANSI Board of Directors, March 30, 1983)" (typescript, 1983). The procedures for canvass by an accredited sponsor basically involve: (1) developing a list of all interests known to be directly and materially affected by the standard, (2) having ANSI review the list and solicit other interested parties to join the proceeding, (3) transmitting the standard along with a brief history of how it was developed to those on the list, (4) attempting to resolve any objections by those canvassed, and (5) reporting the results to ANSI. Those opposed to the canvass method, including some current members of the ANSI Board of Directors, object that it is a "review process," not a method of *developing* standards, so, it is argued, the participants play a much less significant role.

20. Irwin Benjamin, Fire Safety Division, National Bureau of Standards, argued in a letter of June 27, 1979, to UL (on file in the Standards Department at UL headquarters in Northbrook, Illinois) that the proposed standard "does not include any provisions covering a room heater's tendency toward creosoting." Similar arguments were advanced by John Shultz in one of three letters from an NFPA technical committee.

21. C. P. Ramani, of the Open Forum of the ICBO, objected by letter of August 7, 1979, to testing stoves without a grate so long as the manufacturer instructs the consumer accordingly: "We believe that if a conventional grate could be placed in a heater, then it should be tested with one. Use of a cautionary label alone will not insure safe use of the product." Rober Nelson, ASHRAE, objected by letter of June 2, 1979, that "the extent of testing by impact is unreasonable. Six different blows will increase the cost of glass without providing a safer product."

22. On file in the Standards Department at UL headquarters in Northbrook, Illinois.

23. One of the most outspoken critics of UL's "desk standards" is the author of a newsletter called *TMO Update: National and International Developments Concerning Product Certification, Laboratory Accreditation, and Standardization.* See, for example, "NEMA and OSHA and Those UL Desk Standards," *TMO Update* 9, no. 14 (August 15, 1984). For a reply by UL's president, see Jack Bono, "The Role of UL Standards—Published and Unpublished," *Standards Engineering,* March/April 1985, 46–47.

24. Underwriters Laboratories, "Proposed Revisions to Proposed First Edition of UL 1482," 2.

25. See for example, David Hemenway, *Performance vs. Design Standards,* NBS/GCR 80-287 (Springfield, Va.: National Technical Information Service, 1980).

26. UL 1482, sec. 16.2, p. 31.

27. See, for example, ibid., foreword, sec. A, p. 4.

28. Ibid., sec. 15.1, p. 30.

29. For a discussion of these standards (UL 1409 and UL 1410), see Al Gengler, "The UL Investigation of Portable Video Recording Systems," *[UL] Lab Data* 16, no. 1 (1985): 11–15.

30. UL 1482, sec. 11.8, p. 25; sec. 12.10, p. 27; sec. 14.7, p. 29.

31. An internal memorandum dated September 6, 1979, from C. E. Layman, an associate engineer at UL's Santa Clara, California, office (and on file at the Standards Department at UL headquarters in Northbrook, Illinois), states, "We are unable to comment at this time on the 90 and 117F temperature rise."

32. See note 21 above.

33. "Return of the Wood Stove," *Consumer Reports* 46, no. 10 (October 1981): 566, 572.

34. A round-robin study by NBS found "real systematic differences" when different labs used UL 1482 to test the same model stove. In one case, the measured temperature in the same test on the same model stove was 430° F at one lab and 809° F at another. These differences were most likely due to allowable variations in test methods (e.g., moisture content of the wood, air circulation in the test structure). See National Voluntary Laboratory Accreditation Program, National Bureau of Standards, "NVLAP Proficiency Testing, Stove LAP: Round 1" (NVLAP Tech Brief, February 1983), table 1 (and cf. Lab C and Lab D on "center rear stove" measurements for the radiant fire test).

35. For example, UL 1482 leaves considerable latitude to the testing labs in determining the moisture content of the wood and the amount of air circulation in the test structure—two factors that directly affect performance. A small stove manufacturer, who cannot afford to send an engineer to the testing laboratory for a few days, complains that some decisions are influenced by whether the manufacturer has an engineer present during the tests. "You practically need a lobbyist," as he puts it, "or you take the standard as it is." Interviews with manufacturers at a trade show at which most items were certified by either UL or Factory Mutual support the contention that lab technicians occasionally change their interpretations of test procedures to placate an irritated (and often better educated) engineering representative. The waiting room at UL headquarters in Northbrook frequently houses industry representatives seeking through UL's informal appeals process to receive a more favorable interpretation than they received from the technician. Many are apparently successful.

36. The fireplace insert standard is controversial because the safety of the product depends directly on the type of masonry chimney (specifically, the number and location of wooden headers). Not only is there considerable variance in existing chimneys, but most do not comply with the code requirements normally used in product testing—NFPA's. Metal chimneys are controversial because UL, in a very unusual tactic, certifies them to two different standards: UL 103 and UL 103HT. The HT standard requires a higher tolerance than UL 103, one high enough to withstand the damage from a typical chimney fire. The CPSC and many others believe that UL 103 should adopt the HT requirements.

37. A small manufacturer complained that "UL lost its credibility when it certified [an inexpensive brand imported from Taiwan]." No one else interviewed in connection with this study, however, including safety advocates at the

National Bureau of Standards and in the consulting business, agreed with the assertion that this particular brand is a threat to anything but competition.

38. In a letter seeking financial support for a research project to improve various aspects of UL 1482, noted woodstove expert Jay Shelton argued: "In addition to lacking a measure of creosote, UL 1482 may have features which indirectly increase creosote accumulation. Specifically, the temperature limits for flue gas are sometimes difficult to pass. A common design modification is to use an air inlet stop to limit the maximum amount of combustion air which can enter the combustion chamber. The reduced amount of combustion air can increase creosote accumulation" (Letter from Shelton Energy Research to, among others, the National Bureau of Standards, the Society of Fire Protection Engineers, and the Wood Heating Alliance, dated November 13, 1984, p. 2).

39. NVLAP, "NVLAP Proficiency Testing for Stoves: Rounds 1 and 2."

40. 15 U.S.C. sec. 2056 (d) (1976) (repealed 1981). For a detailed discussion of the offeror process, see Schwartz, "The Consumer Product Safety Commission," 32, 57–72.

41. Peacock, *A Review of Fire Incidents*, 15.

42. Statement of Irwin Grief, Office of Program Management, Consumer Product Safety Commission, in Public Hearing before the Consumer Product Safety Commission, Washington, D.C., March 14, 1979.

43. The three trade associations were GAMA (the Gas Appliance Manufacturers Association), the Fireplace Institute, and the Wood Energy Institute. GAMA had been in the business the longest, but only as a sidelight to its main activities and a courtesy to gas appliance manufacturers who also made woodstoves. The other associations were new and between them had a small portion of the market. In 1982 an agreement was reached forming the Wood Heating Alliance in place of these uncoordinated efforts.

44. For a discussion of the lawn mower proceedings, see Schwartz, "The Consumer Product Safety Commission," 77–95 (Appendix A: "A Case Study— The Lawn-Mower Standard"). See also W. Kip Viscusi, *Regulating Consumer Product Safety* (Washington, D.C.: American Enterprise Institute, 1984), 93– 96. For a discussion of the chain saw proceedings, see Elaine Thomas, C. E. Benton, and Werne L. Roberts, *Safe Chain Saw Design* (Durham, N.C.: Institute for Product Safety, 1983).

45. "Briefing Paper on Proposed CPSC 27(e) Labeling Rule for Coal and Wood Burning Appliances" (Office of Program Management, CPSC, September 1980), 3.

46. Beatrice Harwood and Paul Kluge, "Hazards Associated with the Use of Wood or Coal-Burning Stoves or Free-Standing Fireplaces" (Directorate for Hazard Identification and Analysis, CPSC, February 1980), table 1, p. 11.

47. For example, the assumption that all firms would select the lowest-cost testing laboratory. The staff also assumed that increases in the price of woodstoves would not affect industrywide sales. See T. R. Karels, CPSC, memorandum of March 27, 1981, on Coal and Wood Stove Label Rule, p. 2 (located at Tab E of May 1981 briefing package to the commission).

48. T. R. Karels, Division of Special Economic Studies, CPSC, "Coal and

Woodburning Stoves, Section 27(e) Labeling Rule: Preliminary Economic Impact Analysis," February 1980, 4.

49. *Federal Register* 48 (May 16, 1983): 21898, 21912 (final rule).

50. Robert S. Adler and R. David Pittle, "Cajolery or Command: Are Education Campaigns an Adequate Substitute for Regulation?" *Yale Journal on Regulation* 1, no. 2 (1984): 159–93.

51. See note 3 above.

52. Stephen E. Taub, technical division chief, Consumers Union, letter of December 19, 1980 to the CPSC (Comment #CC9-80-27).

53. Eleanor Perry, CPSC, "Provisions for Labeling and Instruction Manuals in the Underwriters Laboratories Standards for Fireplace Stoves (UL737) and Solid Fuel Room Heaters (UL1482)" (Memorandum to Margaret Neily, program representative, for James Hoebel, Fire and Thermal Burn Program manager, May 25, 1982).

54. *Federal Register* 47 (April 6, 1982): 14711 (deferral of consideration of final rule).

55. Elizabeth Gomilla and Eileen Keisler, CPSC, "Report on the Coal and Woodburning Stove Survey Conducted in February 1982" (n.d.; transmitted to the Office of Program Management by memorandum of July 14, 1982).

56. Only the CPSC, for example, requires information about venting through a wall or ceiling.

57. Eleanor Perry, CPSC, "Provisions for Labeling and Instruction Manuals," 2.

58. The Enforcement Directorate reported in 1985 that 31 percent of the three hundred firms responding to the CPSC's request for information were "clearly in violation of the rule." Another 29 percent had "relatively minor violations." If the incidence of violations is larger among those not responding to the CPSC, it is likely that at least 40 or 50 percent of all firms are "clearly in violation." See CPSC, "FY 1984 Wood and Coal Heating Equipment Report," 77.

59. *Aqua Slide 'n' Dive v. Consumer Product Safety Commission,* 569 F.2d 831 (5th Cir. 1978).

60. 16 C.F.R. sec. 1406.4(a)(1) ("The appliance shall bear a legible notice containing the following performance and technical data"); 16 C.F.R. sec. 1406.4(a)(3) ("the written information required . . . shall be readily visible during normal use"); 16 C.F.R. sec. 1406.4(b)(1) ("This statement shall be conspicuous").

61. CPSC, "FY 1984 Wood and Coal Heating Equipment Report," 78.

CHAPTER SIX

1. See, generally, Consumer Product Safety Commission, Directorate for Hazard Identification and Analysis, "Unvented Gas Space Heaters: HIA Hazard Analysis Report," July 1978.

2. The amount of ventilation depends on the size of the heater and the rate of air infiltration. With a 40,000 BTU heater, for example, the largest allowed

under Z21.11.2, a standard-sized window should be opened at least two inches to ensure sufficient ventilation.

3. See, for example, "Minutes of Meeting of Subcommittee on Standards for Unvented Gas-fired Space Heating Appliances" (Cleveland, November 10–11, 1970), item 6, p. 6 (cases involving clothing ignition cited in letter forwarded by the secretary of commerce); "Minutes of Meeting of Subcommittee on Approval Requirements for Unvented Gas-fired Heating Appliances" (Cleveland, September 11–12, 1962), item 5, p. 19 (newspaper clipping sent by NFPA about fire incident involving an open-front room heater).

4. The CPSC list, now in general disrepute, purported to combine the frequency and severity of reported injuries into a single index. A major criticism, aside from problems with the quality of the data collection, was the failure to factor out injuries that could not possibly be reduced through regulation. Stairs, for example, topped the list for many years. Five of the next seven products were sports-related.

5. CPSC, "Unvented Gas Space Heaters: HIA Hazard Analysis Report," p. 12.

6. The most likely explanation is that between 1974 and 1975 the CPSC received seventy death certificates "attributed to carbon monoxide emissions from gas space heaters," but these covered an eighteen-month period and did not distinguish between vented and unvented gas space heaters. Based on seven reported fatalities related to unvented heaters, the CPSC estimated a national total of fifty-six in 1977. This extrapolation is subject to the same well-known criticisms of CPSC's NEISS system.

7. Max Singer, "The Vitality of Mythical Numbers," *The Public Interest* 23 (Spring 1971). See also Peter Reuter, "The (Continued) Vitality of Mythical Numbers," *The Public Interest* 75 (Spring 1984).

8. The CABO (Conference of American Building Officials) One and Two Family Dwelling Code provides, for example, that "only unvented fuel burning heaters equipped with oxygen depletion sensors and listed in accordance with ANSI Standard 'Z21.11.1' 1978 shall be permitted."

9. UL, which began by testing electric appliances, now has six departments: Electrical; Burglary Protection and Signaling; Casualty and Chemical Hazards; Fire Protection; Heating, Air Conditioning, and Refrigeration; and Marine. A few of UL's standards cover gas appliances, overlapping directly with some of AGA's standards. This can create a serious problem if the competition is not just in price, as is the case when smaller labs offer to certify products to UL standards. In these rare instances, the laboratories "compete" on safety as well. Such competition tends to reduce safety requirements.

10. Because of the extensive review and comment procedures utilized by AGA, most standards are submitted to ANSI as "uncontested cases." For example, Z21.11.2 was approved by the Board of Standards review on October 12, 1984, without discussion.

11. American Gas Association, "Procedures for Accredited Standards Committee Z21 on Performance and Installation of Gas Burning Appliances and Related Accessories" (approved by ANSI on July 18, 1984; mimeographed, n.d.).

12. See, for example, "A Resume of the Voluntary Standards Development Procedures for Z21, Z83, and Z223 Standards" (AGA Labs, July 1981; mimeographed), 5.

13. American Gas Association, *American Standard Approval Requirements for Gas-fired Room Heaters. Volume II, Unvented Room Heaters,* 14th ed. (New York: American Gas Association, 1962), sec. 1.5.4, p. 3 (ANSI Z21.11.2-1962; UDC 644.1:696.2).

14. Ibid., sec. 1.6.3.

15. Ibid., sec. 1.7.8, p. 4.

16. Ibid., sec. 1.9.4.

17. AGA Labs, "Minutes of Meeting of Subcommittee on Approval Requirements for Unvented Gas-fired Heating Appliances" (Cleveland, December 8, 1964), item 5, p. 3.

18. AGA, *Unvented Room Heaters,* sec. 2.15, p. 15.

19. AGA Labs, "Minutes of Meeting of Subcommittee on Approval Requirements for Unvented Gas-fired Heating Appliances" (Cleveland, January 11, 1962), item 8, pp. 6–7.

20. For information about the proposal to eliminate these standards, see John Herbers, "U.S. Plans to End Nationwide Code for Construction," *New York Times,* August 18, 1985, 1.

21. Philadelphia Electric Gas System, "Unvented Room Heater and Decorative Indoor Appliance Installation Standard: Final Report" (photocopy, n.d.; attached as appendix to American Gas Association Labs, "Compilation of Comments Received on Proposed Revisions to American National Standard for Gas-fired Room Heaters, Volume II, Unvented Room Heaters," December 1975), 3.

22. American Gas Association, *American National Standard for Gas-fired Room Heaters. Volume II, Unvented Room Heaters,* 19th ed. (Cleveland: American Gas Association Laboratories, 1983), preface, p. i (ANSI Z21.11.2-1983).

23. Other examples from the case studies of the unusual interaction between installation codes and product standards include wall pass-through systems for woodstoves and flexible nozzles for aviation fire extinguishers.

24. American Gas Association Laboratories, "Compilation of Comments Received on Proposed Revisions to American National Standard for Gas-fired Room Heaters," September 1979, p. 2 (R. C. Swangler, The Peoples Natural Gas Company).

25. The severity of burn injuries is a function of both the surface temperature and the time of exposure (or the "response time" before ending the exposure). According to a report prepared for the CPSC, contact with a bare metal surface 140° hotter than room temperature will not produce a third-degree burn unless contact is maintained for at least twenty seconds. Therefore, by lowering surface temperatures, a longer response time is necessary for the same type of injury to result from contact with the heater.

26. Bond paper is nonporous and, therefore, unlikely to ignite under the old test method, even though a similar exposure might actually ignite clothing. Minutes of the subcommittee indicate that someone argued as early as 1963

that "it would be desirable to use a material of greater porosity than bond paper so that oxygen could get to the charring surface." Selecting an appropriate level of porosity for test materials is one of those seemingly "technical" decisions that has significant real-world effects and often cannot be answered scientifically. Porosity is really a correlate of safety. Bond paper, for example, lacks the porosity to reflect the hazards of clothing ignition. Cheesecloth, on the other hand, may be too porous. "The air goes right through it," argues a representative of Consumers Union. By using muslin instead of cheesecloth, CU concluded that an electric space heater approved by UL (using cheesecloth) was unsafe.

27. Z21.11.2 did not ban the model by name, but by features—that is, by requiring such features as automatic ignition.

28. *Federal Register* 40 (September 5, 1975): 4112.

29. In industry's eyes, an unvented heater must be so by design; "vented" heaters installed without venting are nevertheless "vented." The CPSC wasn't sure. Injury data often do not include reliable information on venting, causing considerable disagreements in data interpretation. In a study of 533 death certificates related to gas-fired heaters, for example, the CPSC classified 72 as unvented, 82 as vented, 64 as "judged to be unvented," and 277 as "venting condition not specified." The remaining 38 were located in campers, vans, or trailers. See CPSC, "Unvented Gas Space Heaters: HIA Hazard Analysis Report," 15. A trade association representative familiar with the CPSC "in-depth investigations" claims that many of the injuries categorized as "un-vented" heater cases actually involved vented heaters that were not properly vented.

30. One reason is the limited background and training of CPSC personnel in accident investigation. The agency has since improved its training program and increased its use of expert consultants to conduct investigations.

31. *Federal Register* 42 (September 14, 1977): 46072 (notice that it is not necessary at this time to address any hazards that may be associated with vented gas-fired space heaters); *Federal Register* 42 (February 14, 1978): 6253 (proposed ban on unvented gas-fired space heaters).

32. The unvented heater was one of sixteen products identified by the National Commission on Product Safety as warranting federal standards. Naturally, this created an impression among many in industry that the CPSC was predisposed to regulate the gas heater. See National Commission on Product Safety, *Final Report Presented to the President and Congress* (Washington, D.C.: Government Printing Office, 1970), 12–34.

33. For a detailed description of the devices, see Charles S. Lamar, "Oxygen Depletion Sensor Improves Safety of Gas-fired Heating Equipment," *Appliance Engineer* 5, no. 1 (1971): 21–28.

34. AGA Labs, "Minutes of Meeting of Subcommittee for Unvented Gas-fired Heating Appliances," Cleveland, January 20, 1972, item 6, p. 2.

35. Consumer Product Safety Commission, "Briefing Paper: Proposal to Ban Unvented Gas-fired Space Heaters" (prepared by the Fire and Thermal Burns Program Staff, CPSC, December 21, 1977), p. 3.

36. Firms are so worried about grading safety that they generally refuse to

have their gas appliances tested for efficiency—something required by other laws—at the same laboratories that test their products for safety, even though doing so would certainly be less expensive.

37. Esher Kweller, National Bureau of Standards, "Response to Request for Support: Unvented Space Heater Project" (Memorandum for Walter Leight, through Andrew Fowell, dated January 16, 1979), 2–5.

38. Letter from Esher Kweller, National Bureau of Standards, to Stanley Blachman, chief methods engineer, American Gas Association Laboratories, March 16, 1979, attachment F, an excerpt from American Conference of Government Industrial Hygienists, *Documentation of the Threshold Limit Values for Substances in Work Room Air*, 3d ed., 1971.

39. Memorandum from Leo T. Duffy, M.D., to George Anikis, Office of Program Management, CPSC, October 3, 1977.

40. Memorandum from Dr. Peter Preuss to Bert Simson, Office of Program Management, CPSC, July 3, 1979, p. 2. Concern for health effects prompted Esher Kweller of the Product Performance Engineering Division of the National Bureau of Standards to argue for a 19 percent shutoff level. (As explained earlier, a higher shutoff level for oxygen means that the heater will shut off at a lower carbon monoxide level.) See Kweller, letter to Blachman, March 16, 1979, p. 2.

41. Letter from Frank E. Hodgon, AGA senior vice president for consumer affairs and safety, to George Anikis, Office of Program Management, CPSC, July 26, 1978, p. 3.

42. American Gas Association Laboratories, "Notice to Manufacturers of Unvented Room Heaters," August 9, 1979.

43. *Federal Register* 45 (January 18, 1980): 3762 (proposed rule).

44. CPSC, "Briefing Paper: Proposal to Ban Unvented Gas-Fired Space Heaters," 3.

45. See, for example, the following discussion of labeling in the CPSC's *Federal Register* notice: "Several commenters still prefer the ANSI label wording which specifies a minimum 'fresh air opening' depending on the output size of the heater rather than the proposed label's suggestion to 'open a window an inch or two for fresh air.' . . . The Commission considers that the proposed label's wording . . . is clearer and more readily understood than the ANSI label" (*Federal Register* 45 [September 17, 1980]: 61918).

46. Petition for Exemption, in the Matter of Petition of City of Victorville, State of California, for Exemption for 15 U.S.C. 2075(a) as It Applies to Commission Safety Standards Requiring Oxygen Depletion Safety Shutoff Systems (ODS) for Unvented Space Heaters (16 CFR Part 1212), April 16, 1982, p. 4 (CPSC Application no. SH 82-12).

47. The CPSC staff disagreed about whether the standard even had preemptive effect in the first place. See "Briefing Package on Petition SH 82-1 through SH 82-23: Requesting Exemption from Preemption by the Safety Standard Requiring Oxygen Depletion Safety Shutoff Systems (ODS) for Unvented Gas-fired Space Heaters; 16 C.F.R. Part 1212" (transmitted to the commission by memorandum from Douglas Noble, Office of Program Management, January 19, 1983).

48. Letter from Joe Beck, Kilpatrick & Cody, representing Atlanta Stove Works, to Nancy Steorts, CPSC chair, April 22, 1983.

49. Dissenting Opinion of Vice Chairman Saundra Brown Armstrong, in the Matter of Revocation of the Mandatory Standard for Unvented Gas-fired Space Heaters, 16 CFR 1212.

50. In his critical examination of five CPSC regulations, W. Kip Viscusi concluded that "more than any other standard . . . the standard for unvented gas-fired space heaters may be desirable (*Regulating Consumer Product Safety,* 99).

51. The clear trend in legal decisions affecting consumer products is toward strict liability, minimizing the role of any negligence on the part of the consumer. But that depends on the product being considered unreasonably dangerous. Unless the gas space heater was considered defective for failing to have an ODS device—a line of argument that has been tried unsuccessfully with cars not equipped with airbags—then fatalities caused by carbon monoxide would not be considered the manufacturer's fault.

52. Space heaters equipped with an ODS would have to be considered "unreasonably dangerous" in order for liability to attach. Since this phrase has been stretched to include a variety of "reasonably foreseeable" mishaps and failures, however, the fear is not misplaced.

CHAPTER SEVEN

1. Charles E. Lindblom and David K. Cohen, *Usable Knowledge: Social Science and Social Problem Solving* (New Haven, Conn.: Yale University Press, 1979), 50.

2. Eugene Bardach, "Problems of Problem Definition in Policy Analysis," *Research in Public Policy Analysis and Management* 1 (1981): 161, 163.

3. UL tests kerosene heaters, for example, using certified K-1 kerosene fuel as specified in the manufacturer's instructions. Testing for "flare up" would require the addition of at least trace amounts of gasoline to the fuel.

4. Henry E. Collins, UL vice president, government relations, Hearing Before the Consumer Product Safety Commission, Washington, D.C., October 27, 1982 (transcript), 261.

5. CPSC, "Memorandum to the Commission from the Office of Program Management on Criteria for Endorsement of Publications Developed by Outside Organizations," August 22, 1984.

6. See, for example, Hemenway, *Performance vs. Design Standards.*

7. For a survey of programs utilizing "technology-forcing," see Richard B. Stewart, "Regulation, Innovation, and Administrative Law: A Conceptual Framework," *California Law Review* 69, no. 5 (September 1981): 1256, 1296–1306.

8. This example is set forth in a letter dated June 11, 1979, from R. J. Finegan, Liberty Mutual Insurance Company, to Sava Sherr, ANSI, included in a preliminary report of the ANSI Safe Work Practices Task Group, June 1985.

9. Ibid.

10. NFPA 408-1980, sec. A-5-3.3.

11. The other categories—careerists and politicians—have less application in the private sector. Other than at UL, there are few careerist standards-setters. Participants "volunteer" for standards-setting but make their careers elsewhere. At UL, professional influences are dominant among most careerists. Finally, there are few, if any, politicians, in the sense of employees "who see themselves as having a future in elective or appointive office outside the agency" (Wilson, *The Politics of Regulation*, 374–82).

12. Frederick C. Mosher, *Democracy and the Public Service* (New York: Oxford University Press, 1982), 113, 122.

13. Thomas M. Deitz and Robert W. Rycroft, *The Risk Professionals* (New York: Russell Sage Foundation, 1987).

14. Hamilton, "The Role of Nongovernmental Standards," 1350.

15. Earl F. Cheit, *The Useful Arts and the Liberal Tradition* (New York: McGraw-Hill, 1975), 57–82.

16. See, for example, Richard L. Meehan, *The Atom and the Fault: Experts, Earthquakes, and Nuclear Power* (Cambridge, Mass.: MIT Press, 1984) (geologists versus structural engineers).

17. Unlike in medicine, law, and many other professions, there is no centralized professional engineering organization. Engineering societies are organized around the special fields of engineering: civil, chemical, electrical, and nuclear, for example. Fire protection engineering is another specialty with its own professional society. Fire protection engineers also constitute a significant percentage of the NFPA membership.

18. Human factors engineering, a relatively new specialty with roots in psychology, attempts to "fit the machine to the person." In the 1950s, through applied research on human responses to various aircraft instrumentation, human factors engineers assisted the Air Force in improving the safety of airplanes. When applied to questions about motor capability, ergonomics, or human reflex, the field is well accepted. See, generally, Ernest McCormick, *Human Factors Engineering*, 2d ed. (New York: McGraw-Hill, 1955). A few engineers purport to apply this field to a broader gamut of human behavior, often in a manner that directly challenges existing notions of fault and responsibility. See, for example, R. Matthiew Seiden's discussion of "error-provocative" product designs; those that, in his words, "provoke, seduce, invite, mislead, or otherwise trap a user into making a mistake" (*Product Safety Engineering for Managers* [Englewood Cliffs, N.J.: Prentice-Hall, 1984], 114). This philosophy is widely rejected by most engineers and may account for the skeptical view many have of human factors engineering.

19. Samuel C. Florman, *The Existential Pleasures of Engineering* (New York: St. Martin's Press, 1976), 26. Florman is one of the few outspoken critics of the revolution in professional engineering ethics. He opposes the notion, now expressed in slightly different terms in several professional codes, that an engineer owes a special duty to protect public health and safety. Codes enacted at the turn of the century provided that an engineer's sole responsibility was to the employer. See also Edwin T. Layton, *Revolt of the Engineers: Social Responsibility and the Engineering Profession* (Cleveland: Case Western Reserve University Press, 1971).

20. Florman, *The Existential Pleasures of Engineering,* 26. The distinction, by no means a clear one, is suggested by Florman's discussion of the engineer's role of "creator" and "guardian." He advocates a "balance" between the two, but clearly favors erring on the side of the former.

21. In the gas space heater proceedings, for example, an NBS engineeer informed the CPSC that "there is no apparent reason why a separate ODS pilot cannot be used in addition to the current pilot (except economics)" (Esher Kweller, NBS, memorandum of January 16, 1979).

CHAPTER EIGHT

1. Leland L. Johnson, *Cost-Benefit Analysis and Voluntary Safety Standards for Consumer Products* (Santa Monica, Calif.: RAND Corporation, 1982), 32–35.

2. Unfortunately, the language of safety debates often clouds the real issues. It would be inopportune for UL to say that a significant hazard scenario is "the consumer's fault." Similarly, few people outside of the economics profession are comfortable arguing that a proposed safety measure might be effective but still not worth the cost. As a result, many arguments are cloaked in technical terms. Stated opposition to the CPSC's gas space heater standard, for example, concentrated on alleged technical problems with the oxygen depletion sensor. That none of the predicted problems have come to the attention of the Gas Appliance Manufacturers Association in the four years since this rule was adopted suggests that unvoiced concerns were probably most significant. Other arguments are cloaked under the ambiguous rubric of "a false sense of security." This argument manages to come up on both sides of many safety arguments. Opponents asserted that each of the four public sector standards in this study would lead to "a false sense of security." This is an interesting rhetorical device for arguing from a pro-safety point of view against proposed improvements in safety standards. The argument, in my view, is really directed at the philosophy (or "sense") of safety (or "security") that underlies the standard, not the perceptions that consumers might have.

3. The five-page "worksheets" provided by the NGFA to allow operators to "better understand the financial impact of the standard" included various assumptions that inflated the results. For example, under housekeeping—the most expensive category—the worksheet combined the estimated cost of pneumatic dust control and manual dust removal, even though the rule would require only one. See National Grain and Feed Association, "The OSHA Grain Handling Safety Standard: Understanding the Financial Impact on Your Operations" (mimeographed, n.d.).

4. Viscusi, *Regulating Consumer Product Safety,* 96–99.

CHAPTER NINE

1. Wilson, *The Politics of Regulation,* 374.

2. Of course, there are various degrees of self-regulation ranging from industrywide to intraorganizational. See Ian Maitland, "The Limits of Business

Self-Regulation," *California Management Review* 27, no. 3 (Spring 1985): 132–47.

3. Eads and Reuter, *Designing Safer Products*, 43.

4. This will obviously depend on, among other things, the elasticity of demand for the product and the availability of substitutes.

5. UL often points to its "Consumer Advisory Council," for example. Yet the CAC meets once every two years, and several committee members describe the group as a "public relations gimmick."

6. These organizational problems are well understood. See, for example, Olson, *The Logic of Collective Action*. Lack of interest, a much less popular explanation, also accounts for the minimal participation of various groups in private standards-setting. "You don't capture anyone's imagination with fire extinguishers," explains a lobbyist for the Association of Flight Attendants. The issue is both too specific and too technical. UL had a similar problem with television receivers, finding that some consumers lost interest in the technical discussions (see S. David Hoffman and Janis C. Farr, "Developing a Proposed CPSC Standard for Television Receivers: The UL Experience," *ASTM Standardization News*, May 1977).

7. UL developed the HT (high-tolerance) metal chimney standard largely because the Reinsurance Association of Minnesota, which reinsures most homeowner policies in the state, decided not to insure homes with woodstoves without high-tolerance metal chimneys.

8. Royal Edwards, representative of the National Chimney Sweeps Guild, convinced the Technical Committee for NFPA 211 to prohibit stoves requiring more than a thirty-six-inch clearance. A trade association representative complained that the guild "was on a bit of a do-good crusade" in this respect. The action was eventually overturned by the Standards Council.

9. Robert W. Grant, president, NFPA, "President's Report" (Speech delivered at the NFPA 89th Annual Meeting, Chicago, May 13, 1985).

10. The AGA at large is more concerned with the overall sales and marketing of gas than is AGA Labs. Accordingly, AGA was more concerned that banning the unvented heater would result in the substitution of electric heat in many homes.

11. Hunt, "Trade Associations and Self-Regulation."

12. Garvin, "Can Industry Self-Regulation Work?" 43.

13. UL claims to do some standards on a *pro bono* basis. The only standard that UL officials could point to, however, is the standard for septic tanks.

14. Thomas P. Grumbly, "Self-Regulation: Private Vice and Public Virtue Revisited," in *Social Regulation: Strategies for Reform*, ed. Eugene Bardach and Robert Kagan (San Francisco: Institute for Contemporary Studies, 1982), 97.

15. See, for example, Louis Lasagna, "Who Will Adopt the Orphan Drugs?" *Regulation*, November/December 1979, 27–32.

16. The creosote tests conducted by the National Bureau of Standards were done over a period of several months in order to most closely replicate creosote production during a typical heating season. Obviously, in order to be economically practical a commercial creosote test would have to be accelerated or the

results would have to be extrapolated. Either way, there would likely be criticisms that the accelerated test method is not realistic.

17. Interview data from members of UL's Consumer Advisory Council.

18. Anthony Downs, *Inside Bureaucracy* (Boston: Little, Brown, 1967), 7.

19. American National Standards Institute, *1984 Progress Report* (New York: ANSI, 1984), 9.

20. "National Fire Protection Association Statement of Revenues and Expenses, 1984," *Fire Journal*, May 1985, 82.

21. Staber and Aldrich, "Trade Association Stability and Public Policy," 4.

22. This embarrassing incident prompted criticism and review of NFPA's rules for adopting standards and eventually resulted in changes granting the Standards Council the formal authority for ratifying standards approved by the membership (see NFPA, "Regulation Governing Committee Projects," sec. 13-5). The power does not go unused. The Standards Council recently rejected an amendment to NFPA 211 (Venting for Woodstoves) that was adopted by the general membership over the objection of the sponsoring committee. (The provision would have essentially banned stoves requiring a clearance of more than thirty-six inches.)

23. Wilson, *The Politics of Regulation*, 371.

24. Maitland, "The Limits of Business Self-Regulation," 136–37.

25. See, for example, *Milk and Ice Cream Can Institute v. F.T.C.*, 152 F.2d 478 (7th. Cir. 1946); *United States v. Institute of Carpet Manufacturers*, CCH Trade Reg. Service (9th ed.), par. 52,517 (S.D.N.Y.); *Bond Crown and Cork Co. v. F.T.C.*, 176 F.2d 974 (4th. Cir. 1949).

26. *Radiant Burners v. Peoples Gas Co.*, 364 U.S. 656 (1961).

27. Kahn, "Cartels and Trade Associations."

28. *American Society of Mechanical Engineers v. Hydrolevel Corp.*

29. Floor votes still occur, but standards cannot be adopted in final form by the membership at large. The Standards Council has the ultimate authority to issue standards. It acts as a check on "political" floor votes. Moreover, objections from the floor usually result in a remand of the issue to committee.

30. See, for example, *Structural Laminates Inc. v. Douglas Fir Plywood Assoc.*, 261 F. Supp. 154 (D.Or. 1966), aff'd 399 F.2d 155 (9th Cir. 1968), cert. denied 393 U.S. 1094 (1969).

31. Muris, in ANSI, *Standards and the Law*, 7.

32. *Roofire Alarm Co. v. Royal Indemnity Co.*, 202 F.Supp. 166 (E.D.Tenn. 1962), aff'd, 313 F.2d 635 (6th Cir. 1963), cert. denied 373 U.S. 949. See also *Roofire Alarm Co. v. Underwriters Laboratories*, 188 F.Supp. 753 (E.D.Tenn.), aff'd per curiam, 284 F.2d 360 (6th Cir. 1960).

33. Interview data from three sources at UL.

34. Interview data from a member of the NFPA Standards Council.

35. "Misuse" has been interpreted rather narrowly in many jurisdictions. In Illinois, for example, "misuse" is a defense only if the product was used "for a purpose neither intended nor foreseeable (objectively reasonable) by the defendant" (*Williams v. Brown Mfg. Co.*, 45 Ill.2d 418, 425, 261 N.E.2d 305, 309 [1970]). See also Restatement (Second) of Torts, sec. 402A, comment n (1965) (seller not liable where injury results from "abnormal use").

36. Several members of the Z21.11.2 committee mentioned this concern privately, but none wanted to be quoted.

37. Schwartz, "The Consumer Product Safety Commission," 73.

38. *Aqua Slide 'n' Dive v. Consumer Product Safety Commission*, 569 F.2d 831 (5th Cir. 1978).

39. *D. D. Bean & Sons v. Consumer Product Safety Commission*, 574 F.2d 643 (1st Cir. 1978).

CHAPTER TEN

1. Lave, *The Strategy of Social Regulation*, 26–27.

2. For example, AGA Labs is trying to cut the cost of standards-writing by calling fewer meetings. The result will be cheaper standards that are longer in the making.

3. The one time that UL engaged in cost-benefit analysis—as an "offeror" to the CPSC on television receivers—it spent over $300,000 on the standard. Even though some considered the effort a public relations ploy, it demonstrated that an extraordinarily expensive standard by UL's own standards would still be an inexpensive one to OSHA.

4. Compliance costs, as distinguished from the cost of developing a standard, are often much higher in the private sector because manufacturers must pay to have their products tested. The certification process assures higher compliance, but at a significant cost. In the case of woodstoves, for example, one manufacturer reports paying $70,000 a year for UL labels. With total industry production of several hundred thousand units annually, this adds a considerable private cost to UL 1482. In some cases, particularly for large firms that have engineering departments and conduct their own testing, this cost may be unreasonable. It is most justified for products that vary in the production process in ways that directly affect safety. In the case of woodstoves, however, the private sector, surprisingly, imposes compliance costs far in excess of the most stringent government inspection system.

5. Harold L. Wilensky, *Organizational Intelligence: Knowledge and Policy in Government and Industry* (New York: Basic Books, 1967).

6. Injury data often do not include reliable information on venting, causing considerable disagreements in data interpretation. See chapter 6, note 29.

7. The program was officially called the National Field Observation Program (or NFOP).

8. Eads and Reuter, *Designing Safer Products*, 42 n. 52.

9. For an example of the criticisms lodged against the CPSC's hospital survey information, see Edward Heiden, Allan Pittaway, and Rosalind O'Connor, "Utility of the U.S. Consumer Product Safety Commission's Injury Data System as a Basis for Product Hazard Assessment," *Journal of Products Liability* 5 (1982): 295.

10. For a fifteen-page memo detailing the issues and evidence on this point, see S. L. Blachman, interoffice memorandum (AGA Labs) to D. T. King, November 2, 1979.

11. Edwin I. Colodny, chairman and president, USAir Group Inc., in "Proceedings of Cabin Safety Conference," p. 165.

12. Douglas and Wildavsky, *Risk and Culture*, 196–97.

13. Lave, *The Strategy of Social Regulation*, 8–28.

14. Eugene Bardach and Robert A. Kagan, *Going by the Book: The Problem of Regulatory Unreasonableness* (Philadelphia: Temple University Press, 1982), 184–213.

15. Dissenting Opinion of Vice Chairman Saundra Brown Armstrong, in the Matter of Revocation of the Mandatory Standard for Unvented Gas-fired Space Heaters, 2 n. 2.

16. The Enforcement Directorate sought to obtain an informal agreement among all testing laboratories to require certain detailed information not specifically required by the CPSC rule. Ironically, the Enforcement Directorate used as a "model" an instruction booklet already used by a major UL client. In other words, even in this effort the CPSC was deferring to the private sector.

17. Bardach and Kagan, *Going by the Book*, 184–213.

18. For example, the dust-control and housekeeping recommendations offered in 1980 by representatives of USDA and OSHA were held over "for further study" and rejected without discussion in 1985. NFPA, *Technical Committee Reports: 1986 Fall Meeting*, Comment 61B-61-Chapter 8 (Log #72), 12.

CHAPTER ELEVEN

1. See, for example, Ackerman and Hassler, *Clean Coal/Dirty Air;* Stewart, "The Reformation of American Administrative Law."

2. 5 U.S.C. secs. 551–59 (1976).

3. Administrative Conference of the United States, Recommendation 78-4 (adopted December 14–15, 1978), 7.

4. For example, Executive Order 12291, 1981.

5. This prescription, common on the public side, has recently been applied to the private sector as well. See Johnson, *Cost-Benefit Analysis and Voluntary Safety Standards*, sec. 4.

6. Stewart, "The Reformation of American Administrative Law."

7. For the traditional "capture" theory, see Bernstein, *Regulating Business by Independent Commission*. For the revised theory that includes capture by environmental groups, see R. Shep Melnick, *Regulation and the Courts: The Case of the Clean Air Act* (Washington, D.C.: Brookings Institution, 1983).

8. Stewart, "The Reformation of American Administrative Law," 1807.

9. Herbert Simon, "Rationality as Process and Product of Thought" (Richard T. Ely Lecture to the American Economics Association), *Proceedings of the American Economics Association*, May 1978, 14.

10. S. John Byington, CPSC chairman, "Transcript of Public Meeting on Unvented Gas-fired Space Heaters, March 6, 1978, Washington, D.C.," 68.

11. In March 1982, for example, draft revisions of Z21.11.2 were sent by AGA Labs to 416 potentially interested parties for comment, including 11 manufacturers, 185 gas companies, and 220 other groups, primarily state and local jurisdictions.

12. The FAA received hundreds of postcards and letters supporting a rule it already planned to adopt. OSHA, on the other hand, received thousands of objections from farmers it knew were opposed to the rule, but the agency remained committed to it.

13. See chapter 8, especially pp. 177–78.

14. They might still be influenced, of course, by the knowledge that a "balanced" committee will review their work. Based on the attitudes of those interviewed for this study, however, this does not seem likely. Technical committee members openly refer to the Z21 committee as a "rubber stamp." It is hard to imagine how this committee, meeting only once a year, could exercise meaningful review over the forty-seven standards under its jurisdiction. Those canvassed about UL's standards carry even less clout, since UL admits that it submits its standards to ANSI only as a courtesy. If that "reviewing" body rejected a UL standard, the organization would simply publish it without the ANSI imprimatur. Only the review processes at NFPA appears likely to affect technical committee decisionmaking.

15. The standard, Hydraulic Institute 100, was challenged by ASME at the ANSI Board of Standards Review meeting of November 15, 1984.

16. Robert Lacey, *Ford: The Man and the Machine* (Boston: Little, Brown, 1986), 579.

17. 5 U.S.C. sec. 553 (1976).

18. John H. Young, "Direct Interest Participation in the Regulatory Decision Process" (Staff paper prepared for the Office of Technology Development, May 5, 1983), 12.

19. Membership on UL's Industry Advisory Conferences (IAC) is limited "to employees of manufacturers who are subscribers to UL's Follow-up Service in the product category." At a two-day gathering in November 1978, for example, UL engineers met with representatives of ten woodstove manufacturers and seven "invited guests," either trade association representatives or manufacturers of related products such as fireplace inserts and venting equipment.

20. American National Standards Institute, "Procedures for the Development and Coordination of American National Standards," April 1983, appendix A, sec. A7, p. 14.

21. Basically, critics complain that outside participation comes too late in the UL process. First, there is no outside participation in the drafting of informal "desk standards." Second, the canvass process takes place after there have been give-and-take sessions between UL and industry interests. The latter do not shape the standard nearly so much as the former.

22. On the creosote issue, UL told concerned commenters that it expected current research "within the scientific and technical community [to] provide a data base upon which a [creosote] test might be developed" (UL letter of November 26, 1979, to John Schulz, NFPA Technical Committee member). In fact, UL did not (and does not) intend to develop a creosote test, even though a test method has been developed by a woodstove consultant who operates a testing lab.

23. See chapter 10, note 18.

24. John H. Young, "Direct Interest Participation in the Regulatory Decision Process," 69.

25. David Braybrooke and Charles E. Lindblom, *A Strategy of Decision: Policy Evaluation as a Social Process* (New York: Free Press, 1970).

26. Johnson, *Cost-Benefit Analysis and Voluntary Safety Standards*, 37–51.

27. Actually, UL did it once, when it acted as an "offeror" in the CPSC's proceedings on television receivers. UL spent several hundred thousand dollars on that standard, conducting a full-blown cost-benefit analysis and trying to encourage consumers to participate. By most accounts, the venture failed. The CPSC never adopted the standard prepared by UL. The proceedings were marked by hostile exchanges between UL and the CPSC, leading some observers to conclude that UL set out with the intention to demonstrate that this technique of standards-setting would not work. A UL engineer, citing the case of television receiver, says that UL should "never again do cost-benefit analysis."

28. The "Report of the NFPA Systems Concepts Committee on Cost/Benefit Statements" was circulated to all Technical Committee members by order of the Standards Council in July 1985 (NFPA Standards Council Meeting Minutes, Item 84-20, reprinted in *Fire Journal,* January 1986, 77).

29. See, generally, Serge Taylor, *Making Bureaucracies Think: The Environmental Impact Statement Strategy of Administrative Reform,* (Palo Alto: Stanford University Press, 1984).

30. Breyer, *Regulation and Its Reform,* 98.

31. McConnell, *Private Power and American Democracy,* 138.

CHAPTER TWELVE

1. The CPSC's official policy on employee membership and participation in voluntary standards is published in 16 C.F.R., Part 1031. The commission debated a proposal in 1985 to "acknowledge" private standards and allow for "formal voting" by CPSC participants.

2. Young, "Direct Interest Participation in the Regulatory Process."

3. Timothy J. O'Neill makes a related and fascinating argument, in an entirely different context, about the educational value of *amicus* briefs and the "classroom of litigation" (*Bakke and the Politics of Equality: Friends and Foes in the Classroom of Litigation* [Middletown, Conn.: Wesleyan University Press, 1985]), introduction.

4. OMB Circular no. A-199, sec. 6(a) (October 26, 1982).

5. 15 U.S.C. sec. 2056(b).

6. Steven M. Spivak, *Implementation of OMB Circular A-119,* U.S. Department of Commerce, National Bureau of Standards, Office of Product Standards Policy, March 1985, 2.

7. As Thomas Dietz and Robert Rycroft (*Risk Professionals,* 112) explain: "The risk policy system is clearly a 'transcientific' domain. The term was first coined by Alvin Weinberg to describe problems characterized by great uncertainty for which adequate solutions could not be supplied by science alone, and it has been applied to environmental problems for some time."

8. For an interesting, but tentative, effort, see Susan Bartlett Foote,

"Beyond the Politics of Federalism: An Alternative Model," *Yale Journal on Regulation* 1, no. 2 (1984): 217–25. See also Advisory Commission on Intergovernmental Relations, *Regulatory Federalism: Policy, Process, Impact, and Reform* (Washington D.C.: ACIR, 1984).

9. For example, the "stringency" of UL's warning label and the overall level of compliance with UL standards.

10. See Lasagna, "Who Will Adopt the Orphan Drugs?"

11. See, for example, Cornell, Noll, and Weingast, "Safety Regulations," in *Setting National Priorities,* 457–503.

12. John H. Shenefield, "Standards for Standards-Makers" (Remarks before the American National Standards Institute, Washington, D.C., March 29, 1978), 7.

13. The major firms "complied" with the FDA's request for voluntary rating, but different companies used different systems for rating! ("Are Tampons Safer Now?" *Consumer Reports,* May 1986, 333). Three years later, prompted by a lawsuit, the FDA promulgated a mandatory federal rule ("Judge Orders U.S. to Require Tampon Absorbency Labels," *New York Times,* August 31, 1989, B8; Warren E. Leary, "Tampons to Get Standard Labels," *New York Times,* October 27, 1989, A12).

14. Philip J. Harter and George C. Eads, "Policy Instruments, Institutions, and Objectives: An Analytical Framework for Assessing 'Alternatives' to Regulation," *Administrative Law Review* 37, no. 3 (Summer 1985): 221–58.

15. Ibid., 223

16. See, for example, Peter Huber, "Safety and the Second Best: The Hazards of Public Risk Management in the Courts," *Columbia Law Review* 85, no. 2 (March 1985): 277–337.

17. S. David Hoffman and Mathew E. Hoffman, "Use of Standards in Products Liability Litigation Revisited—*Déjà Vu,* but Even More So" (mimeographed, 1985).

18. See, for example, Peter Huber, "The Old-New Division in Risk Regulation," *Virginia Law Review* 69, no. 6 (September 1983): 1025–1107.

19. *Allied Tube and Conduit Corp. v. Indian Head,* 56 U.S.L.W. 4539 (June 13, 1988), 4545 (Justice White dissenting with Justice O'Connor).

20. For example, the majority in *Indian Head* decided that this case differed from other cases involving governmental immunity because "the context and nature of [NFPA's] activity make it the type of commercial activity that has traditionally had its validity determined by the antitrust laws themselves" (ibid., 4542).

21. Maitland, "The Limits of Business Self-Regulation."

22. Perrow, *Normal Accidents,* 166.

23. Edwin T. Layton, Jr., "Engineering Needs a Loyal Opposition: An Essay Review," *Business and Professional Ethics Journal* (1985): 51–59.

24. The agency's total budget in 1986 was $124 million ("Bureau of Standards Is Pinched Too," *New York Times,* April 28, 1986).

25. See, generally, George S. Emmerson, *Engineering Education: A Social History* (New York: Crane Russak, 1973). For a description of recent changes

aimed at addressing the problem, see Edward Fiske, "M.I.T. Widens Engineer Training," *New York Times*, June 1, 1987, 1.

26. These possibilities include improved state regulation, changes in the agent reward system, and the promotion of purchasing groups. See David Hemenway, "Private Insurance as an Alternative to Protective Regulation: The Market for Residential Fire Insurance," *Policy Studies Journal* 15, no. 3 (March 1987): 433.

27. Ibid.

Bibliographies

Note: Sources pertaining directly to particular case studies are listed in separate bibliographies below.

Adler, Robert S., and R. David Pittle. "Cajolery or Command: Are Education Campaigns an Adequate Substitute for Regulation?" *Yale Journal on Regulation* 1, no. 2 (1984): 159–93.

American National Standards Institute. *Standards and the Law.* Papers presented at the Public Conference on Standards and the Law of the American National Standards Institute, Arlington, Va., March 27, 1984.

Bacow, Lawrence S. *Bargaining for Job Safety and Health.* Cambridge, Mass.: MIT Press, 1980.

Bardach, Eugene. "Problems of Problem Definition in Policy Analysis." *Research in Public Policy Analysis and Management* 1 (1981): 161–71.

Bardach, Eugene, and Robert A. Kagan. *Going by the Book: The Problem of Regulatory Unreasonableness.* Philadelphia: Temple University Press, 1982.

———, eds. *Social Regulation: Strategies for Reform.* San Francisco: Institute for Contemporary Studies, 1982.

Beardsley, Charles W. "The Hydrolevel Case: A Retrospective." *Fire Journal,* May 1985. (First published in *Mechanical Engineering,* June 1984.)

Bernstein, Marver H. *Regulating Business by Independent Commission.* Princeton: Princeton University Press, 1955.

Brand, Donald R. *Corporatism and the Rule of Law: A Study of the National Recovery Administration.* Ithaca: Cornell University Press, 1988.

Breitenberg, Maureen. *Need for Economic Information on Standards Used in Regulatory Programs: Problems and Recommendations.* Prepared for the Office of Standards Information, Analysis, and Development, National Bureau of Standards, U.S. Department of Commerce. NBSIR 80-2123. Springfield, Va.: National Technical Information Service, 1980.

Breitenberg, Maureen, and Robert G. Atkins. *Consumer Representation in Standards Development: Literature Review and Issue Identification.* Prepared for the Office of Engineering Standards, National Bureau of Standards, U.S. Department of Commerce. NBSIR-81-2336. Springfield, Va.: National Technical Information Service, 1981.

Breyer, Stephen. *Regulation and Its Reform.* Cambridge, Mass.: Harvard University Press, 1984.

Caves, Richard E., and Marc J. Roberts, eds. *Regulating the Product: Quality and Variety.* Cambridge, Mass.: Ballinger Publishing, 1975.

Cheit, Earl F. *The Useful Arts and the Liberal Tradition.* New York: McGraw-Hill, 1975.

Cornell, Nina W., Roger G. Noll, and Barry Weingast. "Safety Regulation." In *Setting National Priorities.* Washington, D.C.: Brookings Institution, 1976.

Curran, William J., III. "Volunteers . . . Not Profiteers: The Hydrolevel Myth." *Catholic University Law Review* 33 (1983): 147–62.

DeLong, James V. "Informal Rulemaking and the Integration of Law and Policy." *Virginia Law Review* 65 (1979): 257–356.

Dery, David. *Problem Definition in Policy Analysis.* Lawrence: University Press of Kansas, 1984.

Diver, Colin S. "Policymaking Paradigms in Administrative Law." *Harvard Law Review* 95, no. 2 (December 1981): 393–434.

Dixon, Robert G., Jr. *Standards Development in the Private Sector: Thoughts on Interest Representation and Procedural Fairness.* Boston: National Fire Protection Association, 1978.

Douglas, Mary, and Aaron Wildavsky. *Risk and Culture.* Berkeley and Los Angeles: University of California Press, 1982.

Downs, Anthony. *Inside Bureaucracy.* Boston: Little, Brown, 1967.

Eads, George, and Peter Reuter. *Designing Safer Products: Corporate Responses to Product Liability Law and Regulation.* Santa Monica, Calif.: RAND Corporation (Institute for Civil Justice), 1983.

Florman, Samuel C. *The Existential Pleasures of Engineering.* New York: St. Martin's Press, 1976.

———. "Standards of Value." *Harper's,* February 1980, 62–70.

———. *Blaming Technology: The Irrational Search for Scapegoats.* New York: St. Martin's Press, 1981.

Garvin, David A. "Can Industry Self-Regulation Work?" *California Management Review* 25, no. 4 (Summer 1983): 37–52.

Hamilton, Robert W. "The Role of Nongovernment Standards in the Development of Mandatory Federal Standards Affecting Safety or Health." *Texas Law Review* 56, no. 8 (November 1978): 1329–1484.

Harter, Philip J. *Regulatory Use of Standards: The Implications for Standards Writers.* Prepared for the Office of Standards Information, Analysis, and Development, National Bureau of Standards, U.S. Department of Commerce. NBS-GCR-79-171. Springfield, Va.: National Technical Information Service, 1979.

Harter, Philip J., and George C. Eads. "Policy Instruments, Institutions, and Objectives: An Analytical Framework for Assessing 'Alternatives' to Regulation." *Administrative Law Review* 37, no. 3 (Summer 1985): 221–58.

Hemenway, David. *Industrywide Voluntary Product Standards.* Cambridge, Mass.: Ballinger Publishing, 1975.

_____. *Standards Systems in Canada, the U.K., West Germany, and Denmark: An Overview.* Prepared for the Office of Standards Information, Analysis, and Development, National Bureau of Standards, U.S. Department of Commerce. NBS-GCR-79-172. Springfield, Va.: National Technical Information Service, 1979.

_____. *Performance vs. Design Standards.* Prepared for the Office of Standards Information, Analysis, and Development, National Bureau of Standards, U.S. Department of Commerce. NBS/GCR 80-287. Springfield, Va.: National Technical Information Service, 1980.

Hoffman, S. David, and Dennis O. Duda. *A History of the Development of the Proposed Federal Mandatory Safety Standard for Television Receivers.* Northbrook, Ill.: Underwriters Laboratories, 1980.

Hoffman, S. David, and Mathew E. Hoffman. "Use of Standards in Products Liability Litigation." *Drake Law Review* 20 (1980–81): 283–97.

Jaffe, Louis J. "Law Making by Private Groups," *Harvard Law Review* 51, no. 2 (December 1937): 201–53.

Johnson, Leland L. *Cost-Benefit Analysis and Voluntary Safety Standards for Consumer Products.* Santa Monica, Calif.: RAND Corporation (Institute for Civil Justice), 1982.

Kolb, John, and Steven S. Ross. *Product Safety and Liability: A Desk Reference.* New York: McGraw-Hill, 1980.

Lave, Lester B. *The Strategy of Social Regulation: Decision Frameworks for Policy.* Washington, D.C.: Brookings Institution, 1981.

Lindblom, Charles E., and David K. Cohen. *Usable Knowledge: Social Science and Social Problem Solving.* New Haven: Yale University Press, 1979.

Litan, Robert E., and William D. Nordhaus. *Reforming Federal Regulation.* New Haven: Yale University Press, 1983.

McConnell, Grant. *Private Power and American Democracy.* New York: Alfred A. Knopf, 1966; Vintage Books, 1970.

Madden, M. Stuart. "Admissibility of Past-Incident Remedial Measures: A Pattern Emerges." *Journal of Products Liability* 5 (1982): 1–21.

Maitland, Ian. "The Limits of Business Self-Regulation." *California Management Review* 27, no. 3 (Spring 1985): 132–47.

Meager, Stephen W. "The ANSI Conveyor Standards: A Critical Review." *Journal of Products Liability* 5 (1982): 63–67.

Meehan, Richard L. *The Atom and the Fault: Experts, Earthquakes, and Nuclear Power.* Cambridge, Mass.: MIT Press, 1984.

Mendeloff, John. *Regulating Safety: A Economic and Political Analysis of Occupational Safety and Health.* Cambridge, Mass.: MIT Press, 1979.

Mosher, Frederick C. *Democracy and the Public Service.* 2d ed. New York: Oxford University Press, 1982.

Owen, Bruce M., and Ronald Braeutigam. *The Regulation Game: Strategic Use of the Administrative Process.* Cambridge, Mass.: Ballinger Publishing, 1978.

Pertschuk, Michael. *Revolt Against Regulation: The Rise and Pause of the Consumer Movement.* Berkeley and Los Angeles: University of California Press, 1982.

Petroski, Henry. *To Engineer Is Human: The Role of Failure in Successful Design.* New York: St. Martin's Press, 1985.

Poole, Robert W., Jr., ed. *Instead of Regulation: Alternatives to Federal Regulatory Agencies.* Lexington, Mass.: Lexington Books, 1981.

Quirk, Paul J. *Industry Influence in Federal Regulatory Agencies.* Princeton: Princeton University Press, 1981.

Rawie, Carol Chapman. *A Guide to Papers Citing Antitrust Cases Involving Standards or Certification.* Prepared for the Office of Engineering Standards, National Bureau of Standards, U.S. Department of Commerce. NBSIR 79-1921. Springfield, Va.: National Technical Information Service, 1979.

_____. *Economics of the Product Certification Industry: Some Research Needs.* Prepared for the Office of Engineering Standards, National Bureau of Standards, U.S. Department of Commerce. NBSIR 80-2001. Springfield, Va.: National Technical Information Service, 1980.

Reich, Robert B. "Toward a New Consumer Protection." *University of Pennsylvania Law Review* 128, no. 1 (November 1979): 1–40.

Schwartz, Teresa M. "The Consumer Product Safety Commission: A Flawed Product of the Consumer Decade." *The George Washington Law Review* 51, no. 1 (November 1982): 32–95.

Sevart, John Bart, and R. Lewis Hull. *Power Lawn Mowers: An Unreasonably Dangerous Product.* Durham, N.C.: Institute for Product Safety, 1982.

Spivak, Steven M. *Implementation of OMB Circular A-119: An Independent Appraisal of Federal Participation in the Development of Voluntary Standards.* Prepared for the Office of Product Standards Policy, National Bureau of Standards, U.S. Department of Commerce. NBS-GCR-85-495. Springfield, Va.: National Technical Information Service, 1985.

Stewart, Richard B. "The Reformation of American Administrative Law." *Harvard Law Review* 88, no. 8 (June 1975): 1667–1813.

_____. "Regulation, Innovation, and Administrative Law: A Conceptual Framework." *California Law Review* 69, no. 5 (September 1981): 1256–1377.

Swankin, David A. *Rationale Statements for Voluntary Standards—Issues, Techniques, and Consequences.* Prepared for the Office of Standards Information, Analysis, and Development, National Bureau of Standards, U.S. Department of Commerce. NBS-GCR-81-347. Springfield, Va.: National Technical Information Service, 1981.

Thomas, Elaine, C. E. Benton, and Verne L. Roberts. *Safe Chain Saw Design.* Durham, N.C.: Institute for Product Safety, 1983.

Till, Derek, David Gleicher, and William Kriegsman. "The Role of the Voluntary Standards System in Relation to Mandatory Standards." Report to the Committee on Research and Technical Planning, American Society for Testing and Materials. July 31, 1973.

U.S. Department of Commerce. National Bureau of Standards. *Standards Activities of Organizations in the United States.* NBS Special Publication 681. Washington, D.C.: Government Printing Office, August 1984.

U.S. Federal Trade Commission. "Self-Regulation—Product Standardization, Certification, and Seals of Approval. Preliminary Staff Study, Precis." Photocopy. 1971.

_____. Bureau of Consumer Protection. *Standards and Certification: Proposed Rule and Staff Report.* Washington, D.C.: Government Printing Office, December 1978.

_____. *Standards and Certification: Final Staff Report.* Washington, D.C.: Government Printing Office, April 1983.

_____. *Standards and Certification: Report of the Presiding Officer on Proposed Trade Regulation Rule.* Washington, D.C.: Government Printing Office, June 1983.

Viscusi, W. Kip. *Regulating Consumer Product Safety.* Washington, D.C.: American Enterprise Institute, 1984.

Walkowiak, Vincent S. "Reconsidering Plaintiff's Fault in Product Liability Litigation: The Proposed Conscious Design Choice Exception." *Vanderbilt Law Review* 33 (1980): 651–61.

Woods, Henry. "Product Liability: Is Comparative Fault Winning the Day?" *Arkansas Law Review* 36 (1982): 374–82.

Young, John H. "Direct Interest Participation in the Regulatory Decision Process: Lessons Learned from Two LNG Safety Standards." Staff Paper, Office of Technology Assessment, U.S. Congress. May 5, 1983.

_____. "Consensus: A Better Approach to Regulatory Reform." Photocopy. February 1984.

GRAIN ELEVATORS

The written record of the OSHA rule (Docket H-117) consists of several thousand pages, including comments and hearing transcripts. These documents are available in microfiche form for public viewing at the OSHA Public Reading Room in Washington, D.C. This material was examined for four days and photocopies were obtained of (1) representative samples of hearing testimony and (2) reports prepared for OSHA (for example, by Arthur D. Little and Booz, Allen) and those submitted by such organizations as the National Grain and Feed Association and the AFL-CIO. Some of these documents are cited specifically in the notes to chapter 3. Only the reports are cited below.

The *Occupational Safety and Health Reporter,* a loose-leaf service published by the Bureau of National Affairs, reports extensively on current developments at OSHA. Various stories from 1978 through 1985 provided background for this case study.

The official record of NFPA standards is published in technical committee reports (TCRs) and technical committee documentation (TCDs), which are circulated to the general membership before the semiannual meetings. The TCRs and TCDs for both the 1980 and 1986 versions were obtained directly from NFPA. Earlier versions of the standard were examined at the NFPA Technical Library in Quincy, Massachusetts.

The following documents were the primary written sources, other than those described above, for the grain elevator case study:

Barringer, Felicity. "OSHA's Grain Elevator Rule Delayed." *Washington Post,* August 1, 1983.

Bluhm, Delwyn D. "Grain Elevator Explosions: A University View." In *International Symposium on Grain Elevator Explosions.* National Materials Advisory Board, Washington, D.C., July 11–12, 1978. Ames: Iowa State University, 1978.

"Deadlock over Explosive Dust." *Science* 222 (November 4, 1983): 485–87.

Drapkin, Larry. "OSHA's General Duty Clause: Its Use Is Not Abuse—A Response to Morgan and Duvall." *Industrial Relations Law Journal* 5 (Spring 1983): 322–33.

Factory Insurance Association. "Preventing and Minimizing the Effects of Dust Explosions in Manufacturing Plants." Special Hazard Study, no. 5. Hartford, Conn.: Factory Insurance Association, 1940.

Kauffman, C. W., and Robert F. Hubbard. "An Investigation of Fourteen Grain Elevator Explosions Occurring Between January 1979 and April 1981." Prepared for the Directorate of Safety Standards, Occupational Safety and Health Administration. May 1984.

Kelman, Steven. *Regulating Sweden: A Comparative Study of Occupational Safety and Health Policy.* Cambridge, Mass.: MIT Press, 1981.

Lublin, Joann S. "Grain-Elevator Rule Forges Unusual Link as AFL-CIO Backs Labor Agency's Plan." *Wall Street Journal,* August 24, 1983, 50.

Minter, Stephen G. "Grain Dust: OSHA Proposes a Controversial New Standard." *Occupational Hazards,* March 1984, 59–62.

Morgan, Dan. *Merchants of Grain.* New York: Penguin Books, 1980.

Morgan, Donald L., and Mark N. Duvall. "OSHA's General Duty Clause: An Analysis of Its Use and Abuse." *Industrial Relations Law Journal* 5 (Spring 1983): 283–321.

_____. "Reply to Drapkin." (Article on OSHA's general duty clause.) *Industrial Relations Law Journal* 5 (Spring 1983): 334–37.

National Academy of Sciences. National Materials Advisory Board. Panel on Causes and Prevention of Grain Elevator Explosions. *Prevention of Grain Elevator and Mill Explosions.* NMAB 367-2. Springfield, Va.: National Technical Information Service, 1982.

_____. *Pneumatic Dust Control in Grain Elevators: Guidelines for Design Operation and Maintenance.* NMAB 367-3. Springfield, Va.: National Technical Information Service, 1982.

National Grain and Feed Association. *Dust Control for Grain Elevators.* Papers presented at the Dust Control Seminar, St. Louis, Mo., May 7–8, 1981. Washington, D.C.: NGFA, 1981.

_____. *Retrofitting and Constructing Grain Elevators . . . for Increased Productivity and Safety.* Papers presented at the Five Years of Progress Conference, New Orleans, La., September 27–28, 1984. Washington, D.C.: NGFA, 1985.

Theimer, O. F. "Cause and Prevention of Dust Exposions in Grain Elevators." *Powder Technology* 8 (1973): 137–47.

Townsend, A. S. "Reduction of Explosion Hazard in Grain Risks." *Best's Review* (Prop/Casualty) 83, no. 3 (July 1982): 48–56.

Underwriters Laboratories. "Electrical Equipment for Hazardous Locations." Typescript. N.d.

———. *Control of Floating Dust in Terminal Grain Elevators*, UL Bulletin of Research, no. 1. Fifth Printing. Chicago: UL, 1964.

———. *UL 1604, Electrical Equipment for Use in Hazardous Locations (Class I and Class II, Division 2, and Class III, Divisions 1 and 2)*. Northbrook, Ill.: UL, 1982.

———. *UL 844, Electric Lighting Fixtures for Use in Hazardous (Classified) Locations*. 9th ed. Northbrook, Ill.: UL, 1984.

U.S. Department of Health and Human Services. National Institute for Occupational Safety and Health. *Occupational Safety in Grain Elevators and Feed Mills*. DHHS (NIOSH) Publication no. 83-126. Washington, D.C.: Government Printing Office, September 1983.

U.S. Office of Management and Budget. Executive Office of the President. "OSHA's Proposed Standards for Grain Handling Facilities: April 1984." Attached to letter from Christopher DeMuth, administrator for information and regulatory affairs, to Francis Lilly, solicitor, Department of Labor, April 11, 1984.

U. S. Senate. Committee on Labor and Human Resources. Subcommittee on Labor. "Hearing an Oversight of OSHA Regulations for Grain Handling Facilities, 1984." 98th Cong., 2d. sess. Washington, D.C.: Government Printing Office, 1984.

Verkade, M., and P. Chiotti. "An Overview of Grain Explosion Problems." Ames: Energy and Mineral Resources Institute, Iowa State University, 1976.

Viscusi, W. Kip. *Risk by Choice: Regulating Health and Safety in the Workplace*. Cambridge, Mass.: Harvard University Press, 1983.

AVIATION FIRE SAFETY

The written record of the FAA rule (Docket no. 24073) consists largely of the official regulatory analysis—reproduced in the *Federal Register*—and several hundred comments received from the public. These documents are available for public inspection at the FAA Public Reading Room in Washington, D.C. This material was examined for several hours and photocopies were obtained of relevant public comments from NFPA, UL, and several airlines. There were no public hearings on this standard. Various FAA guides to economic analysis were obtained from the regulatory impact analysis staff. Some of these documents are cited in the notes to chapter 4. None are cited below.

The official record of NFPA standards is published in technical committee reports (TCRs) and technical committee documentation (TCDs), which are circulated to the general membership before the semiannual meetings. The TCRs and TCDs for the 1984 annual meeting were obtained directly from NFPA. Earlier versions of the standard were examined at the NFPA Technical Library in Quincy, Massachusetts.

The following documents were the primary written sources, other than those described above, for the aviation fire-safety case study:

Brenneman, James J. "In-Flight Fire: Smoke Detection and Control, Interior Design, Fire Proofing, Occupant Protection, Cabin Fire Protection and Use." Paper presented at the Flight Safety Foundation Conference on Cabin Safety, Arlington, Va., December 13, 1984.

Burke, James M. "Aviation Exposures Climbing, Experts Say." *Business Insurance,* May 9, 1983, 18.

Ehrich, Lisa. "The Kind of Plane Fire I Survived Could Kill Again." *Washington Post* (National Weekly Edition), June 3, 1985, 24.

Hopkins, Thomas D. "Economics of Safety." Paper presented at the Flight Safety Foundation Conference on Cabin Safety, Arlington, Va., December 13, 1984.

Johansen, Robert J. "Using Statistics in Aviation Underwriting." *Best's Review (Prop/Casualty),* February 1982, 40–46.

Klem, Thomas J. "Investigation Report: Air Canada DC-9 Aircraft Fire, Greater Cincinnati Airport, June 2, 1983." National Fire Protection Association, Fire Investigations and Applied Research Division. Photocopy. N.d.

Krasner, L. M. "Study of Hand-held Fire Extinguishers Aboard Civil Aviation Aircraft." Prepared for Federal Aviation Administration Technical Center. Contract no. DTFA03-81-00029. Norwood, Mass.: Factory Mutual Research Corp., May 1982.

Nance, John J. *Blind Trust: How Deregulation Has Jeopardized Airline Safety and What You Can Do About It.* New York: William Morrow, 1986.

Perrow, Charles. *Normal Accidents: Living with High-Risk Technologies.* New York: Basic Books, 1985.

Quinn, Hal. "A Burning Nightmare at 31,000 Feet." *Maclean's,* June 13, 1983, 19.

Shapiro, Stacy. "Increased Competition Cuts Most Aviation Rates." *Business Insurance,* July 11, 1983.

———. "London Insurer's Tough Terms Boost Airline Deductibles, Rates." *Business Insurance,* May 28, 1984.

———. "Aviation Insurance Costs Taking Off." *Business Insurance,* February 11, 1985.

———. "Aviation Capacity May Be Cut in Half." *Business Insurance,* December 9, 1985.

Sun, Marjorie. "Airplane Fire Safety Debate Rekindled." *Science,* July 1, 1983.

U.S. Congress. House. Committee on Science and Technology. Subcommittee on Transportation, Aviation, and Materials. "Aircraft Maintenance and Fire." 98th Cong., 1st sess. (1983).

U.S. Congress. House. Committee on Public Works and Transportation. Subcommittee on Aviation. "Legislation to Improve Airlines Safety: Hearings on H.R. 1333, H.R. 2088, H.R. 2142, H.R. 2636, H.R. 3264, H.R. 3793, H.R. 5428, H.R. 5518, and S. 197." 98th Cong., 2d sess. (1984).

Witkin, Richard. "Why Fewer Airliners Crash These Days." *New York Times,* April 28, 1985.

_____. "On Airline Safety, the Record is Reassuring." *New York Times,* September 15, 1985.

_____. "Lawmaker Says FAA Cuts Would Harm Key Programs." *New York Times,* January 24, 1986.

WOODSTOVES

The public docket of the CPSC's proceedings on woodstove labeling consists of ten folders, available for public inspection at the CPSC offices in Bethesda. These files were examined by the author for several days in October 1984. Several hundred pages of documents were subsequently obtained through the Freedom on Information Act. A random sample of twenty-five "in-depth investigations" of woodstove incidents was also obtained directly from the CPSC Epidemiology Directorate. Some of these documents are specifically cited in the notes to chapter 5. None are cited below.

All meetings of the CPSC are tape-recorded and these tapes are also available for public listening at the CPSC offices in Bethesda. Copies of the tapes for the following meetings (at which the Banner petition was discussed) were obtained from the CPSC and transcribed in rough form by the author: March 14, May 30, and June 7, 1979. A few of the quotations from these meetings are cited in the notes to chapter 5.

The *Product Safety and Liability Reporter,* a loose-leaf service published by the Bureau of National Affairs, reports extensively on current developments at the CPSC. Various stories from 1978 through 1985 provided background for this case study.

The primary source of written information about UL 1482 is Underwriters Laboratories. Various versions of the standard, from the original proposal to the version officially adopted several years later, along with communications from UL to both the Industry Advisory Council and those participating in the canvass process are contained in files at the Standards Department at UL headquarters in Northbrook, Illinois. All of these documents were examined by the author and many were included in the documents obtained from the CPSC. Some of these documents are cited specifically in the notes to chapter 5. None are cited below.

The following documents were the primary written sources, other than those described above, for the woodstove case study:

Berger, Harvey W., ed. *NVLAP Seventh Annual Report and Directory of Accredited Laboratories.* Office of Product Standards Policy, National Bureau of Standards. NBS Special Publication 677. Springfield, Va.: National Technical Information Service, 1984.

Hall, John R., Jr. "Update on the Auxiliary Heating Fire Problem." *Fire Journal,* March 1986.

Hoebel, James F. "CPSC Projects Involving Residential Auxiliary Heating Equipment Fires." *Fire Journal,* March 1983.

Jones, Jon C., and Michael P. Heck. "A Study of Fires Involving Alternative Heating Equipment." *Fire Journal,* September 1983.

Loftus, Joseph J. *Evaluation of Wall Protection Systems for Wood Heating*

Appliances. Center for Fire Research, National Bureau of Standards, U.S. Department of Commerce. NBSIR 82-2506. Springfield, Va.: National Technical Information Service, 1982.

Maxwell, T. T., D. F. Dyer, G. Maples, and T. Burch. *An Investigation of Creosoting and Fireplace Inserts.* Prepared by Auburn University for the Center for Fire Research, National Bureau of Standards. NSB-GCR-81-365. Springfield, Va.: National Technical Information Service, 1981.

National Fire Protection Association. *NFPA 211: Chimneys, Fireplaces, Vents, and Solid Fuel Burning Appliances 1984.* Quincy, Mass.: NFPA, 1984.

Peacock, Richard D. *A Review of Fire Incidents, Model Building Codes, and Standards Related to Wood-burning Appliances.* Center for Fire Research, National Bureau of Standards. NBSIR 79-1731. Springfield, Va.: National Technical Information Service, 1979.

_____. *Intensity and Duration of Chimney Fires in Several Chimneys.* Center for Fire Research, National Bureau of Standards, U.S. Department of Commerce. NBSIR 83-2771. Springfield, Va.: National Technical Information Service, 1983.

Sciacca, Michael C. "Solid-Fuel Industry Launches Cooperative Safety Program." *Fire Journal,* March 1983.

Shelton, Jay. *Wood Heat Safety.* Pownal, Vt.: Garden Way Publishing, 1979.

_____. *Jay Shelton's Solid Fuels Encyclopedia.* Pownal, Vt.: Garden Way Publishing, 1982.

Sunset Homeowner's Guide to Wood Stoves. Menlo Park, Calif.: Lane Publishing, 1979.

Terpstra, W. R., M. L. Jorgenson, and L. J. Dosedlo. *Investigation of Fire Hazards of Fireplace Inserts in Factory-built and Masonry Fireplaces.* Prepared by Underwriters Laboratories for the Center for Fire Research, National Bureau of Standards, U.S. Department of Commerce. NBS-GCR-82-368. Springfield, Va.: National Technical Information Service, 1982.

Underwriters Laboratories. *Clearances and Insulation of Heating Appliances.* Bulletin of Research no. 27. Northbrook, Ill.: Underwriters Laboratories, 1943; reprint September 1972.

U.S. Department of Commerce. National Bureau of Standards. National Voluntary Laboratory Accreditation Program. "NVLAP Stove LAP Handbook." Gaithersburg, Md., February 1983.

_____. "NVLAP Proficiency Testing, Stove LAP, Round 1." NVLAP Proficiency Testing, Stove LAP, Round 1." NVLAP Tech Brief. Gaithersburg, Md., February 1983.

_____. "NVLAP Proficiency Testing, Stove LAP, Round 2." NVLAP Tech Brief. Gaithersburg, Md., October 1984.

GAS SPACE HEATERS

The public docket of the CPSC's proceedings on gas space heaters consists of eleven folders, available for public inspection at the CPSC offices in Bethesda. These files were examined by the author for several days in October 1984. Several hundred pages of documents were subsequently requested through the

Freedom of Information Act. Some of these documents are cited specifically in the notes to chapter 6. None are cited below.

All meetings of the CPSC are tape-recorded and these tapes are also available for public listening at the CPSC offices in Bethesda. Copies of the tapes for the following meetings (at which gas space heaters were discussed) were obtained from the CPSC and transcribed in rough form by the author: July 27 and November 16, 1978. A few of the quotations from these meetings are cited in the notes to chapter 6.

The *Product Safety and Liability Reporter,* a loose-leaf service published by the Bureau of National Affairs, reports extensively on current developments at the CPSC. Various stories from 1975 through 1985 provided background for this case study.

Minutes of the Subcommittee on Standards for Unvented Gas-fired Space Heating Appliances were the primary written source for the case study of AGA/ANSI Z21.11.2. These minutes are on file in the library of the American Gas Association Laboratories in Cleveland, Ohio. The subcommittee met fifty-two times between January 14, 1960 (when a separate standard for unvented heaters was first developed), and January 16, 1985 (the cutoff date for this research). All of these documents were examined and some are cited specifically in the notes to chapter 6. None are cited below.

The following documents were the primary written sources, other than those described above, for the gas space heater case study:

American Gas Association. Engineering Services Department. *Fundamentals of Gas Appliances.* Arlington, Va.: AGA, 1976.

_____. *Fundamentals of Gas Appliance Venting and Ventilation.* Arlington, Va.: AGA, 1976.

_____. *Fundamentals of Gas Controls.* Arlington, Va.: AGA, 1976.

"Are Kerosene Heaters Safe?" *Consumer Reports,* October 1982, 499–507. (Discussion of carbon monoxide poisoning and various federal and private emission standards applicable to kerosene and gas space heaters.)

Belkin, Lisa. "Devices to Detect Lethal Gas." *New York Times,* December 14, 1984, 16.

Bullerdick, W. A., and R. D. Adams. "Investigation of Safety Standards for Flame-fired Space Heaters." Calspan Report no. YG-5569-D-4. February 1976.

Lamar, Charles S. "Oxygen Depletion Sensor Improves Safety of Gas-fired Heating Equipment." *Appliance Engineer 5,* no. 1 (1971): 21–28.

Index

Compositor: Braun-Brumfield, Inc.
Text: 10/13 Sabon
Display: Sabon
Printer: Braun-Brumfield, Inc.
Binder: Braun-Brumfield, Inc.

3-1ᴅ-91